Dividing Citizens

DIVIDING CITIZENS

Gender and Federalism in New Deal Public Policy

Suzanne Mettler

CORNELL UNIVERSITY PRESS

ITHACA AND LONDON

First published 1998 by Cornell University Press
First printing, Cornell Paperbacks, 1998

Printed in the United States of America

Library of Congress Cataloging-in-Publication Data

Mettler, Suzanne.
Dividing citizens : gender and federalism in New Deal public
policy / Suzanne Mettler.
p.   cm.
Includes index.
ISBN 0-8014-3329-0 (alk. paper). — ISBN 0-8014-8546-0 (pbk. :
alk. paper)
1. New Deal, 1933–1939.   2. Sex discrimination against women—
United States—History—20th century.   3. United States—Politics
and government—1933–1945.   4. United States—Social policy.
I. Title.
HQ1426.M48   1998
323.3'4'0973—dc21   98-18218

Cornell University Press strives to use environmentally responsible
suppliers and materials to the fullest extent possible in the publishing of its books.
Such materials include vegetable-based, low-VOC inks and acid-free papers that are
recycled, totally chlorine-free, or partly composed of nonwood fibers.

Cloth printing   10   9   8   7   6   5   4   3   2   1

Paperback printing   10   9   8   7   6   5   4   3   2   1

For Wayne

Contents

Illustrations

Figures

Maps

Tables

Preface

In the United States today, many lament the apparent decline of civic participation since the middle of the twentieth century and call for a revitalization of social trust and public spiritedness. Citizenship is typically construed in this discourse as if it were a set of attitudes and activities generated solely by society, through the transmission of particular values and ideas. Strikingly absent is any consideration of how governing institutions, public policies, and politics might themselves shape civic and social life.

My questions about this relationship prompted me to wonder how a major transformation in American governance, the New Deal, affected the organization and character of American citizenship. In this book, I investigate how the particular design and institutional arrangements for social and labor policies shaped the manner in and extent to which groups of citizens were incorporated within the polity. Other scholars have examined how naturalization and immigration policies have defined the boundaries of membership in the political community; my focus here is on "social citizenship," how public provisions for economic security and welfare have shaped the experience of citizenship for those who are already, by law, considered to be citizens.

I argue that policy and institutional developments in the New Deal divided Americans, as social citizens, under two distinct forms of governance. Men, particularly white men, were endowed with national citizenship, incorporated into policies to be administered in a centralized, unitary manner through standardized, routinized procedures. Women and minority men were more likely to remain state citizens, subject to policies whose development was hindered by the dynamics of federalism and which were administered with discretion and variability. In effect, the new welfare state treated men and women like members of separate sovereignties. Those within the ranks of national citizenship were governed as rights-bearing individuals, members of a liberal regime. The states ruled, conversely, in a nonliberal manner, regarding citizens in relational, role-oriented, or difference-based terms that perpetuated women's gender roles and status. Differential incorporation of citizens led, in turn, to different kinds of participation in politics.

My analysis builds on the work of historical institutionalists, who have shown how particular institutional configurations and historical precedents in policymaking have shaped subsequent policy developments. But while most prior studies concentrate on the *origins* of policy, I turn attention to the civic and social *consequences* that emerge through institutional arrangements. In the process, I develop a structured-governance approach to policy analysis, examining how citizens are incorporated into public policies administered through particular institutions that operate according to particular norms and procedures.

I am concerned in this book not only with outcomes, however, but also with the politics through which gender inequality became institutionalized in citizenship. Most scholarship on gender and welfare state development assumes a relatively direct correspondence between intentions of policymakers and policy outcomes. But New Deal policies were not simply the result of a deliberate or conscious agenda for elevating men's status and marginalizing women. Rather, citizenship was rendered gender specific through a complex interplay of decisions by policymakers, institutional factors, political imperatives, and the unintended consequences of policy design which emerged in the course of implementation.

Today, as the bounds of U.S. federalism and public policy are once again being negotiated, policy analysts need to consider the potential implications for civic and social life. Most Americans now disapprove of the sort of state-level policies established in the late nineteenth century and early twentieth, such as Jim Crow segregation laws and protective labor laws, which overtly treated people in distinct ways based on race or gender. Instead, they expect policymakers to foster at least a modicum of equality and community in public life. Yet even the best intentioned contemporary policymakers, acting without knowledge of the more subtle and complicated political dynamics that emerged with New Deal policies, are engaging in risky endeavors as they overhaul the welfare state. Their actions are threatening to structure governance, once again, in a way that stratifies the citizenry.

The intellectual contributions and moral support of many people have helped to bring this book to fruition. In my graduate training, Berenice Carroll at the University of Illinois and Mary Beth Norton at Cornell University taught me how to do "gender analysis" in a manner that takes history seriously. My initial training in American political development came from Martin Shefter, in his renowned course at Cornell. I am especially indebted to the committee members who supervised my dissertation: Theodore Lowi, who served as chair; Mary Katzenstein; Isaac Kramnick; and Elizabeth Sanders. Each of them offered valuable advice, careful criticism, and constant enthusiasm, and each one's scholarship has left an indelible mark on my analysis.

As I continued my research and transformed this project into a book, several colleagues at Syracuse University read parts or all of the manuscript and offered useful comments and suggestions. For such assistance, I especially thank Kristi Anderson, Rogan Kersh, Steve Macedo, and Marie Provine. My students in the Maxwell School of Citizenship and Public Affairs have listened patiently as I developed many of the ideas for this book, and I have learned a great deal from them as they have undertaken their own explorations of public policy and U.S. political development. Undergraduate research assistants hunted down numerous documents for me: my thanks go to Laura Jaworski, Bonnie Kordana, Clayton Rosati, Joseph Shanley, and Demietra Williams. One graduate student, McGee Young, rendered invaluable research assistance as I worked through the loose ends in the penultimate version.

Many scholars who work in the field of American political development have read portions of this manuscript, particularly in the form of conference papers that I presented over the past few years. For particularly useful comments that have contributed to the final version, I thank Judith Baer, Eileen Boris, Donald Brand, James MacGregor Burns, Vivien Hart, Marc Landy, Robert Lieberman, Joseph Luders, Gwendolyn Mink, Ann Shola Orloff, David Brian Robertson, and Rogers Smith. Three anonymous reviewers, who read an early draft of the manuscript, gave incisive comments and suggestions. As well, Richard Valelly offered his time with exceptional generosity, reading two full versions of the manuscript. I am especially grateful to him for his profound understanding of what I wanted to accomplish in this book and for the trenchant insights he provided to help make the final version approximate that hope.

Staff at several libraries and archives have lent assistance, including those at the National Archives in Washington, D.C., particularly at the College Park, Maryland, branch; the Franklin D. Roosevelt Library in Hyde Park, N.Y.; the Oral History Collection at Columbia University; the Labor-Management Documentation Center at Cornell University; and the Department of Special Collections at the University of Chicago Library. An Appleby-Mosher grant at Syracuse University helped to fund the research.

Peter Agree, my editor at Cornell University Press, believed in this book from its early stages, and his expertise and encouragement have enabled it to progress to its final form. Janet Mais performed a superb job of copyediting, and Teresa Jesionowski offered valuable advice as I made the last revisions.

Dear friends and family members have sustained me throughout. In particular, my sister, Jody, and her husband, Tony Bosnick, made my research trips to the National Archives a delight by welcoming me in their home for lengthy stints. My sisters Jeanne, Meg, and Sally lent moral support. My parents, John and Elinor Mettler, followed the progress of this book with the constant love and support they have always offered me. My daughter Sophie has grown simultaneously with the project, and she has made the period of working on it full of joy. Wayne Grove has influenced this book in countless ways, and he has given me steadfast encouragement and love. This book is dedicated to him.

SUZANNE METTLER

Syracuse, New York

Abbreviations Used in the Text and Notes

AALL	American Association of Labor Legislation
ACWA	Amalgamated Clothing Workers of America
ADC	Aid to Dependent Children
AFDC	Aid to Families with Dependent Children
AFL	American Federation of Labor
BPA	Bureau of Public Assistance
CCC	Civilian Conservation Corps
CES	Committee on Economic Security
CIO	Congress of Industrial Organizations
CWA	Civil Works Administration
ERA	Equal Rights Amendment
FDR	Franklin D. Roosevelt Library, Hyde Park, N.Y.
OF	Official File of the President
PPF	President's Personal File
PSF	President's Secretary's File
FERA	Federal Emergency Relief Administration
FLSA	Fair Labor Standards Act of 1938
FSA	Family Support Act of 1988
ILGWU	International Ladies Garment Workers' Union
LMDC	Labor-Management Documentation Center, Cornell University
NA	National Archives, Washington, D.C.
RG	Record Group
NCL	National Consumers' League
NLRA	National Labor Relations Act
NLRB	National Labor Relations Board
NRA	National Industrial Recovery Act
NRPB	National Resources Planning Board
OAA	Old Age Assistance

OAI	Old Age Insurance
OASI	Old Age and Survivors' Insurance
OHC	Oral History Collection, Columbia University
PWA	Public Works Administration
SSB	Social Security Board
SSI	Supplemental Security Income
UAW	United Auto Workers
UC	Regenstein Library, University of Chicago
UE	United Electrical, Radio, and Machine Workers of America
UI	Unemployment Insurance
WPA	Works Progress Administration
WTUL	Women's Trade Union League
YWCA	Young Women's Christian Association

CHAPTER ONE

Structured Governance and Citizenship in the New Deal

Next winter we may well undertake the great task of furthering the security of *the citizen and his family* through social insurance.
—President Franklin D. Roosevelt, "Message to Congress, June 8, 1934"

From the viewpoint of industrial democracy the pending measure will
offer to these unfortunate victims of our existing economic system an
opportunity to rise to *industrial citizenship.* . . . It marks the beginning
of an industrial bill of rights for workers as against industry, just as the
so-called Bill of Rights in our political Constitution guarantees personal
and civil liberties of the citizen or individual as against our State or Federal Governments.
—John L. Lewis, *Hearings on the Fair Labor Standards Act,* 1937

During the century and a half preceding the New Deal, under the unique
system of federalism hammered out at the Constitutional Convention of
1787, the actual content of American citizenship was defined primarily by
the individual states rather than by national government. State governments determined the rights and privileges and the duties and obligations
of those living within their borders by enacting the vast majority of policy
decisions that affected their residents' daily lives. They legislated on subjects as diverse as property, family, morality, education, commerce and
labor, banking, and criminal procedure. The national government was restricted from interfering in such activities because its powers were understood to be relatively limited, extending primarily to the promotion of
commercial activity through such means as subsidies and tariffs.[1] As a
patchwork of laws developed, the character of American citizenship evolved

[1] Edward S. Corwin, "The Passing of Dual Federalism," *Virginia Law Review* 36 (February 1965): 1–24; Theodore J. Lowi, *The Personal President* (Ithaca: Cornell University Press,
1985), p. 24; see also Harry N. Scheiber, "The Conditions of American Federalism: An His-
torian's View," in *American Intergovernmental Relations,* ed. Laurence J. O'Toole, Jr. (Washington, D.C.: Congressional Quarterly, 1993), pp. 67–74.

in a manner inextricably bound to the political geography of this variegated system of federalism.

National government began to acquire a role in the governance of the general welfare in the late nineteenth and early twentieth centuries, yet the primacy of states in shaping citizenship remained intact. The Fourteenth Amendment, ratified in 1868, seemed at first to nationalize the rights of citizenship, but within five years the Supreme Court denied that possibility.[2] Pensions for Civil War veterans and their dependents involved national government in what became a widespread and generous social policy, but patronage-style administration undercut the ability of the benefits to incorporate broad classes of Americans as social citizens.[3] In the early twentieth century, state builders with nationalizing tendencies worked to establish regulatory laws and agencies,[4] but the new federal police power clung to a fairly traditional, narrow understanding of national governing authority. In 1918, for example, the Court declared Congress's two-year-old prohibition on child labor to be an unconstitutional invasion of the affairs of the individual states.[5] Meanwhile, most social and labor policies from the Progressive Era, such as mothers' pensions and protective labor legislation, did not involve national government at all. They marked the elevation of responsibility for social citizenship upward from municipal to state

---

[2] In the *Slaughterhouse Cases* (1873), the Supreme Court interpreted the Fourteenth Amendment as pertaining solely to the rights of freed slaves and negated the broader power of the amendment. 16 Wallace 36 (1873). In subsequent decisions, such as *Plessy v. Ferguson*, 163 U.S. 537 (1896), which affirmed the establishment of "separate but equal" facilities as a valid use of a state's police powers, the meaning of the amendment became even more restricted. On national state-building and its possibilities and limitations for citizenship from the Civil War through the end of the nineteenth century, see esp. Robert J. Kaczorowski, "To Begin the Nation Anew: Congress, Citizenship, and Civil Rights after the Civil War," *American Historical Review* 92 (1987): 45–68. More generally, see Eric Foner, *Reconstruction: America's Unfinished Revolution, 1863–1877* (New York: Harper and Row, 1988), esp. pp. 18–34; Morton Keller, *Affairs of State: Public Life in Late Nineteenth Century America* (Cambridge: Harvard University Press, 1977), esp. chaps. 4 and 12; and Richard Franklin Bensel, *Yankee Leviathan: The Origins of Central State Authority in America, 1859–1877* (New York: Cambridge University Press, 1990). On the rise and fall of the Fifteenth Amendment as a means of nationalizing electoral rules during the era, see Richard M. Valelly, "Party, Coercion, and Inclusion: The Two Reconstructions of the South's Electoral Politics," *Politics and Society* 21 (1993): 37–67.

[3] Theda Skocpol, *Protecting Soldiers and Mothers: The Political Origins of Social Policy in the United States* (Cambridge: Harvard University Press, 1992), pp. 82–87, 102–51; see also Theodore J. Lowi, "American Business, Public Policy, Case Studies, and Political Theory," *World Politics* 16 (1964): 677–715.

[4] Stephen Skowronek, *Building a New American State: The Expansion of National Administrative Capacities, 1877–1920* (New York: Cambridge University Press, 1982); Robert H. Wiebe, *The Search for Order, 1877–1920* (New York: Hill and Wang, 1967), pp. 185–95.

[5] Alfred H. Kelly, Winfred A. Harbison, and Herman Belz, *The American Constitution: Its Origins and Development*, 7th ed. (New York: Norton, 1991), 2:416–19, 447–48; *Hammer v. Dagenhart*, 247 U.S. 251 (1918).

government but still conformed to tradition by varying both in form and in extent of implementation between and within individual states.

The New Deal constituted the decisive break of the American polity with the old regime of dual federalism, and the transformation toward a more centralized administrative state whose reach extended into the lives of ordinary citizens. Spurred by the worst depression in U.S. history and the demands of social movements that government respond to the crisis, New Deal policymakers sought to ease the plight of the sort of person President Roosevelt called the "forgotten man at the bottom of the economic pyramid"[6] by forging regulatory labor policies and redistributive social policies that would previously have been forbidden within institutions of the national government. Whereas even most political and civic dimensions of citizenship had been left to the individual states beforehand, in the New Deal the national government endowed Americans with new social and economic dimensions of citizenship. The right of workers to organize and to engage in collective bargaining was institutionalized under the National Labor Relations Act of 1935; social provisions for the unemployed, elderly, and solo mothers with children were solidified through the Social Security Act of 1935; and minimum wages were guaranteed by the Fair Labor Standards Act of 1938. New rights were accompanied by new obligations, of course, as citizens began to pay more taxes to national government to finance social programs and to tolerate the increased government intervention in private life that accompanied new regulatory policies. The metamorphosis embodied by such policies has been widely regarded a "constitutional revolution," a permanent expansion of the scope and an alteration of the subject matter of national government authority.[7]

These changes in governance beg the question, "How would the governing arrangements of the New Deal affect the character and experience of American citizenship?" This question inquires about a relationship among public policies, institutional arrangements, and society which has barely been explored despite the current interest in welfare state development and matters of citizenship generally. The dominant approach to policy analysis treats policy outcomes as simple reflections of the preferences of voters, politicians, or interest groups, with little heed to the role of institutional and political dynamics.[8] "New institutionalist" studies have challenged

---

[6] Franklin D. Roosevelt, *The Public Papers and Addresses of Franklin D. Roosevelt*, comp. Samuel I. Roseman (New York: Random House, 1938), 1:625.

[7] On the implications of New Deal administrative state development for party politics, see Sidney M. Milkis, *The President and the Parties: The Transformation of the American Party System since the New Deal* (New York: Oxford University Press, 1993).

[8] The formal model for this approach is presented in David L. Weimer and Aidan R. Vining, *Policy Analysis: Concepts and Practice*, 2d ed. (Englewood Cliffs, N.J.: Prentice-Hall, 1992).

this paradigm by demonstrating, through what Theda Skocpol calls "structured polity" analysis, how institutional arrangements, political processes, and historical precedents shape policy outcomes.[9] But while historical institutionalists have done much to explain the origins or determinants of public policies, less attention has been given to the civic and social consequences of policies.[10] This book thus seeks not only to explain much about the New Deal but, more important, to illuminate a vital and largely overlooked aspect of state-society relations: the implications of institutionalized patterns of governance for citizenship.

The structural arrangements through which policies are administered shape the character and experience of citizenship for those covered by the policies. Governance may legitimate the formation of certain social identities, determine the civic status attached to particular social roles, and produce particular organizational arrangements in society, creating unity or division among the citizenry. As well, governing arrangements can shape the extent and form of subsequent political activity by those affected by policies. This book aims to explain and describe these consequences of public policy through what can be termed *structured-governance analysis*.

As illustrated in Figure 1, this approach examines how citizens are incorporated within public policies designed in certain ways and administered through institutions that operate according to distinct norms and procedures, and the civic and social implications that result. The questions used to probe the relationship between policy design and institutional administrative arrangements are: On what basis is the policy bestowed on individuals? Who is included and who is not? How is the policy administered? What organizational arrangements are used? What manner of rules and procedures are applied? Through what political processes are such

---

[9] Skocpol, *Protecting Soldiers and Mothers*, pp. 41–60. For additional studies of American welfare state development in this vein, see Theda Skocpol and John Ikenberry, "The Political Formation of the American Welfare State in Historical and Comparative Perspective," *Comparative Social Research* 6 (1983): 87–148; Theda Skocpol and Kenneth Finegold, "State Capacity and Economic Intervention in the Early New Deal," *Political Science Quarterly* 97 (1982): 255–78; Ann Shola Orloff, "The Political Origins of America's Belated Welfare State," in *The Politics of Social Policy in the United States*, ed. Margaret Weir, Ann Shola Orloff, and Theda Skocpol (Princeton: Princeton University Press, 1988), pp. 37–80; and *The Politics of Pensions* (Madison: University of Wisconsin Press, 1993); Theda Skocpol and Edwin Amenta, "Did Capitalists Shape Social Security," *American Sociological Review* 50 (1985): 572–75; and Margaret Weir, *Politics and Jobs:The Boundaries of Employment Policy in the United States* (Princeton: Princeton University Press, 1992).

[10] Several of the studies in note 9 do explore one dimension of how "policies shape politics": through "policy feedback," policy officials build incrementally on preexisting policies or reject policies that resemble past failures. Yet to be explored are the wider array of dynamics that occur when policy acts as an independent variable, with consequences not only for policy officials but for civil society more generally. On this point, see Paul Pierson, "When Effect Becomes Cause: Policy Feedback and Political Change," *World Politics* 45 (July 1993): 595–628.

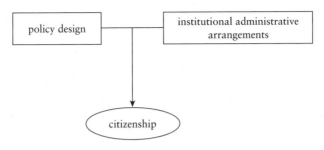

Figure 1. Structured governance

measures defined? What is the locus of subsequent policy development?
What are the mechanisms for such development? Combined, the answers
to these questions can reveal how groups of people are incorporated within
the polity, shaping the character of civic and social life.

The task that constitutes the body of this book is the examination of the
formation and early implementation of key social and labor policies of
the New Deal which have endured through much of the twentieth century:
the major components of the Social Security Act, including Old Age Insurance (OAI), Old Age Assistance (OAA), Unemployment Insurance (UI),
and Aid to Dependent Children (ADC), as well the Fair Labor Standards
Act (FLSA).[11] These case studies reveal that through the New Deal, American citizenship, specifically in its social and economic dimensions, became
divided by two distinct forms of governance separated in terms of gender.
Men, particularly white men, were endowed with national citizenship as
they were incorporated into policies to be administered through standardized, routinized procedures by the national government, such as OAI and
the FLSA. New Deal policymakers built several programs, however, atop
the traditional arrangements of federalism, retaining and in many ways
bolstering the important role of state and local governance.[12] Women and
minority men were the persons most typically relegated to those social and
labor policies to be administered primarily by the individual states, such as
the grants-in-aid public assistance programs, OAA and ADC, as well as
protective labor legislation for women beyond the reach of the FLSA. Divided citizenship emerged as white men were incorporated into the uniform domain of national government and women and nonwhite men were

[11] In 1939, OAI was amended to become Old Age and Survivors' Insurance (OASI) and
later, in 1956, to include disability insurance (OASDI). It is now generally referred to simply
as "social security." In 1974, OAA was merged with state programs for the blind and disabled
to become the Supplemental Security Income (SSI) program. ADC became known as Aid to
Families with Dependent Children (AFDC) and survived until it was abolished in 1996.

[12] Barry D. Karl, *The Uneasy State: The United States from 1915 to 1945* (Chicago: University of Chicago Press, 1983).

left under the auspices of the states, subject to highly variable forms of citizenship inherently tied to the politics of place.

The New Deal as a case reveals much about the role of institutions and public policies in relation to American citizenship. This book, then, is like an onion with its layers embedded each within another. The largest argument of the book is that public policies and governing institutions shape citizenship in critical ways, most centrally by organizing the incorporation of citizens within the polity. The second argument follows: U.S. federalism, as illustrated by the New Deal case, has had tremendous implications for citizenship by enabling distinct forms of governance to coexist and by constraining state-level citizenship in particular ways.

Peel off these outer layers, and the two central arguments of the book are found. First, New Deal policymakers and administrative officials shaped social and labor policies in some gender-specific ways. They reflexively incorporated gendered traditions of policymaking inherited from the Progressive Era and, in the course of implementation, elevated programs that targeted men to the detriment of programs in which women found coverage. Second, policymakers shaped policies in a manner that partially transformed federalism. Through the overlapping of gender-specific designs with national policy plans on the one hand and state-administered strategies on the other, two distinct forms of citizenship, inscribed by gender, were established. Then, in the course of implementation, divided—and unequal—citizenship emerged, carrying with it important implications for the status of men and women in U.S. democracy.

Inlaid within these arguments are explanations of the politics of New Deal policymaking and implementation. Divided citizenship and the gendered character of the New Deal were the result of a combination of intended and unintended consequences of policymaking efforts, influenced by the predominant focus of New Dealers on replacing the wages of unemployed male breadwinners; the battle between old-guard policymakers partial to state-level administrative authority and a new guard favoring uniform, national standards; the side effects of efforts in Congress to preserve "states' rights" and local autonomy; and the dynamics of policy implementation in a highly decentralized governing system.

At its heart, this book takes a stand on the nature of American political development. Contrary to the predominant interpretations of the United States as dominated, for good or ill, by liberalism, this retelling of the New Deal reveals the perpetuation, long after the "constitutional revolution," of a nonliberal realm of governance.[13] The individual states served tradition-

---

[13] This perspective on American political development bears close resemblance to those articulated by Rogers M. Smith, "Beyond Tocqueville, Myrdal, and Hartz: The Multiple Traditions in America," *American Political Science Review* 87 (1993): 549–66; and Karen Orren, *Belated Feudalism: Labor, Law and Liberal Development in the United States* (New York: Cambridge University Press, 1991).

ally as the political institutions wherein nonliberal rule could most easily flourish, and has tended to do so most readily. Throughout much of American history, the states have functioned as safe havens for community values, preserving local, ascriptive versions of the social order and values at odds with individual rights. Even in the Progressive Era, when some states developed precocious social policies that rewarded the civic value of women's work as mothers, they tended to condition eligibility on narrowly defined cultural models of the "good citizen" or "good mother" rather than to apply broad, rights-based standards. Though many policymakers in the Roosevelt administration and executive branch agencies intended otherwise, New Deal policies actually empowered state governments, throughout the mid-twentieth century, to extend the reach of their nonliberal rule. In the 1960s and 1970s, policymakers acted to broaden national citizenship to incorporate persons previously excluded, and the particularities of state-level governance faded as the states improved their administrative capacities and were pushed to comply with stronger national standards. At century's close, however, the patterns of citizenship divided by gender seem reinvigorated once again, as governance in particular policy areas is being restored to the states.

Understanding Citizenship

In the contemporary United States, the revitalized interest in matters of citizenship has been guided predominantly by a society-centered model that gives little attention to the governing context in which citizens dwell. Seeking to understand what prevents modern citizens from being sufficiently "civic minded," scholars have focused on how different forms of societal arrangements, education, or values might prompt greater engagement in public life. Robert Putnam, for example, probes for the causes of a seeming malaise in civil society which is characterized by declining social trust and involvement in civic associations.[14] Educators and some social scientists investigate how to develop curricula to educate students to become "good citizens."[15] Benjamin Barber argues for a shift in values to

---

[14] Robert D. Putnam, "Tuning In, Tuning Out: The Strange Disappearance of Social Capital in America," *PS: Political Science and Politics* 28 (1995): 664–83; see also Michael Walzer, "The Civil Society Argument," in *Theorizing Citizenship*, ed. Ronald Beiner (Albany: State University of New York Press, 1995), pp. 153–74.

[15] Ernest L. Boyer and Fred M. Hechinger, *Higher Learning in the Nation's Service* (Washington, D.C.: Carnegie Foundation for the Advancement of Teaching, 1981); Bernard Murchland, ed., *Higher Education and the Practice of Democratic Politics* (Dayton: Kettering Foundation, 1991); Suzanne W. Morse, *Renewing Civic Capacity: Preparing College Students for Service and Citizenship* (Washington, D.C.: ERIC Clearinghouse on Higher Education, 1989); Paul Gagnon, *Democracy's Half-Told Story* (Washington, D.C.: American Federation of Teachers, 1989).

enable the development of "strong democracy," a participatory form of politics in which citizens would actively engage in deliberation over public issues.[16] Citizenship is most typically construed, in other words, as if it were a commodity generated solely and voluntarily by society, as a function of associational activity and collective values. Strikingly absent in this portrayal of citizenship is what Stephen Skowronek refers to as a "sense of the state."[17]

Citizenship is, fundamentally, a relationship between citizens and government. Therefore, besides asking about whether people participate in public life, scholars need to investigate how governance affects citizenship.[18] Citizenship is shaped and defined, after all, by public policies and institutional arrangements through which rights and privileges are bestowed on citizens, duties and obligations are imposed on them, and public life is organized. On the basis of their particular design and coverage, public policies function to provide citizens with what Lawrence Mead calls an "operational definition of citizenship," or what Marc Landy terms "a civic teaching."[19] They do this, write Helen Ingram and Anne Schneider, by conveying important messages to citizens about "what government is supposed to do, which citizens are deserving and undeserving, and what sorts of participation is appropriate in democratic societies."[20] Equally important, but most overlooked in contemporary analyses of citizenship, governance is carried out in the context of particular political institutions, and those institutions serve to organize the citizenry in certain ways, to provide a particular context for the implementation of policies, and to shape the path of subsequent policy development.[21]

The significance of governance for citizenship can be studied effectively,

---

[16] Benjamin Barber, *Strong Democracy: Participatory Politics for a New Age* (Berkeley: University of California Press, 1984).

[17] Skowronek, *Building a New American State*, p. 3.

[18] For a related argument, see Theda Skocpol, "Unravelling from Above," *American Prospect* (March–April 1996): 20–25. See also Lowi's call to examine how "policy shapes politics" in his "American Business, Public Policy" and a call to examine how "policies shape citizenship" by Steven Rathgeb Smith and Helen Ingram, "Public Policy and Democracy," in *Public Policy for Democracy*, ed. Helen Ingram and Steve Rathgeb Smith (Washington, D.C.: Brookings, 1993), pp. 1–17.

[19] Lawrence Mead, *Beyond Entitlement: The Social Obligations of Citizenship* (New York: Free Press, 1986), p. 7; Marc Landy, "Public Policy and Citizenship," in *Public Policy for Democracy*, ed. Ingram and Smith, p. 26.

[20] Helen Ingram and Anne Schneider, "Constructing Citizenship: The Subtle Messages of Policy Design," in *Public Policy for Democracy*, ed. Ingram and Smith, p. 68.

[21] Institutionalists have pointed scholars in this direction; see Theda Skocpol, "Bringing the State Back In," in *Bringing the State Back In*, ed. Peter B. Evans, Dietrich Rueschemeyer, and Theda Skocpol (Cambridge: Cambridge University Press, 1985), pp. 3–37; Margaret Weir, Ann Shola Orloff, and Theda Skocpol, "Introduction: Understanding American Social Policies," in *Politics of Social Policy*, ed. Weir, Orloff, and Skocpol, pp. 16–27; and James G. March and Johan P. Olsen, *Rediscovering Institutions: The Organizational Basis of Politics* (New York: Free Press, 1989).

therefore, by examining how public policies and institutional arrangements organize the citizenry and shape the meaning and character of citizenship. First, and most fundamental, naturalization and immigration policies define the *membership* of the citizenry, thus establishing the boundaries of the political community.[22] Second, policies shape *participation* among citizens, affecting the character of their participation in public life. Whereas some policies might encourage citizens to act as rights-bearing individuals, others might render them "dependents" on the state, without a sense of obligation or agency in the public realm.[23] Third, governance affects what can be called *incorporation*, the manner and extent to which people are included, consolidated, and organized as members of the political community.[24] "Incorporation," a fundamental task of state-building, encompasses what has been identified by Judith Shklar as "inclusion" in the political community and by T. H. Marshall as a three-step process through which civil, political, and social rights are extended.[25] A critical dimension of incorporation and the central concern of this book is "social citizenship," meaning citizens' entitlement, as an extension of their membership in the political community, to the basic necessities of economic security and social well-being.[26]

Some contemporary scholars portray "rights" and "access," aspects of incorporation, as if they were unrelated, or even contradictory to other qualities of citizenship they perceive as most essential, such as "participation" or "obligation."[27] Yet incorporation establishes the very basis on which citizens can participate in public life at all. Inclusion in the citizenry

[22] See Rogers M. Smith, *Civic Ideals: Conflicting Visions of Citizenship in U.S. History* (New Haven: Yale University Press, 1997); Virginia Sapiro, "Women, Citizenship, and Nationality: Immigration and Naturalization Policies in the United States," *Politics and Society* 13 (1984): 1–26; and Candice Dawn Bredbenner, "Toward Independent Citizenship: Married Women's Nationality Rights in the United States, 1855–1937" (Ph.D. diss., University of Virginia, 1990).

[23] See the essays in Ingram and Smith, *Public Policy for Democracy*, most notably Landy, "Public Policy and Citizenship," pp. 19–44; Ingram and Schneider, "Constructing Citizenship," pp. 68–94; Sallie A. Marston, "Citizen Action Programs and Participatory Politics in Tucson," pp. 119–35; and Richard M. Valelly, "Public Policy for Reconnected Citizenship," pp. 241–67. See also Robert B. Reich, "Policy Making in a Democracy," in *The Power of Public Ideas*, ed. Robert B. Reich (Cambridge: Harvard University Press, 1988), pp. 123–56; Michael Sandel, *Democracy's Discontent: America in Search of a Public Philosophy* (Cambridge: Harvard University Press, 1996); and Mead, *Beyond Entitlement*.

[24] Francisco Ramirez and Jane Weiss, "The Political Incorporation of Women," in *National Development and the World System*, ed. John W. Meyer and Michael T. Hannan (Chicago: University of Chicago Press, 1979), pp. 238–39.

[25] Judith N. Shklar, *American Citizenship: The Quest for Inclusion* (Cambridge: Harvard University Press, 1991); T. H. Marshall, "Citizenship and Social Class," in *Class, Citizenship, and Social Development* (New York: Doubleday, 1965), pp. 65–122.

[26] Marshall, "Citizenship and Social Class."

[27] For the fullest articulation of this view, see Sandel, *Democracy's Discontent*; see also Mead, *Beyond Entitlement*.

may not, as noted by Jürgen Habermas, be sufficient to compel participation, but it is nonetheless an essential prerequisite with various implications for civic life.[28]

First, the manner in which groups of citizens are incorporated into the nation imbues them with a particular form of *status* or, in Shklar's terminology, "standing" in society, as members of the political community. Full inclusion in such aspects of citizenship as the suffrage, for example, bestows public respect on citizens.[29] Broad standards for social citizenship are a critical dimension of democracy, assuring citizens of not only a modicum of well-being but also a measure of dignity that is understood to befit those with the franchise.[30] As Michael Walzer explains, "Communal provision [of security and welfare] . . . teaches us the value of membership" in the community.[31]

Second, the incorporation of citizens in turn shapes the *organization* of the citizenry. Broad incorporation may unite citizens in the polity, fostering the shared identity and sense of solidarity so essential, particularly in a diverse and multicultural society, to community life, political allegiance, and social peace.[32] Alternatively, narrow or differentiated incorporation can stratify and divide the citizenry into groups that understand their place in public life to be distinct from that of others, promoting the pursuit of self-interest over the common good. Incorporation of social citizens involves not only the extension of rights and privileges but the bestowal of obligations and duties as well, and the balance between those may vary for different groups within the polity.[33]

---

[28] Jürgen Habermas, "Citizenship and National Identity," in *Theorizing Citizenship*, ed. Beiner, p. 268.

[29] Shklar, *American Citizenship*, p. 2.

[30] Reflections on the relationship between social standards and solidarity within the polity appear in Fred Block, "Social Policy and Accumulation: A Critique of the New Consensus," in *Stagnation and Renewal in Social Policy: The Rise and Fall of Policy Regimes*, ed. Martin Rein, Gosta Esping-Andersen, and Lee Rainwater (Armonk, N.Y.: Sharpe, 1987); Albert O. Hirshman, *The Rhetoric of Reaction* (Cambridge: Harvard University Press, 1991); and Theda Skocpol, "The Limits of the New Deal System and the Roots of Contemporary Welfare Dilemmas," in *Politics of Social Policy*, ed. Weir, Orloff, and Skocpol, esp. pp. 307–11.

[31] Michael Walzer, *Spheres of Justice* (New York: Basic Books, 1983), p. 64.

[32] Ronald Beiner, "Why Citizenship Constitutes a Theoretical Problem in the Last Decade of the Twentieth Century," pp. 1–28, and Will Kymlicka and Wayne Norman, "Return of the Citizen: A Survey of Recent Work on Citizenship Theory," pp. 283–322, both in *Theorizing Citizenship*, ed. Beiner.

[33] Gosta Esping-Andersen, *The Three Worlds of Welfare Capitalism* (Princeton: Princeton University Press, 1990); Marilyn Lake, guest ed., "Citizenship: Intersections of Gender, Race, and Ethnicity," special issue of *Social Politics* 2 (summer 1995); Ann Shola Orloff, "Gender and the Social Rights of Citizenship: The Comparative Analyses of Gender Relations and Welfare States," *American Sociological Review* 58 (1993): 303–28; Ursula Vogel, "Is Citizenship Gender-Specific?" in *The Frontiers of Citizenship*, ed. Ursula Vogel and Michael Moran (New York: St. Martin's, 1991); Diane Sainsbury, ed., *Gendering Welfare States* (London: Sage, 1994).

Third, incorporation establishes the ground on which *participation* in the polity occurs and affects the form it takes. For example, as shown by Theda Skocpol, the early universal suffrage of men in the United States affected participation by promoting gender-specific political identities and activism on the part of men and women in the late nineteenth and early twentieth centuries.[34] In other words, the stratified incorporation of men and women in the polity in turn fostered different forms of participation.

To understand how citizens have been incorporated through American citizenship, key public policies must be examined with particular attention to both historical, political development and the institutional context for policy implementation. Some scholars have begun to sketch the idiosyncratic historical development of inclusion with particular attention to divisions of race and gender.[35] They observe that African Americans remained in slavery until the 1860s and were not fully incorporated through civil and political rights until the 1960s; women achieved the vote in 1920, only after seventy years of struggle, and remnants of the common-law principle of coverture remained in place into the twentieth century, limiting the basic civil rights of married women.[36] Scholars have yet to examine, however, the significance of political institutions for the incorporation of citizens. Inclusion in the polity through distinct political institutions, each organized in particular ways and governed according to varying rules and procedures, may accentuate stratification of the citizenry in terms of gender, race, or class.

Citizenship and American Federalism

The arrangements of American federalism, according to many scholars, enhance the participatory dimensions of citizenship. Federalism provides multiple loci for political mobilization and participation and can thus foster policy development in a uniquely decentralized fashion. Theda Skocpol,

---

[34] Skocpol, *Protecting Soldiers and Mothers*, pp. 47–57.

[35] Eileen Boris, "The Racialized Gendered State: Construction of Citizenship in the United States," *Social Politics* 2 (summer 1995): 160–80; Nancy Fraser and Linda Gordon, "Civil Citizenship against Social Citizenship? On the Ideology of Contract-versus-Charity," in *The Condition of Citizenship*, ed. Bart van Steenbergen (London: Sage, 1994), pp. 90–107; Jill Quadagno, *The Color of Welfare: How Racism Undermined the War on Poverty* (New York: Oxford University Press, 1994), pp. 17–31.

[36] Linda K. Kerber, "A Constitutional Right to Be Treated Like Ladies: Women and the Obligations of Citizenship," in *U.S. History as Women's History: New Feminist Essays*, ed. Linda K. Kerber, Alice Kessler-Harris, and Kathryn Kish Sklar (Chapel Hill: University of North Carolina Press, 1995), pp. 17–35; Rogers M. Smith, "'One United People': Second-Class Female Citizenship and the American Quest for Community," *Yale Journal of Law and Humanities* 1 (1989): 229–93.

for example, has detailed in *Protecting Soldiers and Mothers* how "widespread federated interests" in the United States have worked precisely through the federal structure to promote the development of social policies, especially mothers' pensions and protective labor legislation, across the individual states.[37] Richard Valelly has shown how federalism, at least into the 1930s, provided a ripe climate for state-level radicalism by third parties, and such parties helped spur the development and implementation of public policies.[38] From the Progressive Era to the present, many have lauded the states as "laboratories of democracy" that permit policy experimentation as well as the adaptation of nationally planned programs to local purposes.

But although decentralized governing arrangements may provide multiple points of access for the participatory dimensions of citizenship, the incorporation of citizens in the context of American federalism has tended to undercut possibilities for full inclusion, in turn curtailing more complete opportunities for participation in public life. This becomes evident when policy analysis turns from the deliberative and formative stages of policymaking amid state-level governance to policy outcomes. For example, though the movement for mothers' pensions studied by Skocpol did indeed spread "like wildfire," the implementation of such laws proved much less auspicious. Although forty-five states had enacted mothers' pensions laws by 1934, fewer than half of the local units empowered to administer the statutes actually had programs in operation.[39] Those programs that were in effect made assistance conditional on the willingness of recipients, often immigrant women, to adapt to restrictive cultural norms of child rearing and housekeeping that were measured through "fit-mother" and "suitable-home" criteria.[40] The particular manner in which these state-level programs extended social citizenship to women, then, failed to provide them with a sufficient means to inclusion in public life, and it constrained beneficiaries to a role in the polity that was attached to their ascribed status as mothers.

Social citizenship determined by the states, judging by its ability to incorporate citizens on a broad and equal basis, has generally tended to be

---

[37] Skocpol, *Protecting Soldiers and Mothers*, pp. 54–57; see also Samuel H. Beer, "The Modernization of American Federalism," *Publius* 3 (fall 1973): 49–95, and, "Federalism, Nationalism, and Democracy in America," *American Political Science Review* 72 (1978): 9–21; and Jack L. Walker, "The Diffusion of Innovations among the American States," ibid. 63 (1969): 880–99.

[38] Richard M. Valelly, *Radicalism in the States: The Minnesota Farmer-Labor Party and the American Political Economy* (Chicago: University of Chicago Press, 1989).

[39] See Eveline Burns, *Toward Social Security* (New York: McGraw-Hill, 1936), pp. 111–12.

[40] Gwendolyn Mink, *The Wages of Motherhood: Inequality in the Welfare State, 1917–1942* (Ithaca: Cornell University Press, 1995).

inferior to social citizenship with national standards for eligibility and administration. If political parties or associations are well organized and active at the state level, as in the case of the Townsend movement in western states and the labor movement in various states in the late 1930s and 1940s, they may be able to promote successful policy development and implementation.[41] More typically, however, when social and labor policies have been left in the hands of states and localities, standards have been lowered or neglected in more areas than not. Other nations characterized by federalism have also developed social programs later, more slowly, and less completely than nations with more centralized governing arrangements, but particular aspects of U.S. federalism have served to accentuate those tendencies.[42]

Political-institutional factors explain some of the differences in national and state-level citizenship in the United States. Contrary to the pervasive assumption that decentralized governance is more democratic than centralized governance, the states in the U.S. system, well into the twentieth century, often fostered domination of the political process by narrow interests. At the national level, by contrast, such factions were, at least on occasion, countered and diffused. E. E. Schattschneider and Grant McConnell suggested a connection between, on the one hand, the relatively small size of the constituency and scope of conflict in the American states and, on the other hand, limitations on the expansion of democracy in the context of U.S. federalism.[43] But McConnell and Schattschneider neglected to identify a significant institutional feature primarily at the disposal of the states in that era, which combined with their narrow political scope to give state governance an inherently inegalitarian character: the police power.

The U.S. constitutional system traditionally endowed the states with the police power, a governing capacity with communitarian roots that predate liberal conceptions of the rule of law. "Policing" in the eighteenth century meant promoting the public good or the life of the community as opposed to the modern emphasis on maintaining order and preserving security.[44]

---

[41] This theme emerges in Chapters 4 and 6. See also Valelly, *Radicalism in the States*, and Edwin Amenta et al., "The Political Origins of Unemployment Insurance in Five American States," *Studies in American Political Development* 2 (1987): 137–82.

[42] Robert T. Kudrle and Theodore R. Marmor, "The Development of Welfare States in North America," in *The Development of Welfare States in Europe and America*, ed. Peter Flora and Arnold J. Heidenheimer (New Brunswick: Transaction Books, 1982), pp. 81–121.

[43] E. E. Schattschneider, *The Semisovereign People* (New York: Holt, Rinehart and Winston, 1960), pp. 1–19; Grant McConnell, *Private Power and American Democracy* (New York: Knopf, 1966), esp. pp. 3–8, 91–118, 166–95.

[44] Christopher L. Tomlins, "Law, Police, and the Pursuit of Happiness in the New American Republic," *Studies in American Political Development* 4 (1990): 3–34; William J. Novak, *Intellectual Origins of the State Police Power: The Common Law Vision of a Well-Regulated Society*, Legal History Program, Working Papers, ser. 3 (Madison: University of Wisconsin, Institute for Legal Studies, 1989).

Defined by the mid-nineteenth-century Taney Court as the power to "provide for the public health, safety, and good order" of the community, the police power was interpreted broadly as a "sovereign power" reserved to the states by the Tenth Amendment.[45] Acting on the police power, state legislatures proceeded to define the rights and obligations of those citizens living within their boundaries by creating a broad and eclectic patchwork of laws.[46] But as neither the Bill of Rights nor the Fourteenth Amendment was understood as applying to the states except in the most narrow circumstances, states were relatively unrestrained in their application of the police power.[47] Without liberal guarantees of rights, the potentially communitarian character of life in the states easily dissolved into arrangements that more closely resembled feudalism.

By exercising the police power within a narrow scope of conflict, states tended to become separate and distinct political communities that functioned to preserve the social order—in a multitude of ways—rather than to promote equality. The police power was used effectively and with the approval of the Supreme Court to uphold the dominant social system and political-economic relations within individual states. Maintaining racial segregation under the Jim Crow laws, for example, was justified as an appropriate exercise of the police power.[48] In keeping with the police power, state legislation designed to address the social and economic situation of women tended to be designed in a paternalistic manner. Thus though laws such as Married Women's Property Acts and protective labor legislation were created to improve women's individual lives, they served to institutionalize women's marginal status in society and politics.[49] The states retained their capacity to exercise the police power in a fairly autonomous fashion until the late 1950s and 1960s, when they were restrained by various reforms and court decisions at the national level.

Besides the political-institutional factors, the willingness of the states to enact and carry out broad and inclusive social and labor policies has been and continues to be restrained by the political-economic features of U.S.

---

[45] David B. Walker, *The Rebirth of Federalism* (Chatham, N.J.: Chatham House, 1995), p. 69.

[46] Corwin, "Passing of Dual Federalism"; Scheiber, "Conditions of American Federalism."

[47] Under the traditional system of dual federalism, Americans were formerly considered dual citizens: citizens of both national and state governments, as established by *Barron v. Baltimore*, 7 Peters 243 (1833). The decision was interpreted to mean that the Bill of Rights did not apply to state or local governments. On the limited interpretation of the Fourteenth Amendment before the 1950s, see Kelly, Harbison, and Belz, *American Constitution*, 2:355–61, 689–90.

[48] *Plessy v. Ferguson*, 163 U.S. 537 (1896); C. Vann Woodward, *The Strange Career of Jim Crow*, 3d rev. ed. (New York: Oxford University Press, 1974), pp. 97–102.

[49] Joan Hoff, *Law, Gender, and Injustice* (New York: New York University Press, 1991), pp. 127–31; Smith, "'One United People,'" pp. 249, 253; *Muller v. Oregon*, 208 U.S. 412 (1908); Alice Kessler-Harris, *Out to Work* (New York: Oxford University Press, 1982), pp. 194, 205–14.

federalism. As observed by David B. Robertson and Dennis R. Judd, the Constitution created "the world's largest 'free trade' zone," inasmuch as the individual states lack the power either to prevent businesses from entering and leaving their borders or, unlike the national government, to protect businesses within their borders.[50] Rather, states must compete with one another to establish a favorable "business climate" in order to attract and retain businesses. Thus, even in celebrated periods of social reform at the state level, most notably the Progressive Era, the majority of states have been reluctant to implement policies that may act or be perceived as acting to increase the cost of doing business within their boundaries.[51] As Paul Peterson has shown, when states administer redistributive policies, they tend to neglect standards as they engage in a "race to the bottom," competing to make benefits less generous in amount and more punitive in form. They fear becoming "welfare magnets," or being considered as such by businesses. National government, in contrast, does not have to be as concerned about the outward flow of capital, and it has a greater taxing power than the states. National government is thus far better positioned than state or municipal governments to administer redistributive policies.[52]

In sum, the states have, historically, tended to incorporate citizens in a manner inferior to that of national government. Governance left to the states has been particularly disadvantageous for groups that are relatively lacking in political power. Without the requirements of national standards for eligibility and administration, state-level policies have often institutionalized social and economic inequalities. And when some citizens have been incorporated as national citizens and others as state-level citizens, fragmentation has been inscribed in the heart of the American polity. Such were the implications of the New Deal in terms of gender.

Dividing Citizens in the New Deal

Most scholarship on the implications of New Deal governance has concentrated on how the new regime affected organized labor, a predominantly male domain in the 1930s.[53] A growing body of literature contends

---

[50] David B. Robertson and Dennis R. Judd, *The Development of American Public Policy: The Structure of Policy Restraint* (Glenview, Ill.: Scott, Foresman, 1989), p. 31.

[51] David Brian Robertson, "The Bias of American Federalism: The Limits of Welfare-State Development in the Progressive Era," *Journal of Policy History* 1 (1989): 261–91; William Graebner, "Federalism in the Progressive Era: A Structural Interpretation of Reform," *Journal of American History* 54 (1977): 331–57.

[52] Paul E. Peterson, "Who Should Do What? Divided Responsibility in the Federal System," *Brookings Review* (spring 1995): 6–11, and *City Limits* (Chicago: University of Chicago Press, 1981).

[53] See, e.g., Steve Fraser and Gary Gerstle, eds., *The Rise and Fall of the New Deal Order, 1930–1980* (Princeton: Princeton University Press, 1989); Melvyn Dubofsky, ed., *The New Deal: Conflicting Interpretations and Shifting Perspectives* (New York: Garland, 1992); and

that the welfare state developed in a manner that was "gendered": imbued by particular ideas regarding the proper social organization of sexual difference, such that men and women were treated differently in the policy-making process, with ascribed gender roles and gender inequality perpetuated.[54] The topic of gender and the New Deal welfare state has received surprisingly little attention, but some studies of earlier periods of state building, primarily the Progressive Era, do discuss the implications for New Deal developments.[55]

These analyses show how ideologies rooted in particular views about gender were dominant in shaping New Deal social and labor policies. Specifically, the authors indicate how policies from the Progressive Era served as the foundation on which New Deal policies were built, with the effect of perpetuating beliefs and norms about gender organization inherited from an earlier era. In her intellectual history of U.S. social policy-making, for example, Linda Gordon argues that a female-dominated, social work–oriented, "maternalist" strain of social provision was predominant in the Progressive Era, as epitomized by the creation of mothers' pensions and a maternal and child health program, whereas in the New Deal a "male vision" of social insurance–style policies was central, and the maternalist policies were marginalized.[56] Gwendolyn Mink has shown how the culturally prescriptive character of maternalist policies in the Progressive Era was woven into ADC in the New Deal.[57] In her book on the politics of industrial homework, Eileen Boris traces how cultural interpretations about the proper arrangements of social life have been definitive in shaping a gendered framework for policymaking over the past century, including during the New Deal.[58]

Colin Gordon, *New Deals: Business, Labor, and Politics in America, 1920–1935* (New York: Cambridge University Press, 1994).

[54] For a comprehensive review of this literature, see Ann Shola Orloff, "Gender in the Welfare State," *American Sociological Review* 22 (1996): 51–78.

[55] For book-length studies that include examinations of the New Deal, see Eileen Boris, *Home to Work: Motherhood and the Politics of Industrial Homework in the United States* (New York: Cambridge University Press, 1994); Linda Gordon, *Pitied but Not Entitled: Single Mothers and the History of Welfare, 1890–1935* (New York: Free Press, 1994); Mink, *The Wages of Motherhood*; and Mimi Abramovitz, *Regulating the Lives of Women: Social Welfare Policy from Colonial Times to the Present* (Boston: South End Press, 1988).

[56] Gordon, *Pitied but Not Entitled*; see also Robyn Muncy, *Creating a Female Dominion in American Reform, 1890–1935* (New York: Oxford University Press, 1991); and Alice Kessler-Harris, "Designing Women and Old Fools: The Construction of the Social Security Amendments of 1939," in *U.S. History as Women's History*, ed. Kerber, Kessler-Harris, and Sklar, pp. 87–106. The term *maternalist* refers to reform efforts in the early twentieth century which were conducted by women and which sought to establish social provision for women in their role as mothers. Some also use the term *paternalist* to refer to simultaneous efforts by men to establish social and labor policies for men in their role as breadwinners. These distinctions are treated more thoroughly in Chapter 2.

[57] Mink, *Wages of Motherhood*; see also Molly Ladd-Taylor, *Mother-Work: Women, Child Welfare, and the State, 1890–1930* (Urbana: University of Illinois Press, 1994).

[58] Boris, *Home to Work*.

These rich contributions to the literature on gender and policy development raise "gender analysis" to a new level of sophistication, but their focus—how ideas about gender shape policy and thus produce gendered effects—does not fully illuminate how policymaking and governance shape citizenship in terms of gender. In fact, the politics of New Deal policymaking had less to do with gendered battles over policy priorities than with seemingly "gender-neutral" debates over the shape of policy design and the institutional framework for American politics, namely, federalism. Yet, nonetheless, the welfare state that emerged was inherently gendered. This demonstrates that although some aspects of policy outcomes can be traced directly to the ideas and intentions of policymakers, policies are also affected by critical political and institutional factors in the policymaking context, by particular features of policy design, and by the institutional context of the implementation process. Thus, political debates and institutional dynamics that might appear to have little to do with gender can still affect state development and policy outcomes in "gendered" ways, albeit indirectly and unintentionally.[59]

Political and institutional analysis is particularly necessary for understanding how New Deal policies shaped citizenship in terms of gender. First, whereas earlier in the century, male and female social reformers and policy officials had worked quite separately from one another, the divide between maternalists and paternalists had blurred significantly by the 1930s. Franklin D. Roosevelt appointed an unprecedented number of women to key posts in his administration.[60] For example, Frances Perkins, who as secretary of labor was the first woman cabinet member in U.S. history, spearheaded the formation of all the critical New Deal social and labor policies examined in this book. Besides the fact that women played a critical role in shaping public assistance–type programs in the New Deal, continuing the Progressive Era maternalist tradition, social insurance plans were also engineered by a woman, Barbara Nachtrieb Armstrong. Second, unlike Progressive Era policies, which tended to be very rigidly gender-identified, New Deal policies were characterized for the most part by gender-neutral language and somewhat less definitive ideas about men's and women's proper roles in society. Earlier in the century, the Supreme Court had defined male workers as "independent" and able to take care

---

[59] Only a few examples in the literature on gender and public policy illustrate this perspective, namely, Vivien Hart, *Bound by Our Constitution: Women, Workers, and the Minimum Wage* (Princeton: Princeton University Press, 1994); Theda Skocpol and Gretchen Ritter, "Gender and the Origins of Modern Social Policies in Britain and the United States," *Studies in American Political Development* 5 (1991): 36–93; Skocpol, *Protecting Soldiers and Mothers*; and Barbara J. Nelson, "The Origins of the Two-Channel Welfare State: Workmen's Compensation and Mothers' Aid," in *Women, the State, and Welfare*, ed. Linda Gordon (Madison: University of Wisconsin Press, 1990) pp. 123–51.

[60] Susan Ware, *Beyond Suffrage: Women in the New Deal* (Cambridge: Harvard University Press, 1981).

of themselves in market society; the "protection" of women through protective labor legislation had, in contrast, been construed as a worthy government interest.[61] Social policies geared toward women and children succeeded in the form of mothers' pensions and the Sheppard-Towner Maternity and Infancy Protection Act, but comparable policies aimed toward men as breadwinners failed.[62] In the New Deal, policy officials, the Supreme Court, and the public all recognized a governmental responsibility to provide for the welfare of both men and women. But despite these changes, still the outcome was that citizens became divided by gender between two different forms of governance. Therefore, the analysis of how New Deal policies shaped citizenship in terms of gender clearly does require attention to the politics and institutional dynamics of the era rather than to ideologies alone.

The first of the core arguments of this book is that New Deal policy officials did shape policies in some directly gender-specific ways. In some regards, these actions by policymakers were conscious and intentional. Most policymakers in the Roosevelt administration, for example, were sympathetic to the "family wage" ideal, the notion that men's work in the market economy should enable them to serve as "breadwinners" for their families, so that women could attend to unpaid domestic work and refrain from taking jobs that could otherwise belong to men. Almost reflexively, then, they drew on policy alternatives from the Progressive Era inscribed with assumptions about distinct gender roles.

But not all the direct gendering of policies during the New Deal was, as others have implied, intentional or conscious. Policymakers in the 1930s were not rigidly bound to preexisting policy traditions and ideologies, nor were they guided by an ideological agenda aiming to preserve ascribed gender roles. Rather, they were enmeshed by the politics of the New Deal and preoccupied with serving key constituencies and interests. These political forces coalesced in a manner that confirmed officials' preexisting inclinations to channel men and women into separate and distinct types of policies. As Schattschneider observed, "Organization is itself a mobilization of bias in preparation for action. . . . Some issues are organized into politics while others are organized out."[63]

Although officials in the Women's Bureau of the Department of Labor, some women leaders in the labor movement, and various radicals called for social and labor policies to address women's inferior status in the work force and their dual burden of work for wages and unpaid labor in the home, together they did not constitute a powerful presence in the Demo-

---

[61] *Lochner v. New York*, 198 U.S. 45 (1905); *Muller v. Oregon*, 208 U.S. 412 (1908).
[62] Skocpol, *Protecting Soldiers and Mothers*.
[63] Schattschneider, *Semisovereign People*, pp. 30, 71.

cratic Party. The party's political-economic agenda combined the interests of labor unions, whose ranks were predominantly male, with the demands of urban interests in the North and agricultural interests in the impoverished South, both eager to draw on the largesse of the federal government. Southern members of Congress also insisted, however, on administrative arrangements that would preserve "states' rights" and local autonomy. They had the necessary leverage to accomplish their goals: the unchallenged one-party rule in the prereapportionment, Jim Crow South combined with seniority rules in Congress gave them institutional advantages in securing key committee assignments and chairmanships.[64]

These political forces produced New Deal policies that placed priority on the concerns of men, especially white men. Neither the concerns of workers in low-wage and service-sector jobs nor those of housewives weighed heavily in the minds of many officials, and those who were attentive to them, such as Frances Perkins, considered political obstacles to prohibit their inclusion. In sum, New Deal policymakers were not guided strictly by conscious intentions to treat women differently from men, but the "mobilization of bias" in the Democratic Party worked to yield such results anyway. Similarly, in the course of implementation, political imperatives prompted public officials to improve especially those policies that targeted men, who tended to be represented by organized interests, while neglecting or marginalizing those that affected women, who tended not to be effectively mobilized. New Deal policies thus codified with state power distinct statuses for men and women.

Besides shaping gender directly, policymakers altered American institutions in ways that indirectly but significantly reorganized citizenship in terms of gender. The second core argument posited here is that in the New Deal, policy officials made public policy by reshaping the contours of federalism, enlarging the authority and scope of national government in the system of dual sovereignty while at the same time retaining and even bolstering the power of the individual states. The particular rearrangements of federalism facilitated a gendered division of Americans as social citizens, as programs geared toward men became nationally administered programs and those aimed toward women retained state-level authority. What emerges as truly exceptional about the construction of the welfare state in the New Deal, then, is that citizens became divided by gender between two different sovereignties that govern in very different ways. New Deal policies thus not only institutionalized social organization on the basis of sexual

---

[64] Frank Freidel, *F.D.R. and the South* (Baton Rouge: Louisiana State University Press, 1965). On the political economy of the South in the 1930s and the implications of New Deal policies for the region, see Arthur F. Raper, *Preface to Peasantry* (New York: Atheneum, 1968); and David Eugene Conrad, *The Forgotten Farmers: The Story of Sharecroppers in the New Deal* (Urbana: University of Illinois Press, 1965).

difference but formulated political arrangements of the citizenry on that basis as well.

The case studies that constitute the core of this book point to three primary aspects of the politics of the New Deal that explain the emergence of divided citizenship. First, New Deal policymaking was characterized by battles that pitted an "old guard" of policymakers who favored state-level administrative power, at least for redistributive policies, against a new and insurgent cadre of policymakers who favored national standards and administrative procedures. In the creation of the Social Security Act, the old guard included persons that had previously been actively involved in developing state-level social and labor legislation, namely, Frances Perkins in New York and Arthur Altmeyer and Edwin Witte in Wisconsin. They were predisposed to favor solutions that left substantial autonomy to the states, which they viewed as laboratories for policy experimentation.[65] This old guard won most, but not all, of those battles, with important implications for the subsequent character of programs that already tended to separate women and men. Similarly, when delineating the reach of the Fair Labor Standards Act, legal advisers for the Roosevelt administration, such as Felix Frankfurter, defined the newly expanded realm of "interstate commerce" in a manner that still excluded most women and nonwhite men, although they were the lowest paid sectors of the work force and could have benefited the most from the law's provisions.

Second, the shape of New Deal federalism resulted in part from efforts by members of Congress to preserve "states' rights" and local autonomy in public policy. Southern and western senators and representatives, dominating critical committees and leadership positions, purposefully excluded various categories of workers, including domestic and agricultural workers, from programs to be administered from national government. They also altered programs that administration officials had already planned to be administered primarily at the state level, so as further to restrain national bureaucrats from intervening in policy implementation and to guarantee that state and local officials would instead retain a high degree of discretionary authority. Scholars have noted that Congress thus excluded most African Americans from nationally administered programs and vested local officials with authority that was subsequently used in many southern and western states to omit nonwhite applicants from coverage in public assistance programs.[66] This analysis will show that efforts to preserve state

---

[65] *Reminiscences of Frances Perkins*, vol. 2, pt. 4, p. 631, Oral History Collection of Columbia University (hereafter, OHC).

[66] Robert C. Lieberman, "Race and the Development of the American Welfare State from the New Deal to the Great Society" (Ph.D. diss., Harvard University, 1994); Jill Quadagno, "From Old-Age Assistance to Supplemental Security Income: The Political Economy of Relief in the South, 1935–1972," in *Politics of Social Policy*, ed. Weir, Orloff, and Skocpol, pp. 235–64; Phyllis Palmer, "Outside the Law: Agricultural and Domestic Workers under the Fair Labor Standards Act," *Journal of Policy History* 7 (1995): 416–40.

and local authority had important gender effects as well. Several of the occupational groups that congressional committees dropped from coverage in the national program were disproportionately female. Congressmen also altered the public assistance programs on which women would most rely in ways that rendered them far more subject to provincial rule than they would otherwise have been.

Third, the unintended consequences of policy implementation accentuated divided citizenship. After policy formation is completed, policies are shaped anew through the politics and institutional context surrounding their implementation. Political agendas of bureaucrats may be distinct from those of policymakers, particularly as they attempt to institutionalize the power and authority of their agencies. Such dynamics drove the early implementation of old age insurance and unemployment insurance in the hands of the Social Security Board. Implementation, furthermore, is enormously complicated by federalism. Theodore Lowi and Benjamin Ginsberg have shown that in policies decided by the national government but handed over to state and local officials for implementation, such as the grant-in-aid public assistance programs of the New Deal, the multiplication of layers of responsibility makes for a proliferation of "access points and opportunities for influence."[67] Indeed, during the decades after the New Deal, state and local officials shaped programs in their jurisdiction to reflect cultural norms and local political-economic priorities rather than the goals of national policymakers. Such dynamics further intensified the distinctions between national and state-level citizenship for men and women.

In sum, a combination of deliberate choices and indirect decisions led New Deal policymakers to consolidate the new power of national government by incorporating mostly male wage earners under its jurisdiction, and to leave substantial authority to the states to provide for the welfare and security of most women. Through the subsequent politics of policy implementation, the separateness and gender-specific character of two forms of citizenship, national and state-level, institutionalized gender inequalities and built political barriers against further social change.

Highlighting the political and institutional determinants and effects of policymaking reveals how gender bias can be institutionalized even when policymakers perceive their goals in relatively "gender-neutral" ways. New Dealers did not set out purposefully to establish an inferior type of citizenship for women. Rather, they attempted to meet their constituencies' needs and did so in part by revising federalism far enough to allow for some policy innovations while still preserving the bulwark of American institutional traditions and partisan accord. They expanded the boundaries of national

---

[67] Theodore J. Lowi et al., *Poliscide* (Lanham, Md.: University Press of America, 1990), pp. 27–28; see also Jeffrey L. Pressman and Aaron Wildavsky, *Implementation* (Berkeley: University of California Press, 1973).

government far enough to bring full-time, long-term wage earners in the industrial sector under nationally administered policies but not far enough to include other groups. The gender-specific results were thus less the product of sexist intentions per se than of a combination of institutional and political biases that combined to advantage men.

American Political Development and Citizenship

Most scholars have followed the lead of a long line of noted writers, from Alexis de Tocqueville through Louis Hartz, in viewing American political development as infused by liberalism.[68] Lacking Europe's feudal past, the logic goes, Americans have, from the time of the founding, been able and inclined to embrace the core liberal principles: limited government, individual rights, and a market economy. Challenging this thesis, Rogers Smith has argued that the "liberal tradition" has flourished alongside two distinctly nonliberal traditions: first, a "republican tradition" based on notions of popular sovereignty, civic virtue, and economic regulation for the common good; and second, "ascriptive Americanist traditions" that make race and gender hierarchies legitimate.[69] In a similar vein but with a particular emphasis on the role of law and institutions, Karen Orren has shown how remnants of feudalism persisted in labor relations until the New Deal finally sanctioned the rule of law in such matters and dissolved the old master-servant code from the common law.[70] This book, too, shows how a nonliberal realm of governance persisted, in this case well beyond the New Deal. It was institutionalized through the system of U.S. federalism within the states, the realm in which most women continued to be governed long after the New Deal.

The most innovative development of the New Deal, the aspect of political change that most dramatically qualifies it for the status of a "revolution," was surely the creation of a liberal regime of citizenship within the domain of national government. The founders had established a narrow commercial republic at the national level, which could be described as ostensibly "liberal" but did not much affect the governance of citizens, whose fates were left primarily to the states.[71] New Deal policymakers reconfigured the national government into what can be called a prototypical

---

[68] Louis Hartz, *The Liberal Tradition in America* (New York: Harcourt, Brace, 1955); Alexis de Tocqueville, *Democracy in America*, ed. J. P. Mayer (New York: Doubleday, Anchor, 1969).

[69] Smith, "Beyond Tocqueville, Myrdal, and Hartz," p. 563, n. 4.

[70] Orren, *Belated Feudalism*.

[71] Isaac Kramnick, "The 'Great National Discussion': The Discourse of Politics in 1787," *William and Mary Quarterly* 45 (1988): 3–32.

Table 1. Incorporation of citizens in the New Deal

Administrative jurisdiction	Basis of inclusion	
	Liberal	Nonliberal
National	Old Age Insurance Fair Labor Standards Act	Old Age and Survivors' Insurance
State-level	Unemployment Insurance*	Aid to Dependent Children Old Age Assistance Protective labor laws

* UI eventually bifurcated, belonging in part to the national, liberal realm and in part to the state-level, nonliberal realm.

Lockean liberal state. In its new guise, national government incorporated, through social and labor policies, those whom John Locke might have termed the "Industrious and Rational" persons.[72] To New Dealers, these persons qualified as "independent" citizens, and thus as free and equal bearers of rights, strictly because they were long-term, full-time wage earners. Given the composition of the work force, this meant men, even though, formally, such laws were "gender-neutral," treating individuals abstractly without regard for biological characteristics and ascribed statuses.

New Deal officials also endowed national programs with particular administrative characteristics. Programs were implemented according to fairly standardized, routinized rules and procedures. The federal civil service was in the process of becoming more fully infused with practices for hiring and promoting personnel based on merit, meaning the use of exams and fair and open competition in place of old-style patronage.

Table 1 summarizes the characteristics of the major programs examined in this book. As the case studies show, two New Deal programs most fully combined the ethos of liberalism in their eligibility criteria with the administrative practices most common in national governance: OAI as it was created in 1935 and the FLSA, the two that applied, at least at the outset, primarily to men.

Feminist political theorists have pointed out that the social contract in liberal theory, through its division of the public and private realms, left the domestic sphere beyond the reach of its principles.[73] When classical liberal

[72] John Locke, *Two Treatises of Government*, ed. Peter Laslett (1960; New York: Cambridge University Press, 1980), bk. 2, chap. 5, par. 34.5.
[73] See esp. the work of Carole Pateman, including *The Sexual Contract* (Stanford: Stanford University Press, 1988), and her edited volume, *Feminist Challenges: Social and Political Theory* (Boston: Northeastern Press, 1986), esp. Pateman's "Introduction" and Merle Thornton's "Sex Equality Is Not Enough for Feminists." See also Susan Moeller Okin, *Justice, Gender, and the Family* (Basic Books, 1989), esp. chap. 5; Martha Ackelsburg, "Communities, Resis-

theorists imagined the creation of a public realm by and for free and equal citizens, they assumed the perpetuation of a nonliberal, private realm of the family, wherein a hierarchy based on ascribed roles and status could continue. Long after women were included as citizens in the public sphere, their lives have continued to be defined primarily within the private sphere, without the protection of rights.

Similarly, in the establishment of the "second American republic" beginning with the New Deal, most women remained beyond the purview of the new liberal realm of citizenship.[74] But the lines drawn between men and women in New Deal policies were inscribed not only on the classic liberal divide between public and private but, more important, between national and state-level governance. States tended to incorporate women as social citizens according to nonliberal criteria that regarded them in relational, role-oriented, or difference-based terms, rather than as abstract individuals. These criteria reflect the republican tradition and the ascriptive Americanist traditions detailed by Smith. Old age assistance was rooted in ideas that predated the New Deal: that certain citizens, in this case the elderly, were worthy of social provision simply because of their service to society, as "good citizens," rather than because of their paid labor. Similarly, ADC's predecessor, mothers' pensions, was based on another variant of "good citizenship," the notion that women, as mothers, served the needs of the public sphere by raising future citizens.[75] Left out of the FLSA provisions, women remained dependent on state-level protective labor laws for at least a minimal floor under labor standards; the courts had long found a compelling state interest in the protection of women in the workplace because of their innate function as actual or potential mothers.

State governments also administered programs in a manner distinct from national government. They added layers of eligibility requirements to those stated in federal law and permitted local officials to implement rules with ample discretion. Beneficiaries came to be treated as dependent persons who required supervision and protection rather than as bearers of rights. As the case studies show, state-administered programs were characterized by invasive rules and procedures through which officials monitored and regulated women's moral character. In determining client eligibility for

---

tance, and Women's Activism: Some Implications for a Democratic Polity," in *Women and the Politics of Empowerment*, ed. Ann Bookman and Sandra Morgen (Philadelphia: Temple University Press, 1988), pp. 297–313; and Catharine MacKinnon, *Towards a Feminist Theory of the State* (Cambridge: Harvard University Press, 1989).

[74] The term *second republic* comes from Theodore J. Lowi, *The End of Liberalism*, 2d ed. (New York: Norton, 1979); see pp. 273–74 on the transition toward it in the New Deal.

[75] Ann Shola Orloff, "Gender in Early U.S. Social Policy," *Journal of Policy History* 3 (1991): 249–81; Ladd-Taylor, *Mother-Work*, p. 147; Gordon, *Pitied but Not Entitled*, p. 40; Mink, *Wages of Motherhood*, pp. 27–38.

ADC, for example, suitable-home rules were used to scrutinize the lives of potential ADC beneficiaries, evaluating their child rearing and house-keeping abilities and the school and church attendance of their children. Some states and localities used "man-in-the-house" rules to withdraw aid from women suspected of having or found to have "male callers." Such investigations were often conducted through midnight raids by local officials.[76] While national programs were being infused with the professionalism that accompanied the development of the merit system, states continued to rely on patronage procedures for selecting personnel and oftentimes used overt political influence in the allocation of benefits. These programs perpetuated a form of governance for women that can be described as "semifeudal" because of the ascriptive basis on which people were included within programs and the parochial administrative procedures used in their implementation.

Ironically, the major route through which women did gain access to the national realm of citizenship in the New Deal was through incorporation on a distinctly nonliberal basis. Through the addition of widows' and wives' benefits to OAI in 1939, women who were married to men covered by OAI were included, by virtue of being wives of "independent men," in a program administered according to the professionalism of national governance. Similarly, through pensions to Civil War veterans and subsequently through the G.I. Bill of Rights of 1944, former soldiers were included in national social provisions as a means of honoring their civic virtue, an ideal that emanated from republican rather than liberal ideology.[77]

Unemployment insurance was a hybrid program: inclusion was based on liberal criteria but states played a significant role in administration. The program changed and developed in the course of implementation, and by midcentury, most white men experienced liberal grounds for inclusion and nearly national standards of administration, whereas women and nonwhite men faced nonliberal eligibility rules that varied tremendously from state to state and tended to make the program inaccessible to them.

The development of UI illustrates how women can be twice ostracized under the system of U.S. federalism. First, New Deal liberals at the national level, who viewed the beneficiary pool for UI in gender-neutral, wage-related terms, excluded most women from the policy by limiting coverage to wage earners and, by correlating benefits to prior wages, assured most women workers of lower benefits than men. Next, women who survived

---

[76] Winifred Bell, *Aid to Dependent Children* (New York: Columbia University Press, 1965).

[77] Harold M. Hyman, *American Singularity: The 1787 Northwest Ordinance, the 1862 Homestead and Morrill Acts, and the 1944 GI Bill* (Athens: University of Georgia Press, 1986), pp. 62–76; Skocpol, *Protecting Soldiers and Mothers*, pp. 102–7.

the test at the national level faced a different set of exclusionary rules at the state level: there they were seen in a gender-particular light and frequently excluded because of the notion that their husbands should provide for them. Though either system by itself would have carried substantial disadvantages, women would have been better off with either a purely liberal plan as created by the Roosevelt administration or a nonliberal plan that ascribed roles in the democratic polity based on sex. Instead, the combination of the two in a joint national-state plan inflicted on women the worst of both ideologies. Women lost on both counts, while national administrators proceeded to make UI a respectable policy for men at the high end of the wage scale.

Of course the liberal character of the New Deal meant that its categories of citizenship were neither overtly nor rigidly defined in terms of sex. Women were entitled to the same rights and benefits as men when they fit the mold: as long-term, full-time participants in the paid labor force, as union members, as workers in industry. Accordingly, New Deal policies were potentially expandable, capable of including more and more women as they increased their numbers in the work force and as they entered male-dominated occupations. But women in the late 1930s gained little from the policies: on average, only 25.4 percent participated in the paid labor force at any given time compared with 79 percent of men, and those who did work were frequently rendered ineligible because they were intermittent or part-time workers, workers in the service sector, unemployed owing to pregnancy or family responsibilities, or nonunion workers.[78]

In later decades, the bounds of the national realm of governance were expanded as both the Social Security Act and the FLSA were amended to include women more broadly. By the late 1960s even AFDC, though still the New Deal social policy that allowed states the greatest measure of authority, began to acquire some of the features of an entitlement with national standards. As well, OASI, which had come to be termed simply "social security," was altered so that women and men were covered on a somewhat more equitable basis.

Yet at the close of the century, policymakers are reconstructing divided citizenship by returning control for various policies, particularly those affecting women and the poor, to the states while retaining control of social security and Medicare at the national level. The Family Support Act of 1988 enabled states to obtain waivers from national standards for AFDC as they attempted to fashion their own "workfare" plans. By the mid-

---

[78] Bureau of the Census, *U.S. Census, 1940: The Labor Force* (Washington, D.C.: GPO, 1940), p. 18. Similarly, New Deal policies did not include explicit racial exclusions, although in omitting agricultural and domestic workers, they excluded the majority of African Americans from coverage. As blacks moved into covered occupations, they too received the benefits of the New Deal. See Lieberman, "Race and the American Welfare State."

1990s, as the momentum for "welfare reform" mounted, state legislatures established new eligibility restrictions and coercive procedural rules for women on welfare. In 1996, the Republican Congress passed, and President Clinton signed into law, the Personal Responsibility and Work Opportunity Reconciliation Act, abolishing AFDC and the entitlement to welfare for poor women and children and offering states the option of participating in a block grants program through which they regain more authority than they have known in six decades and in which benefits may vary even more dramatically from state to state than under AFDC. As a result, for poor women with children, the barriers to full incorporation in the polity have once again become nearly insurmountable.

CHAPTER TWO

From Dual Federalism to a New Deal

These unhappy times call for the building of plans that . . . put their
faith once more in the forgotten man at the bottom of the economic
pyramid.

> —President Franklin D. Roosevelt, radio address,
> Albany, N.Y., April 7, 1932

The New Deal was carried out under the most tumultuous economic circumstances in the nation's history and amid turbulent social conflict. After
the stock market crashed on October 29, 1929, the economy began a long
descent lasting for the next four years. Manufacturing output fell by half,
unemployment rose from 3 percent to 25 percent of the labor force, more
than nine thousand banks closed their doors, and personal incomes declined by more than half.[1] Unemployment led to the spread of malnutri-
tion, disease, and shanty towns and, according to sociologists of the era,
threatened family life, in as much as men's authority and stature stemmed
from their roles as breadwinners.[2] Mobs looted stores in search of food;
jobless persons organized through the communist-led Trade Union Unity
League demonstrated in cities across the nation; and groups engaged in
"rent riots" aimed to forestall evictions.[3] The traditional poor-relief apparatus of the states and localities were strained to the breaking point by the
depth of the crisis.[4]

---

[1] American Social History Project, *Who Built America?* (New York: Pantheon, 1992),
2:318–22.

[2] On the threat of unemployment to gender roles in the family, see Mirra Komarovsky,
The Unemployed Man and His Family (New York: Dryden, 1940), pp. 1–48; and E. Wight
Bakke, *Citizens without Work* (1940; reprint, Hamden, Conn.: Shoe String, Archon, 1969),
pp. 109–242.

[3] Frances Fox Piven and Richard A. Cloward, *Poor People's Movements: Why They Succeed, How They Fail* (Random House, New York: Vintage, 1979), pp. 49–55; Michael
Goldfield, "The Influence of Worker Insurgency and Radical Organization on New Deal Labor Legislation," *American Political Science Review* 83 (1989): 1257–82.

[4] James T. Patterson, *The New Deal and the States: Federalism in Transition* (Princeton:
Princeton University Press, 1969), chap. 2; Piven and Cloward, *Poor People's Movements*,
pp. 60–62.

With the country suffering through the "winter of despair" of 1932–33, President Franklin D. Roosevelt was inaugurated. The severity of the economic crisis and the social turmoil of the 1930s provided a context in which Roosevelt could build an unlikely but powerful political coalition through which to carry out unprecedented alterations in the American political economy and the meaning of American citizenship. Preexisting policies and policymaking traditions were important, however, in shaping the direction of the New Deal and providing policymakers with certain openings while constraining other choices. Understanding the shape of precedents in policymaking as well as the character of preexisting social and economic conditions is essential for comprehending both the extent to which the New Deal was new and innovative and the ways it was limited to tasks of incrementalism. The contextual background in this chapter prepares the way for the book's policy analyses, first, by exploring the historical precedents in American welfare state development during the late nineteenth and early twentieth centuries, when citizenship was shaped by the institutions of dual federalism and, second, by examining the social, economic, and political circumstances at the beginning of the New Deal which framed the context for a constitutional revolution that would allow for the birth of national citizenship. A discussion of early New Deal policies and the National Labor Relations Act of 1935 then sets the stage for the policy case studies.

Policymaking and Citizenship under Dual Federalism

Most western nations enacted national social and labor policies around the turn of the century, long before the New Deal. Compulsory, contributory old age insurance was adopted first in Germany in 1889, then in Austria in 1909 and France in 1910; other European nations simultaneously developed more limited plans applying to workers in specific industries. Great Britain established national unemployment insurance in 1911, followed by seven more nations during the 1920s. The minimum wage movement began in Australia and New Zealand in the 1890s, and by the early twentieth century, those nations and most in western Europe had enacted minimum wage legislation.[5]

---

[5] Roy Lubove, *The Struggle for Social Security, 1900–1935* (Cambridge: Harvard University Press, 1968), pp. 27–29; Social Security Board (hereafter SSB), *Social Security in America: The Factual Background of the Social Security Act as Summarized from Staff Reports to the Committee on Economic Security* (Washington, D.C.: GPO, 1937), p. 17; John W. Chambers, "The Big Switch: Justice Roberts and the Minimum-Wage Cases," *Labor History* 10 (winter 1969): 46–47; Theda Skocpol, *Protecting Soldiers and Mothers: The Political Origins of Social Policy in the United States* (Cambridge: Harvard University Press, 1992), p. 9.

During the same period, the United States pursued an independent course. Locally administered poor relief, orphanages, and county poorhouses, as well as assistance from private charities, had long constituted the main sources of aid for those in need, making for a highly uneven and largely inadequate set of arrangements.[6] The nation had begun, as Theda Skocpol has shown, to develop more broad-based forms of social provision in a manner quite distinct from European developments. After the Civil War, the United States had established pensions for veterans and their dependents, and by the early twentieth century those benefits were being distributed fairly widely and generously.[7]

Yet, although the scope of national government had been broadened slightly by the early twentieth century, the arrangements of dual federalism remained intact, and most policies that directly affected citizens' lives were still made and implemented at the state level.[8] Institutional and political features of American government presented obstacles to the development of broadly based regulatory labor policies and redistributive social policies.[9] Only particularistic, ascriptive policies geared toward women in their roles as potential or actual mothers were enacted successfully.

The Failure of Employment-Based Social Reform

Although the United States, like other western nations, experienced intensive industrialization and urbanization in the late nineteenth century, efforts for public policies geared toward persons on the basis of their participation in the work place did not advance as they had in European nations. Early universal male suffrage in the United States had preempted the identification of political consciousness with class consciousness as in Great Britain, where the vote was extended gradually on the basis of social class.[10] Some labor organizations that focused on reform through public policy did emerge in the late nineteenth century,[11] but the labor movement

---

[6] Michael B. Katz, *In the Shadow of the Poorhouse: A Social History of Welfare in America* (New York: Basic Books, 1986).

[7] Skocpol, *Protecting Soldiers and Mothers.*

[8] On national state-building during the period, see above, chap. 1, nn. 2 and 4.

[9] These policy categories appear in Theodore J. Lowi, "American Business, Public Policy, Case Studies, and Political Theory," *World Politics* 6 (1964): 677–715.

[10] Martin Shefter, "Trade Unions and Political Machines: The Organization and Disorganization of the American Working Class in the Late Nineteenth Century," in *Working Class Formation: Nineteenth Century Patterns in Europe and the United States,* ed. Ira Katznelson and Aristide R. Zolberg (Princeton: Princeton University Press, 1986), pp. 197–278.

[11] Leon Fink, *Workingmen's Democracy: The Knights of Labor and American Politics* (Urbana: University of Illinois Press, 1983); David Brody, *In Labor's Cause: Main Themes on the History of the American Worker* (New York: Oxford University Press, 1993), pp. 50–51.

was thwarted by features of the American polity, particularly the power of the judiciary.

Workers were subordinated to employers through what Karen Orren has called "a belated feudalism, a remnant of the medieval hierarchy of personal relations": employees' circumstances remained, at common law, defined according to an ancient code of master-servant relations. Thus, working conditions were understood by courts as largely beyond the reach of legislatures.[12] Public officials approved, and courts sanctioned, the use of violence to repress labor activism, first with the use of police, state militias, and national guardsmen to put down strikes in the 1870s, later by issuing injunctions, backed up with force, beginning with the 1894 Pullman strike.[13]

Through judicial review, furthermore, the courts exercised a broad interpretation of "freedom of contract" and a restrictive interpretation of the commerce clause to forbid nearly all attempts at regulation of the workplace by national or state governments. Some state legislatures had begun to limit the hours of work in particular occupations. In the 1905 decision *Lochner v. New York*, however, the Court restrained individual states from enacting labor regulations for work not deemed dangerous, invalidating maximum-hours laws for workers on the premise that they interfered with freedom of contract.[14] The Erdman Act of 1898, protecting workers' right to join labor unions, was similarly invalidated by the 1908 decision *Adair v. U.S.*[15] Previous to 1900, the Supreme Court interpreted the Congress's power as extending only to a very restricted realm of "interstate commerce," meaning that legislation could only pertain to the literal flow of goods across state lines. When Congress began sparingly, in the early years of the twentieth century, to use the commerce and taxing powers for the general welfare, the Court granted tacit approval in cases pertaining to such diverse objects of state action as lottery tickets, oleomargarine, and prostitutes in "interstate commerce." When it came to labor conditions, though, the Court usually held the line, even finding a prohibition on child labor unconstitutional on the grounds that Congress had attempted to interfere with production processes, properly the domain of the states.[16]

---

[12] Karen Orren, *Belated Feudalism: Labor, the Law, and Liberal Development in the United States* (New York: Cambridge University Press, 1991), p. 2.

[13] Jeremy Brecher, *Strike!* (Boston: South End Press, 1972); Paul Avrich, *The Haymarket Tragedy* (Princeton: Princeton University Press, 1984); Paul Krause, *The Battle for Homestead, 1880–1892* (Pittsburgh: University of Pittsburgh Press, 1992; Melvyn Dubofsky, *We Shall Be All: A History of the Industrial Workers of the World*, 2d ed. (Urbana: University of Illinois Press, 1988), pp. 286, 273–78, 325–26.

[14] 198 U.S. 45 (1905).

[15] 208 U.S. 161 (1908).

[16] *Hammer v. Dagenhart*, 247 U.S. 251 (1918).

Given these factors, the United States did not produce a strong labor movement. Reform-oriented labor organizations dissipated, leaving the American Federation of Labor (AFL) as sole survivor into the twentieth century. Established in 1886, the AFL aimed to unite long-existing crafts unions and to protect the jobs of skilled workers. In time, under the leadership of Samuel Gompers, the organization came to define its mission as "pure and simple unionism," focusing explicitly on negotiating with employers rather than on reform through public policy. Not only did the AFL's national leaders view political efforts as largely futile, but moreover, they feared that engagement in political agreements could result in a loss of autonomy for labor organizations.[17]

Besides its apolitical stance, the narrowness of the range of the work force represented by the AFL made the likelihood that the federation might assume a dominant role in social reform all the more remote. The AFL existed to protect skilled workers, who tended to be white, native-born males. Many AFL union locals formally denied membership to women or charged initiation fees and dues few women could afford. Union practices, such as meeting times and places, also made membership less accessible to women.[18]

Apart from labor organizations, a group of male social scientists established the American Association for Labor Legislation (AALL) in 1905. They sought to promote social-insurance kinds of programs for wage earners which would provide for them when they became ill, unemployed, or old. For the most part, however, the AALL did not achieve its goals. Public officials were reluctant to establish new spending programs that might foster the degree of corruption they associated with Civil War pensions as administered through the patronage system. Nor did government appear to have the capacity to administer new contributory-type programs.[19]

In sum, the United States in the early twentieth century was not poised to develop policies to assist individuals based on their participation in the work force. A wide array of women's organizations and many individual

[17] Brody, *In Labor's Cause*, p. 54; more generally, see David Montgomery, *The Fall of the House of Labor: The Workplace, the State, and American Labor Activism, 1865–1925* (Cambridge: Cambridge University Press, 1987), chaps. 8–9.

[18] Ruth Milkman, "Organizing the Sexual Division of Labor: Historical Perspectives on 'Women's Work' and the American Labor Movement," *Socialist Review* 10 (January–February 1980): 114–17. On various occasions throughout the Progressive Era, the AFL tried to defend itself against charges that it discriminated against women; see the Philip Taft Papers, Labor-Management Documentation Center, Cornell University (hereafter, LMDC) collection 5541, box 14, file 2.

[19] Skocpol, *Protecting Soldiers and Mothers*, pp. 176–204, 261–85; Linda Gordon, *Pitied but Not Entitled: Single Mothers and the History of Welfare, 1890–1935* (New York: Free Press, 1994), 145–82.

female reformers proved quite successful at reform during the early twentieth century, however, establishing the beginnings of what Skocpol has called a "maternalist welfare state."[20]

Maternalist Politics

Whereas political parties and electoral activities in the nineteenth century had been dominated by men, middle- and upper-class women had become increasingly involved in social reform. The early establishment of universal suffrage for all free men left women in a class by themselves politically, prompting them to identify themselves particularly in gender terms and to organize along gender lines, first through the suffrage movement in the mid-1800s. Middle-class women's groups began to capitalize on the ideology of "separate spheres," the notion that women's place is in the home, to engage in what has been call "social housekeeping": efforts to uplift public and civic life.[21] By the twentieth century, their organizations began to work for labor and social provisions for women.

Most women's reform efforts of the period were driven by the ideology that contemporary scholars have termed "maternalism," which can be characterized by three tenets: (1) that women's primary role involved domestic responsibilities, particularly raising children to be future citizens; (2) that all women shared a bond because of their common capacity for motherhood; and thus (3) that they themselves had a particular moral authority with which to call for reforms that would assist other mothers and children.[22] Political strategies of the maternalists were also shaped and constrained by another prevailing belief of the era: the notion of the "family wage," that men's earnings should allow them to serve as sole breadwinner for the family, permitting women and children to remain out of the paid work force and enabling women to spend their time engaged in unpaid domestic work.[23] This ideal overlooked the actual circumstances of women workers, who sought wages not for mere "pin money" but to provide at least for themselves and often to support family members. In 1900, when

---

[20] Skocpol, *Protecting Soldiers and Mothers*, p. 526.

[21] Paula Baker, *The Moral Frameworks of Public Life: Gender, Politics, and the State in Rural New York, 1870–1930* (New York: Oxford University Press, 1991); Kathryn Kish Sklar, "The Historical Foundations of Women's Power in the Creation of the American Welfare State, 1830–1930," in *Mothers of a New World: Maternalist Politics and the Origins of Welfare States*, ed. Seth Koven and Sonya Michel (New York: Routledge, 1993), pp. 43–93; Nancy F. Cott, "Across the Great Divide: Women and Politics before and after 1920," in *Women, Politics, and Change*, ed. Louise A. Tilly and Patricia Gurin (New York: Russell Sage, 1990), pp. 153–76.

[22] Molly Ladd-Taylor, *Mother-Work: Women, Child Welfare, and the State, 1890–1930* (Urbana: University of Illinois Press, 1994), p. 3; Gordon, *Pitied but Not Entitled*, p. 55.

[23] Alice Kessler-Harris, *A Woman's Wage* (Lexington: University Press of Kentucky, 1990), p. 7.

20 percent of all women were participating in the work force, more than one-third of working women in urban areas lived independently, supporting themselves, and three-quarters of those living at home were responsible for supporting other family members.[24] But although the family wage ideal helped to justify lower wages for women, most maternalists accepted the fact that the ideal had broad political appeal, and they sought to improve conditions for women without challenging its limits.[25]

The Protective Labor Law Strategy

Efforts for protective labor laws for women began in various states by the late nineteenth century. In 1908 the Supreme Court heard *Muller v. Oregon*, a case that challenged the constitutionality of an Oregon law that limited the workday of women in laundries and other specific occupations to ten hours. Louis Brandeis presented a brief prepared by the National Consumers' League (NCL) which drew on extensive research on the risks of long hours of work to women's health and utilized the notion that "woman's place" lay in the domestic sphere in order to justify differential treatment on the basis of sex.[26] In a startling departure from *Lochner*, the Supreme Court upheld Oregon's law, reasoning that in the case of women, the state's interest took priority over liberty of contract because, "as healthy mothers are essential to vigorous offspring, the physical well-being of woman becomes an object of public interest and care in order to preserve the strength and vigor of the race." [27] In essence, the reformers had succeeded in piercing a tentative loophole in the doctrine of "freedom of contract" by advancing state-level protective labor legislation for women workers.

Women's reform groups seized the opportunity afforded by the *Muller* decision to commence state-by-state efforts to improve the conditions of women workers through the enactment of protective labor legislation. The NCL led a coalition of women's organizations, such as the Women's Trade Union League (WTUL), the General Federation of Women's Clubs, and the Young Women's Christian Association (YWCA), in the campaign. They sought the regulation of hours and wages and the enactment of seating

[24] Bureau of the Census, *The Statistical History of the United States, from Colonial Times to the Present* (New York: Basic Books, 1976), p. 133; Kessler-Harris, *Woman's Wage*, pp. 10–11.

[25] Gordon, *Pitied but Not Entitled*, p. 59.

[26] Skocpol, *Protecting Soldiers and Mothers*, pp. 375–76; Eileen Boris, *Home to Work: Motherhood and the Politics of Industrial Homework in the United States* (New York: Cambridge University Press, 1994), p. 119.

[27] Justice David A. Brewer, Opinion, *Muller v. Oregon*, 208 U.S. 412 (1908); see also Judith Baer, *The Chains of Protection* (Westport, Conn.: Greenwood, 1978), pp. 51–67.

laws, rest periods, night work prohibitions, and prohibitions of female employment in some occupations.[28]

Although the well-organized and broadly based advocacy groups that worked toward legislative reforms on behalf of women workers remain an impressive example of a social movement, in fact the protective labor legislation approach toward improving working conditions for women proved tedious and obstacle laden. Hours limitations survived court challenges, but minimum wage laws, enacted in sixteen states and the District of Columbia between 1912 and the early twenties, stood on more tenuous ground.[29] All were destroyed with the *Adkins v. Children's Hospital* decision in 1923, in which the Supreme Court declared an unwillingness to waive "freedom of contract" in the case of minimum wage laws.[30]

Most women reformers had become convinced by 1923 that protective labor laws for women were necessary to enable women to achieve social and economic equality with men in the workplace, but in an ironic application of liberal principles, the Supreme Court used women's recent attainment of suffrage against them.[31] Justice George Sutherland, who penned the majority opinion in *Adkins v. Children's Hospital*, took issue with the "protective" attitude of labor legislation by pointing to the "revolutionary" changes that had occurred since the *Muller* decision:

> In the contractual, political and civil status of women, culminating in the 19th Amendment, . . . differences (between the sexes, other than physical) have now come almost, if not quite, to the vanishing point. (Therefore) . . . we cannot accept the doctrine that women of mature age, sui juris, require or may be subjected to restrictions upon their liberty of contract which could not lawfully be imposed in the case of men under similar circumstances. To do so would be to ignore all the implications to be drawn from . . . present day trend[s] . . . by which woman is accorded emancipation from the old doctrine that she must

---

[28] Skocpol, *Protecting Soldiers and Mothers*, pp. 373–423; Susan Lehrer, *Origins of Protective Labor Legislation for Women, 1905–1925* (Albany: State University of New York Press, 1987); Boris, *Home to Work*, pp. 81–122; and Vivien Hart, *Bound by Our Constitution: Women, Workers, and the Minimum Wage* (Princeton: Princeton University Press, 1994).

[29] Irving Bernstein, *Turbulent Years: A History of the American Worker, 1933–1941* (Boston: Houghton Mifflin, 1970), p. 122; Hart, *Bound by Our Constitution*, pp. 66–86; Skocpol, *Protecting Soldiers and Mothers*, pp. 401–21.

[30] 261 U.S. 525 (1923). The hospital involved in the dispute employed women at a rate lower than the minimum wage mandated by the District; when authorities attempted to force compliance, Children's Hospital appealed to the courts on the grounds of unconstitutionality, and the Court agreed with the claim in a 5–4 vote.

[31] Sybil Lipshultz, "Social Feminism and Legal Discourse, 1908–1923," in *At the Boundaries of the Law: Feminism and Legal Theory*, ed. Martha Albertson Fineman and Nancy Sweet Thomadsen (New York: Routledge, Chapman and Hall, 1991), pp. 209–25; Hart, *Bound by Our Constitution*, pp. 108–29.

be given special protection or be subjected to special restraint in her contractual and civil relationships.[32]

Because the Court let other types of protective labor laws stand, *Adkins* left women workers in a paradoxical position: on the one hand, to the extent that they were limited to employment in certain jobs and during certain hours, they were "protected" by the states and denied freedom of contract, but on the other hand, they were simultaneously denied minimum wages on the premise that they were as able to negotiate employment contracts as men. The combined effect of these positive and negative freedoms was that women typically had no choice but to work fewer hours and for less pay than men.

Some married women benefited from mandatory reductions of hours, which assisted them with the double burden of wage earning and domestic responsibilities, but other women resented the policies for preventing them from competing for better paying jobs and sufficient and suitable work hours. In fact, some unions supported protective labor laws as an explicit strategy for ousting women from the best jobs in industry. The labor legislation strategy dissuaded unions, furthermore, from organizing women workers because it reinforced their separate status as workers needing protection rather than as agents capable of bargaining for themselves. The newly formed Women's Bureau in the Department of Labor kept on file hundreds of unsuccessful applications by women seeking to attain work in jobs considered dangerous or membership in unions. Overall, protective labor laws reinforced the separateness of women and men in the workplace, institutionalizing occupational segregation by gender.[33]

Furthermore, the strategy divided women's groups struggling to improve the conditions of women. A small cadre, under the banner of the National Women's Party, echoed the view of Justice Sutherland and opposed protective labor legislation. Trying to move away from distinctions that reinforced women's inferiority and dependence on men, they argued that employee benefits should be applied to workers according to occupation rather than sex. In 1923, the same year as the *Adkins* decision, they called for an equal rights amendment. Opposed to them was a large coalition of women's groups allied with the Women's Bureau, whose work concerned the economic conditions of women workers. Though campaigns for minimum wage laws dissipated for some years after the *Adkins* decision, the proponents continued to lobby for other forms of protective labor legisla-

---

[32] Justice George Sutherland, Majority opinion, *Adkins v. Children's Hospital.*

[33] Judith Sealander, *As Minority Becomes Majority: Federal Reaction to the Phenomenon of Women in the Work Force, 1920–1963* (Westport, Conn.: Greenwood, 1983), pp. 75–78; Alice Kessler-Harris, *Out to Work: A History of Wage-Earning Women in the United States* (New York: Oxford University Press, 1982), pp. 194, 205–14; Baer, *Chains of Protection.*

tion left intact by the ruling, such as night work prohibitions, the eight-hour workday and six-day workweek, weight-lifting limits, and special restroom facilities for women. They opposed the ERA, fearing its enactment would mean the overturning of labor laws for women. Rather, they insisted that improvements in working conditions would gain women social equality, a goal far more necessary, they believed, than legal equality.[34]

Although maternalists had succeeded in establishing the political space in which to create reforms for workers, in the context of dual federalism that space was very narrow, defined by state borders and the judicial delineation of "freedom of contract." Thus reform had to be carried out state by state, meaning that workers' conditions depended on several features of their individual state's politics: the strength of organizations advocating on their behalf, the access those organizations had in the political realm, and the legal and administrative capacity of state institutions. In addition, such laws adhered to the notions of ascribed roles for women based on their sex and thus reinforced gender distinctions. Once established, however, protective labor laws would remain entrenched for several decades, well beyond the New Deal.

Mothers' Pensions

Beginning in the early teens, white, middle-class women's civic organizations worked state by state to achieve the enactment of mothers' pensions laws. Such policies authorized the provision of grants to single mothers in the absence of a male breadwinner. The funds were supposed to enable women to stay at home, caring for their children, rather than to have to participate in the paid work force. Inclusion in the program was also presumed to offer a more dignified form of aid than public relief for those considered to be "worthy" poor.[35] The General Federation of Women's Clubs and the National Congress of Mothers promoted the adoption of such laws through public education and lobbying efforts at the grass-roots level and

[34] Sealander, *As Minority Becomes Majority*, pp. 1–7, 31–33; see also Wendy Sarvasy, "Beyond the Difference versus Equality Policy Debate: Postsuffrage Feminism, Citizenship, and the Quest for a Feminist Welfare State," *Signs* 17 (1992): 329–62.

[35] Grace Abbott, "Recent Trends in Mothers' Aid," *Social Service Review* 8 (June 1934): 192–93. A growing literature examines the development of mothers' pensions, including Robyn Muncy, *Creating a Female Dominion in American Reform, 1890–1935* (New York: Oxford University Press, 1991); Skocpol, *Protecting Soldiers and Mothers*; Ladd-Taylor, *Mother-Work*, chap. 5; Gordon, *Pitied but Not Entitled*, chap. 3; Gwendolyn Mink, *The Wages of Motherhood: Inequality in the Welfare State, 1917–1942* (Ithaca: Cornell University Press, 1995), chap. 2; Barbara J. Nelson, "The Origins of the Two-Channel Welfare State: Workmen's Compensation and Mothers' Aid," in *Women, the State, and Welfare*, ed. Linda Gordon (Madison: University of Wisconsin Press, 1990), pp. 123–51; and Christopher Howard, "Sowing the Seeds of 'Welfare': The Transformation of Mothers' Pensions, 1900–1940," *Journal of Policy History* 4 (1992): 188–227.

succeeded in establishing mother pensions' laws in twenty states during the 1911–13 period alone.[36] By 1920, when only two states had developed old age pension laws and when unemployment insurance laws were still nonexistent, thirty-nine states had already enacted mothers' pensions laws.[37]

The widespread enactment of mothers' pensions was a remarkable achievement under the institutional and political circumstances which still inhibited the development of most social programs. Program implementation, however, was far less impressive, shaped, as it was, by the dynamics of state-level governance and federalism combined with the ideology of maternalism. Distinct from the failed social insurance plans advocated by men's reform groups, the programs were to be delivered through the emerging model of casework as used by social workers, incorporating home visits to beneficiaries for the purposes of personal evaluation and supervision.[38] As a means of establishing the legitimacy of mothers' pensions, reformers enacted highly restrictive laws, requiring mothers who received the benefits to emulate Anglo-Saxon middle-class behavioral norms for women.[39] Sanctioned by the states' police power and implemented with extensive discretion by local officials, these rulings endowed mothers' pensions with its invasive character and allowed local and regional prejudices to be reflected in program coverage.

Though widows maintained the majority of female-headed households in the 1930s, approximately one-third of women who were single parents either had never been married or were divorced or separated from their husbands.[40] Yet although all mothers' pensions laws covered children whose fathers were dead, and most covered those whose fathers were in penal institutions or incapacitated, only 36 states covered families deserted by fathers, 21 of the laws provided coverage in the case of divorce, and only 11 covered children born outside of marriage.[41] States also had a variety of suitable home laws that stipulated particular behavior on the part of mothers in order to remain eligible. Some states and localities required women to exhibit housekeeping and child-rearing methods deemed acceptable by white, Anglo-Saxon standards; most forbade the presence of male boarders; a few required that children attend school and church regularly.[42] Characteristic of social programs implemented at the state and local levels, mothers' pensions developed in a manner that was, in the words of Winifred Bell, "intimately based in parochial and regional values."[43]

[36] Skocpol, *Protecting Soldiers and Mothers*, p. 424.
[37] SSB, *Social Security in America*, p. 160.
[38] Gordon, *Pitied but Not Entitled*, pp. 102–5.
[39] Gordon, *Pitied but Not Entitled*, pp. 27–36; Winifred Bell, *Aid to Dependent Children*, (New York: Cambridge University Press, 1965), chap. 1.
[40] See 1930 Census data, in SSB, *Social Security in America*, p. 240.
[41] Ibid. pp. 234–36.
[42] Mink, *Wages of Motherhood*, pp. 31–41; Gordon, *Pitied but Not Entitled*, pp. 45–46.
[43] Bell, *Aid to Dependent Children*, p. 19.

Owing to the pressures of interstate economic competition and the lack of state-level capacity to raise revenues, furthermore, mothers' pensions fell far short of the goals of the maternalist reform groups that had worked for their enactment. Though forty-five states had enacted such laws by 1934, the statutes typically functioned only to permit rather than to mandate implementation by local governments, and less than half of the localities empowered to administer the statutes actually followed through.[44] Even where programs were in effect, a chronic shortage of funds meant that only a small portion of eligible families received assistance, and benefits were rarely ever sufficient to enable women to refrain from work for wages outside the home.[45] During the depression, need among families without a breadwinner far outweighed available aid, and an estimated 358,000 relied on emergency relief instead.[46]

In sum, though the widespread enactment of mothers' pensions was surprising in the context of dual federalism and can only be explained by the unique status of maternalist organizations at the turn of the century, the less impressive story of their implementation was in keeping with the characteristics and dynamics of state-level governance of that era. Yet despite their early record, mothers' pensions would provide a precedent on which New Deal policymakers would build, perpetuating their legacy throughout the entire twentieth century.

Implications for Citizenship

The emerging welfare state of the late nineteenth and twentieth centuries failed to incorporate citizens broadly and equitably into the polity. Three characteristics typical of policies of the era undermined their potential in this regard. First, most policies were developed state by state, yielding considerable variation between and within states. Thus the character of citizenship depended on where a person resided in the political geography of federalism. Second, state legislatures employed the police power free from the restraints of the equal protection clause of the Fourteenth Amendment, so they could fashion policies that preserved and institutionalized social hierarchies, differentiating between and stratifying the citizenry. Third, most policies were designed in the form of what Theodore Lowi terms "distributive" or "patronage" policies, which are necessarily particularistic—aimed at a specific group to reward particular behavior. They permitted a high degree of discretion to politicians, who could in practice control the

---

[44] SSB, *Social Security in America*, p. 233.

[45] Joanne L. Goodwin, "An American Experiment in Paid Motherhood: The Implementation of Mothers' Pensions in Early Twentieth Century Chicago," *Gender and History* 4 (autumn 1992): 330–34; Gordon, *Pitied but Not Entitled*, pp. 49–50; Paul H. Douglas, *Social Security in the United States* (New York: Whittlesey House, 1936), pp. 187–92.

[46] SSB, *Social Security in America*, p. 241.

timing and targeting of benefits for political purposes. Only regulatory policies, which control the behavior of actors in the private sector, and redistributive policies, which manipulate the environment of conduct, have the potential to affect broad classes of citizens and thus have fundamental implications for the incorporation of citizens.[47]

Civil War pensions, enacted and financed nationally, failed to broaden citizenship because of distributive policy characteristics. As Skocpol has shown, the pensions were established explicitly for those who had proven their civic virtue by serving in the Union Army and their families, and their distribution became even more particularistic as they were allocated through the patronage system.[48] Protective labor laws and mothers' pensions were formulated, respectively, as regulatory and redistributive policies and therefore had the potential to incorporate broader classes of people. The reach of such policies was limited, however, both by their state-level application and the ascriptive character of their eligibility criteria. The maternalist reforms recognized the social value of unpaid work by women but simultaneously reinforced women's inferior status as citizens and their primary civic function as mothers. By offering social provision and workplace protection to some citizens, the nascent welfare state did represent a departure from the previous reliance on private charity, local relief, and the market, but limited coverage and the governing context of federalism blocked the development of a means of assuring citizens of fuller incorporation in the polity.

The Beginnings of a New Deal in Policymaking

The end of the 1920s brought two developments that would establish the context for a transformation of political institutions, policymaking, and citizenship: the Great Depression and a political realignment. But although women had become increasingly present in the work force and party politics, New Deal policymakers would act amid a political economy still segregated in terms of gender.

Gender and the Economy in the Great Depression

Since the mid-nineteenth century, the family model of two parents, a breadwinner father and a homemaker mother, had been gradually replacing the two-parent farm family model. By 1920, the breadwinner-homemaker model represented more than half of all U.S. families, and it re-

---

[47] Lowi, "American Business, Public Policy," pp. 677–715.
[48] Skocpol, *Protecting Soldiers and Mothers*, pp. 82–87, 120–24, 143–48.

mained dominant for four decades. But even during the half century that the breadwinner-homemaker family was most typical, it never accounted for more than 56 percent of all families; for at the same time, another family model was emerging.[49] Since the turn of the century, women had been slowly but steadily increasing their numbers in the paid work force, from 20.6 percent of the female population in 1900 to 23.7 percent in 1920 and 24.8 percent in 1930.[50] During the 1920s, the presence of married women among wage earners grew most dramatically, by 40 percent over the decade, establishing the trend that would in time make dual-earner families the prevalent model.[51]

Although shifts in the economy had led to an increase in white-collar jobs, so that women entering the work force found jobs in new areas of employment, occupational segregation by gender persisted. As professions and office work became more segmented and hierarchically arranged, women were offered jobs at the bottom of the wage and status scale which offered very limited opportunities for advancement.[52] For every ten women workers in 1930, three were in clerical or sales work, two were factory operatives (especially in the low-wage clothing and textile industries), two were employed as domestic servants, one was a professional (usually a nurse or a teacher), and one worked in a personal service job (as a cook, waitress, or beautician, for example).[53] The earnings gap between women and men actually widened during the 1920s, with women earning only 57 percent of men's wages.[54] Outside of jobs covered by protective labor laws, women worked often worked long hours: a study by the Women's Bureau found that one-half of women employed in 1930 worked more than fifty hours per week.[55] Thus, as the depression began, most women still worked in very rigidly defined sectors of the work force, in jobs notorious for low pay, few opportunities for advancement, long hours, and difficult working conditions.

Though unemployment climbed steadily as the depression deepened, women continued to increase their numbers in the work force during the 1930s. Interestingly, the structure of occupational segregation protected many women's jobs from layoffs, because industries employing women

---

[49] Donald J. Hernandez, *America's Children: Resources from Family, Government, and the Economy* (New York: Russell Sage, 1993), pp. 102–3.

[50] Bureau of the Census, *Statistical History of the United States*, p. 133.

[51] Lois Scharf, *To Work and to Wed: Female Employment, Feminism, and the Great Depression* (Westport, Conn.: Greenwood, 1980), pp. 41–42.

[52] Kessler-Harris, *Out to Work*, p. 224.

[53] Susan Ware, *Holding Their Own: American Women in the 1930s* (Boston: Twayne, 1982), pp. 25–26, 30–31; see also Robert S. Lynd and Helen Merrell Lynd, *Middletown in Transition: A Study in Cultural Conflicts* (New York: Harcourt, Brace, 1937), pp. 54–63.

[54] Kessler-Harris, *Out to Work*, p. 227.

[55] Ware, *Holding Their Own*, p. 27.

tended to contract less than those employing men. Consequently, married, middle-class, middle-aged women took jobs in large part to compensate for losses of work or decreased wages for their husbands.[56] The percentage of women who worked grew from 24.8 to 25.8 over the decade, and the female proportion of the work force grew from 21.9 to 24.6 percent.[57]

As unemployment skyrocketed and job competition intensified, however, women working in occupations that employed both men and women became the objects of public animosity and, in many cases, discriminatory policies. The AFL made public statements advocating preferential treatment for men in hiring procedures.[58] In a 1936 Gallup poll, 82 percent of Americans agreed that wives should not work if their husbands had jobs, and national, state, and local public policies, as well as business practices in the private sector, reflected such public antagonism. Public school systems quickly took dramatic measures: a survey conducted by the National Education Association in 1930–31 found that 77 percent of public schools refused to hire married women and 63 percent dismissed women teachers who were married. Congress, over protests from the National Women's Party, included a "married persons clause," Section 213 of the 1932 Economy Act, requiring that women be discharged if their husbands also held government jobs. Within one year, more than 1,500 women employed in departments such as the post office, treasury, war, navy, and veterans administration were dismissed. Subsequently, several state legislatures followed the national government's example and enacted similar bills. Numerous businesses, especially those employing clerical and service workers, also dismissed women employees. The National Industrial Conference Board found in 1939 that 84 percent of insurance companies, 65 percent of banks, and 63 percent of public utility companies restricted the employment of married women. Although in 1937, women's groups had finally succeeded in getting Section 213 repealed, it had provided an example that was emulated widely.[59]

Most nonwhite Americans had lived at or below subsistence levels even before the depression and worked in the lowest paying and most exploited positions in the work force.[60] The worsening economy presented particu-

---

[56] Ruth Milkman, "Women's Work and Economic Crises: Some Lessons of the Great Depression," *Review of Radical Political Economy* 8 (spring 1976): 75–77; Kessler-Harris, *Out to Work*, pp. 251–72.

[57] Bureau of the Census, *Statistical History of the U.S.*, pp. 132–33.

[58] Philip S. Foner, *Women and the American Labor Movement: From World War I to the Present* (New York: Free Press, 1980), p. 257; see also Scharf, *To Work and to Wed*, pp. 43–44, on precedents to such activities during the 1920s.

[59] Ware, *Holding Their Own*, pp. 27–28, 46–53; Foner, *Women and the American Labor Movement*, p. 258; Claudia Goldin, *Understanding the Gender Gap: An Economic History of American Women* (New York: Oxford University Press, 1990), pp. 159–79.

[60] Jacqueline Jones, *Labor of Love, Labor of Sorrow: Black Women, Work, and the Family from Slavery to the Present* (New York: Basic Books, 1985), pp. 46–47; Julia Kirk Black-

larly harsh conditions for nonwhite women. In 1930, 40 percent of African American women participated in the paid work force and only 20 percent of white women.[61] Nine-tenths of African American working women were employed in domestic service or agriculture.[62] As economic conditions deteriorated, more white women sought jobs in domestic service and in the few menial jobs that had been secured by black women in shops and factories. As a result, unemployment was particularly acute for black women: 56 percent lost their jobs in domestic and personal service. In Louisville, Kentucky, for example, more than half of black women were unemployed in 1933, in contrast to fewer than one-fourth of white women.[63] More generally, nonwhite women who did retain jobs were paid at rates far below those paid to white women, often for doing the same work and sometimes through job segregation.[64]

In sum, high unemployment and low production and consumption levels represented only the newest and most striking characteristics of the U.S. economy encountered by policymakers in the 1930s. The increase of married women in the work force had been underway well before the depression began, and patterns of occupational segregation by sex, race, and ethnicity were deeply entrenched. The political significance of such features would depend, however, on the politics of the New Deal.

Early New Deal Policies and Politics

On March 4, 1933, in his inaugural address, Franklin D. Roosevelt spoke with resolve to a nation struggling in the depths of the economic crisis. Poised as a commander-in-chief ready to wage war on the domestic front, the new president announced that he would ask Congress for "broad Executive power to wage a war against the emergency." Specifically, he announced, "Our greatest primary task is to put people to work."[65]

The depression had overwhelmed the local governments' ability to respond to the demands for relief. The finances of state governments were strained to the breaking point, and most states lacked the capacity to raise additional revenues and to implement extensive relief programs.[66] Thus

---

welder, *Women of the Depression: Caste and Culture in San Antonio, 1929–1939* (College Station: Texas A & M University Press, 1984).

[61] Ware, *Holding their Own*, pp. 30–31.

[62] Department of Labor, Women's Bureau, *The Negro Woman Worker*, by Jean Collier Brown, Bulletin 165 (Washington, D.C.: GPO, 1938), pp. 2–3.

[63] Foner, *Women and the American Labor Movement*, pp. 261–62.

[64] Blackwelder, *Women of the Depression*.

[65] Franklin D. Roosevelt, *The Public Papers and Addresses of Franklin D. Roosevelt*, comp. Samuel I. Rosenman (New York: Random House, 1938), 2:15, 13.

[66] *Reminiscences of Bernice Bernstein*, OHC, p.8; *Reminiscences of Frank Bane*, OHC, pp. 7–8; Patterson, *New Deal and the States*, chap. 2.

Roosevelt immediately sought emergency measures to provide federal monies for relief and to spur recovery. In the famous First Hundred Days of his administration, the "alphabet agencies" were established to administer numerous temporary programs, such as the Civilian Conservation Corps (CCC), Works Progress Administration (WPA), Public Works Administration (PWA), Civil Works Administration (CWA), and Federal Emergency Relief Administration (FERA).

As federally financed programs geared toward relief and recovery, the programs of the First New Deal were unprecedented, and their enactment was made possible only through the combination of Roosevelt's leadership and the emergence of a new Democratic Party coalition in Congress. Between 1928 and 1936, a massive party realignment was transforming U.S. politics, dismantling the sectional politics in place since 1896. Democrats began to arise as the majority party for the first time in nearly a decade, as working-class, ethnic voters in northern cities added their votes to those of the traditionally one-party South.[67] Democratic candidates won at all levels and made substantial gains in Congress. Skillfully united by Roosevelt, an unlikely coalition of advocates of organized labor and representatives of agrarian interests emerged in Congress and began to dominate the policymaking process. Though northern and southern Democrats split on civil rights issues, they voted together during the 1930s for an expanded role for national government in issues pertaining to the development of the welfare state and on fiscal, regulatory, and labor matters.[68]

How did women figure into the New Deal coalition? Scholars have generally treated the 1920 achievement of women's suffrage as a nonevent and assumed that women stayed away from the polls and had little influence on politics for several more decades. Kristi Andersen has shown, however, that women did become actively involved in formal politics during the 1920s, increasing their presence not only among voters but as party officials, candidates, and officeholders, albeit usually in circumscribed roles.[69] By the 1928 election, women voters had become a significant portion of the electorate, possibly constituting 49 percent of all voters.[70]

In 1932, the Women's Division of the Democratic National Committee, spearheaded by Molly Dewson, made tremendous efforts to urge women

---

[67] James L. Sundquist, *Dynamics of the Party System* (Washington, D.C.: Brookings, 1983), pp. 198–239; Walter Dean Burnham, *The Current Crisis in American Politics* (New York: Oxford University Press, 1982), pp. 110–13; Kristi Andersen, *The Creation of a Democratic Majority, 1928–1936* (Chicago: University of Chicago Press, 1979).

[68] Ira Katznelson, Kim Geiger, and Daniel Kryder, "Limiting Liberalism: The Southern Veto in Congress, 1933–1950," *Political Science Quarterly* 108 (1993): 283–306.

[69] Kristi Andersen, *After Suffrage: Women in Partisan and Electoral Politics before the New Deal* (Chicago: University of Chicago Press, 1996).

[70] Kristi Andersen, "Women and Citizenship in the 1920s," in *Women, Politics, and Change*, ed. Tilly and Gurin, pp. 177–98.

to participate in the election and to vote for Roosevelt.[71] Once elected, Roosevelt appointed an unprecedented number of women to official positions in his administration, most notably Secretary of Labor Frances Perkins as the first woman ever to serve in the cabinet.[72] Representatives of women's organizations such as the National League of Women Voters and the YWCA were routinely appointed to serve on advisory councils for policymaking matters. The Women's Bureau and the Children's Bureau of the Department of Labor, both established during the Progressive Era in response to maternalist politics, continued to be staffed by women.[73]

Yet despite the increased presence of women in politics by the 1930s, policymakers in the early New Deal did not appear to place priority on women's needs. Still adhering to the family wage ideal, officials tended to assume that policies directed toward male breadwinners would indirectly benefit women as well as children. Relief programs such as the CCC, WPA, and CWA were developed primarily to employ jobless men. Various special corollary programs were created for women, but the number of jobs provided was a small fraction of those offered to men. The few job-training programs for women, moreover, tended to reinforce their traditional roles in the domestic sphere rather than to enable them to gain skills necessary to compete in the labor market.[74]

In any case, although the programs of the First New Deal expanded the fiscal outlays and subject matter of national policy as never before, they perpetuated the tradition of patronage policies that national government had long utilized as a means of sharing resources with particular groups or individuals as determined by Congress.[75] Only the regulatory and redistributive policies of the Second New Deal would truly and permanently

---

[71]Susan Ware, *Partner and I* (New Haven: Yale University Press, 1987), pp. 168–73. Insufficient data exist to determine precisely the extent to which members of either sex contributed to the Democratic victories in the 1930s, but according to Gerald Gamm's study of Boston, men's votes made for Democratic victories in 1932, and women's votes bolstered 1936 and 1938 outcomes. Gerald Gamm, *The Making of New Deal Democrats: Voting Behavior and Realignment in Boston, 1920–1940* (Chicago: University of Chicago Press, 1989), chap. 7.

[72] On the women's network in national politics during the New Deal, see Susan Ware, *Beyond Suffrage: Women in the New Deal* (Cambridge: Harvard University Press, 1981).

[73] On the role of the Women's Bureau in New Deal policymaking, see Sealander, *As Minority Becomes Majority*, pp. 57–84; on the Children's Bureau, see Muncy, *Creating a Female Dominion*.

[74] Scharf, *To Work and to Wed*, pp. 122–25; Ware, *Holding Their Own*, pp. 39–40; Jones, *Labor of Love*, p. 217; Winifred Wandersee, "A New Deal for Women: Government Programs, 1933–1940," in *The Roosevelt New Deal: A Program Assessment Fifty Years After*, ed. Wilbur J. Cohen (Austin: University of Texas, Lyndon B. Johnson School of Public Affairs, 1986); Sealander, *As Minority Becomes Majority*, pp. 63, 69–74; Department of Labor, Women's Bureau, *Women Workers in the Third Year of the Depression*, Bulletin 103 (Washington, D.C.: GPO, 1933).

[75] William E. Leuchtenburg, *Franklin D. Roosevelt and the New Deal* (New York: Harper and Row, 1963), pp. 41–42; Theodore J. Lowi, *The Personal President* (Ithaca: Cornell University Press, 1985), pp. 25, 44–45.

change the character of national governance with respect to citizenship, beginning with the National Labor Relations Act of 1935.

Gender and the National Labor Relations Act

The first major labor policies of the New Deal were included in the National Industrial Recovery Act (NRA), a comprehensive piece of legislation designed during the First Hundred Days primarily to enable industries to circumvent antitrust laws and develop large trade associations that would make market decisions. Besides establishing minimum wage and maximum-hours provisions (treated in Chapter 7), the law included, in Section 7(a), a recognition of the right of workers to join unions and to engage in collective bargaining. Just two years later, though, in *Schecter Poultry Co. v. United States*, the Supreme Court declared the NRA unconstitutional.[76]

Already, however, Senator Robert Wagner (D-N.Y.) and staff attorneys at the National Labor Relations Board (NLRB) had worked together to develop a new, narrower bill that would deal exclusively with organizing and collective-bargaining procedures.[77] Although Roosevelt had previously distanced himself from Wagner's efforts, the *Schecter* decision left his administration without a labor policy, and he willingly agreed to give the bill his support. On July 5, 1935, Roosevelt signed the National Labor Relations Act of 1935 (NLRA), otherwise known as the Wagner Act, into law.[78]

---

[76] 295 U.S. 495 (1935).

[77] The literature on the creation of the National Labor Relations Act is large and contentious. Standard histories of the era emphasize the role of Congress in developing the law, as seen in Leuchtenburg, *Roosevelt and the New Deal*; James MacGregor Burns, *Roosevelt: The Lion and the Fox* (New York: Harcourt, Brace and World, 1956), pp. 216–17; and Murray Edelman, "New Deal Sensitivity to Labor Interests," in *Labor and the New Deal*, ed. Milton Derber and Edwin Young (Madison: University of Wisconsin Press, 1961), pp. 186–87. Thomas Ferguson offers a corporate liberal analysis in Thomas Ferguson, "From Normalcy to New Deal: Industrial Structure, Party Competition, and American Public Policy in the Great Depression," *International Organization* 38 (winter 1984). A critical legal theory analysis appears in Christopher L. Tomlins, *Labor Relations, Law, and the Organized Labor Movement in America, 1880–1960* (New York: Cambridge University Press, 1985). Other analyses emphasize the role of government bureaucrats: see Kenneth Finegold and Theda Skocpol, "State, Party and Industry," in *Statemaking and Social Movements: Esaays in History and Theory*, ed. Susan Bright and Charles Harding (Ann Arbor: University of Michigan Press, 1984), pp. 159–92; and Howell Harris, "The Snares of Liberalism? Politicians, Bureaucrats, and the Shaping of Federal Labor Relations Policy in the United States, ca. 1915–1947," in *Shop Floor Bargaining and the State*, ed. Steven Tolliday and Jonathan Zeitlin (New York: Cambridge University Press, 1985), pp. 148–91. Finally, some emphasize the role of working class insurgency: Piven and Cloward, *Poor People's Movements*, pp. 96–180; and Goldfield, "Influence of Worker Insurgency."

[78] Melvyn Dubofsky, *The State and Labor in Modern America* (Chapel Hill: University of North Carolina Press, 1994), p. 144.

The United States thus became, through the NLRA, the only western nation to regulate industry-labor relations by legal prescription. The central provision of the NLRA, Section 7, constituted a national industrial bill of rights for employees, guaranteeing workers the right to form and participate in labor organizations and to select their own representatives for the purpose of collective bargaining. To guarantee the rights of employees, the statute also defined unfair labor practices by employers, established rules for employee-representation elections, and created a new independent NLRB with three members appointed by the president to administer the policy. The NLRB would be charged with developing a body of precedents pertaining to industry-labor relations to replace the common-law principles, which had finally come to be regarded as extinct.[79]

An earthshaking change of course by the Supreme Court in 1937 sustained the NLRA. Through the key decision, *National Labor Relations Board v. Jones and Laughlin Steel Corp.*, the common-law tenets of "master and servant" were at last displaced, bringing the workplace within reach of legislative activity.[80] Even more broadly, the decision epitomized the "constitutional revolution" of the New Deal: whereas previously, the Court had interpreted the scope of interstate commerce very narrowly, considering the commerce clause to function primarily as a constraint upon Congress, through the NLRB decision nearly all stages of the production process came to be understood as interdependent and thus within the powers of Congress to regulate.[81] In effect, the Court allowed one of the central pillars of dual federalism to be shattered and sanctioned a greatly expanded role of national government in the realm of public policy.

How would the NLRA operate in terms of gender? The new law appeared to have the potential to benefit both men and women workers. Its language was gender neutral, and unlike the Social Security Act and Fair Labor Standards Act which were to follow, it applied to organizations rather than to individuals citizens defined in such terms as occupation or marital status. The law sanctioned a tremendous increase in unionization, strike activity, and collective-bargaining efforts, and initially it appeared that women would be better represented in organizing efforts and workplace activism than previously.

Immediately, the NLRA gave momentum to the newly formed Committee for Industrial Organization (CIO), created by pro-industrial unionists who had broken ranks with the AFL and its tradition of organizing along

---

[79] Frank W. McCulloch and Tim Bornstein, *The National Labor Relations Board* (New York: Praeger, 1974), pp. 18–25; Dubofsky, *State and Labor*, pp. 129–30.

[80] Orren, *Belated Feudalism*, p. 29; 301 U.S. 1 (1937).

[81] 301 U.S. 1 (1937); Dubofsky, *State and Labor*, pp. 144–45.

craft lines. The CIO leaders set out to organize unskilled workers in mass-production industries, regardless of sex, race, or skill.[82] This strategy promoted, in 1937 alone, a 100 percent increase in union membership and made the CIO far more inclusive of women than the AFL had been.[83] Just one-third of the CIO's member organizations represented male-dominated occupations and industries, in contrast to more than half of the AFL groups. About one-fifth of the CIO membership, furthermore, came from industries employing high proportions of women, such as the garment and textile trades.[84] Expressing awareness of the needs of women workers, John L. Lewis, president of the CIO, advocated equal pay for "substantially the same work." The WTUL and the Women's Bureau both affirmed the advantages of the new approach for women workers.[85]

Strike activity soared after the creation of the NLRA, and women assumed new prominence in the mobilization. In Richmond, Virginia, in 1936, four hundred black female stemmers in the tobacco industry walked out to protest wages of three dollars per week and poor working conditions, the first strike by the union in thirty years under the AFL. After winning their demands, the members voted to change their affiliation to the CIO.[86] Women made up 60 percent of the nine thousand strikers in a United Electrical, Radio, and Machine Workers of America (UE) strike in Camden, New Jersey. In 1937, two weeks after a victory in Flint, Michigan, by the United Auto Workers (UAW), which had engaged in a sit-down strike, some three thousand women in Detroit staged sit-downs to win union recognition in industries ranging from pie making to cigar making. Retail clerks in department stores and five-and-tens in Detroit, Chicago, and New York used the same strategy.[87]

Yet once the initial upsurge abated, the benefits of the law for women workers appeared to be marginal at best. Labor organizations, outside of the realm of a few industries, remained primarily a male enterprise for several decades. Though the numbers of organized women had more than tripled from the pre-NLRA days, women continued to account for less than one-tenth of all union members: their numbers grew only from about

[82] Foner, *Women and the American Labor Movement*, pp. 301–2.

[83] Dubofsky, *State and Labor*, pp. 137; Robert H. Zieger, *American Workers, American Unions, 1920–1935* (Baltimore: Johns Hopkins University Press, 1986), pp. 46–55.

[84] Department of Labor, Women's Bureau, *The Woman Wage Earner: Her Situation Today*, by Elisabeth D. Benham, Bulletin 172 (Washington, D.C.: GPO, 1939), pp. 42–43.

[85] Foner, *Women in the American Labor Movement*, pp. 301–2.

[86] Dolores Janiewski, "Seeking a New Day and a New Way: Black Women and Unions in the Southern Tobacco Industry," in *"To Toil the Livelong Day": America's Women at Work, 1780–1980*, ed. Carol Groneman and Mary Beth Norton (Ithaca: Cornell University Press, 1987), pp. 161–78.

[87] Sharon Hartman Strom, "Challenging 'Woman's Place': Feminism, the Left, and Industrial Unionism in the 1930s," *Feminist Studies* 9 (summer 1983): 365; Foner, *Women in the American Labor Movement*, pp. 311–16, 321–22.

260,000 in 1930, to 800,000 in 1940, from 7.7 percent to 9.4 percent of all union members.[88] The trends persisted although through unionization, women tended to experience greater wage increases than men, and they more readily described themselves as interested in joining unions.[89] Men continued to be twice as likely as women to belong to labor unions for the next several decades. In 1956, for example, only 15.7 percent of women workers were union members, compared with 32.3 percent of the male work force.[90]

The CIO did continue to be more open to women than the AFL, but the initial promise of broad inclusivity faded as leaders narrowed their organizing efforts to the sectors of basic industry or manufacturing where mostly men were employed and limited their goals to contract negotiations. The CIO's efforts to organize women workers were primarily in those industries that both employed large numbers of men and had a women's employment sector considered strategic for the industrial union movement, through such organizations as the International Ladies Garment Workers' Union (ILGWU), the Amalgamated Clothing Workers of America (ACWA), and the UE.[91] The perpetuation of occupational segregation meant, however, that such instances were rare. In some cases, women in female-dominated sectors of manufacturing or in other employment sectors such as office work, retail, and service occupations organized themselves, but the CIO tended to be, as Sharon Strom has shown, "indifferent at best and hostile at worst" to such efforts.[92]

Not only was the membership of women in CIO unions low, but their presence in the leadership was even smaller. Few women unionists were among the leaders at the local level, and even fewer held posts at the regional and international levels. In surveying the leadership of unions in industries with high proportions of women employees, the Women's Bureau found that women constituted only nine out of forty-five council members for the Actors Equity Association, one board member on the ACWA, one

---

[88] Gladys Dickason, "Women in Labor Unions," *Annals of the American Academy of Political and Social Science* 251 (May 1947): 71; see also Department of Labor, *Woman Wage Earner*, p. 42.

[89] Ruth Milkman, "The New Deal, the CIO, and Women in Industry," in *Roosevelt New Deal*; ed. Cohen, p. 169; Richard B. Freeman and James L. Medoff, *What Do Unions Do?* (New York: Basic Books, 1984), pp. 28–29.

[90] Francine D. Blau and Marianne A. Ferber, *The Economics of Women, Men, and Work* (Englewood Cliffs, N.J.: Prentice-Hall, 1986), p. 273.

[91] Milkman, "Organizing the Sexual Division of Labor," p. 127; Sharon Hartman Strom, "'We're No Kitty Foyles': Organizing Office Workers for the Congress of Industrial Organizations, 1937–1950," in *Women, Work, and Protest*, ed. Ruth Milkman (Boston: Routledge and Kegan Paul, 1985), p. 213.

[92] Strom, "Challenging 'Woman's Place,'" quotation on p. 373, see also pp. 369–73; Nancy F. Gabin, *Feminism in the Labor Movement: Women and the United Auto Workers, 1935–1975* (Ithaca: Cornell University Press, 1990), pp. 17, 20, 38.

out of eight vice-presidents in the American Federation of State, County, and Municipal Employees, five out of 15 vice-presidents in the American Federation of Teachers, and one board member on the ILGWU.[93] At the CIO's annual convention in 1938, 4 out of 519 delegates were women. Even unions with high portions of female members sent male delegates. The only resolution at the convention which specifically mentioned women did not concern women as workers but acknowledged the significance of the involvement of female relatives of members in supporting unionism.[94] In a declaration of purpose, the CIO, now the Congress of Industrial Organizations, did state its intention "to bring about the effective organization of the workingmen and women of America regardless of race, creed, color or nationality, and to unite them into labor unions for their mutual aid and protection."[95] Yet in 1946 only twenty women numbered among the six hundred delegates at the annual convention.[96]

With so few women in leadership positions, the particular concerns of women were usually neglected in collective-bargaining efforts, and contracts often included discriminatory features. Outright wage differentials by sex appeared in many contracts. Unions efforts to establish job security based on both seniority and job classification tended to make divisions between male-typed and female-typed jobs more rigid and to undercut women's opportunities for advancement.[97] Unions in industries hiring large numbers of both men and women were most likely to support the CIO's call for equal pay for equal work regardless of sex to prevent employers from using female substitution for jobs previously held by men as a means of cutting wages. As a case in point, the UE's constitution stated that the organization intended to unite "all workers in our industry . . . regardless of craft, age, sex, nationality, race, creed, or political belief."[98] In most occupations, however, women's underrepresentation in the new unions and

[93] Department of Labor, *Woman Wage Earner*, pp. 44–47; on the career of the ACWA board member, see Nina Lynn Asher, "Dorothy Jacobs Bellanca: Feminist Trade Unionist, 1894–1946" (Ph.D. diss., State University of New York at Binghamton, 1982).

[94] Foner, *Women in the American Labor Movement*, pp. 326–27.

[95] *Proceedings of the First Constitutional Convention of the Congress of Industrial Organizations, Pittsburgh, November 14–18, 1938* (n.p.: Congress of Industrial Organizations, 1938), pp. 123–24.

[96] Strom, "Challenging 'Woman's Place,'" p. 370; Foner, *Women in the American Labor Movement*, pp. 331–32.

[97] Gabin, *Feminism in the Labor Movement*, pp. 31–34; Wandersee, "New Deal for Women," pp. 188–89; Foner, *Women in the American Labor Movement*, p. 332; Milkman, "Organizing the Sexual Division of Labor," p. 126; Patricia Cooper, "The Faces of Gender: Sex Segregation and Work Relations at Philco, 1928–1938," in *Work Engendered: Toward a New History of American Labor*, ed. Ava Baron (Ithaca: Cornell University Press, 1991), p. 330.

[98] Foner, *Women in the American Labor Movement*, quotation on p. 314; Ruth Milkman, *Gender at Work* (Urbana: University of Illinois Press, 1987), pp. 42–48.

their marginal status in those unions to which they did belong meant that the method of resolving industrial conflict by collective bargaining did little to improve the circumstances of their lives as workers.

Thus, in effect, the NLRA had bestowed new nationally guaranteed rights of social or industrial citizenship primarily on men, particularly those employed in basic, nonagricultural industries. Regardless of the shortcomings of the NLRA even for unionized men, at least the law did grant government sanction to the activities of their labor organizations. Men could henceforth turn to collective bargaining for improvements in wages, hours, benefits, and working conditions; their activism would develop along a particular trajectory as a result. The circumstances of most women's lives remained out of the reach of the Wagner Act, except to the extent to which they would benefit indirectly from the improvements in wages and working conditions won by their husbands through collective bargaining.

Was the NLRA itself, though seemingly gender neutral, biased against women workers, and if so, how? Some scholars have explained the low levels of unionization by women as an effect of job segmentation or occupational segregation itself, rather than as an unintended consequence of public policy.[99] Others have argued that the particular design of the NLRA fostered a hierarchical and narrow unionism, in turn exacerbating the already male-dominated character of labor organizations.[100] Still other analysts reason that the politics of the late 1930s and 1940s, driven by disenchantment with the NLRA on the part of business, southerners, and the AFL, pushed Roosevelt to make more conservative appointments to the NLRB and that those bureaucrats in turn shaped the implementation of the law in a fashion that marginalized women workers.[101] For example, the NLRB handed down several decisions during the late 1930s and 1940s that forbade clerical and manufacturing employees from being part of the same bargaining units, undermining the solidarity of workers across gender.[102] In any case, the explanation for why the NLRA bore such paltry effects for

---

[99] Milkman, *Gender at Work*, p. 7; Freeman and Medoff, *What Do Unions Do?* p. 28.

[100] David Montgomery, *Workers' Control in America: Studies in the History of Work, Technology, and Labor Struggles* (New York: Cambridge University Press, 1979), pp. 165–66; Piven and Cloward, *Poor People's Movements*, pp. 155–61; Elizabeth Faue, "Paths of Unionization: Community, Bureaucracy, and Gender in the Minneapolis Labor Movement of the 1930s," in *Work Engendered*, ed. Baron, pp. 296–319.

[101] Christopher L. Tomlins, "The New Deal, Collective Bargaining, and the Triumph of Industrial Pluralism," in *The New Deal: Conflicting Interpretations and Shifting Perspectives*, ed. Melvyn Dubofsky (New York: Garland, 1992), pp. 318–19; James A. Gross, *The Reshaping of the National Labor Relations Board: National Labor Policy in Transition, 1937–1947* (Albany, N.Y.: State University of New York Press, 1981), p. 43; McCulloch and Bornstein, *National Labor Relations Board*, pp. 29–30.

[102] Strom, " 'We're No Kitty Foyles,' " p. 214.

women workers for the next several decades after its enactment lies beyond the scope of this analysis; rather, its relative insignificance for women underscores the importance of how subsequent New Deal policies would shape citizenship in terms of gender.

Because the NLRA had so little immediate relevance for women, they would have to continue to look toward government to establish programs for economic security as well as labor standards. The Social Security Act and the Fair Labor Standards Act, held out the possibility that women, too, might become endowed with rights of social citizenship bestowed by the national government.

CHAPTER THREE

The Formation of Old Age Insurance and Old Age Assistance

Among our objectives I place the security of the men, women and children of the Nation first. . . . Fear and worry based on unknown danger contribute to social unrest and economic demoralization. If, as our Constitution tells us, our Federal Government was established among other things, "to promote the general welfare," it is our plain duty to provide for that security upon which welfare depends.

—President Franklin D. Roosevelt, "Message to Congress, June 8, 1934"

With these words, Roosevelt made public his preliminary plans for legislation to provide lasting measures of economic security to Americans. Anxious about his prospects for reelection in 1936, Roosevelt wanted to proceed quickly on the development and passage of a bill for social provision. By the end of June 1934, he appointed a cabinet committee called the Committee on Economic Security (CES) to study economic security concerns, develop recommendations, and draft legislative proposals that could be sent to Congress within six months. The Social Security Act, which Roosevelt signed into law in August 1935, was unprecedented in scope by American standards and remains today the most comprehensive social policy creation in U.S. political history. By combining several programs into one law, the act effectively established an entire social welfare apparatus, intended to reach, eventually, the lives of the majority of citizens. The major components of the statute include contributory Old Age Insurance (which has come to be called "social security"), noncontributory Old Age Assistance for the elderly, Unemployment Insurance, and Aid to Dependent Children.[1]

---

[1] The Social Security Act also included several smaller programs, such as Aid to the Blind, a maternal and child health program fashioned after the Sheppard-Towner Act, support for state programs for crippled children, and some funds for state-level public health programs. Comprehensive health insurance was also intended to be part of the bill, until it became clear that it was not politically feasible, primarily owing to opposition by the American Medical Association. See Arthur J. Altmeyer, *The Formative Years of Social Security* (Madison: University of Wisconsin Press, 1966), pp. 27–28, 33, 56–57; Edwin E. Witte, *The Development of the Social Security Act* (Madison: University of Wisconsin Press, 1962), pp. 173–89; and *Reminiscences of Arthur J. Altmeyer*, pp. 28–31, OHC.

In contrast to European social insurance plans and the American mothers' pensions from the Progressive Era, New Deal statebuilders created social programs that were ostensibly gender neutral. Examination of the policies reveals, however, that the Social Security Act established American social citizenship in a manner that was deeply stratified by gender. Such divisions occurred as, first of all, policymakers built on the gendered legacies of Progressive Era reform traditions: social insurance and social work. In creating distinct programs for the "able-bodied employables" and those who were deemed "unable to take care of themselves," they effectively sorted potential beneficiaries by sex. Second, policymakers compounded the distinctions between programs with the national-state administrative split, so that implementation created separate forms of citizenship.

Neither the framework for the Social Security Act nor the design of its particular programs were foreordained, however, and even after the law's creation, the implications for citizenship were still unclear. To understand how the law shaped citizenship in terms of gender, it is necessary to examine the politics of both the formation and the implementation of its major programs. This chapter begins with how the Roosevelt administration began to shape the framework for what was called the "Economic Security Bill" in its early stages, and proceeds to the politics of policymaking for the elderly in both the CES and Congress.

The Roosevelt Administration's Approach to Social Provision

In the 1930s, many voices proposed plans for social insurance. A widespread grass-roots populist movement known as the Townsendites championed monthly payments of two hundred dollars, drawn from taxes, to every individual sixty and older on the condition that the money be spent within the month as a means to spur the economy.[2] Left-wing supporters of the Lundeen Bill, or "workers' bill," believed that a universal unemployment compensation plan should be financed by general taxation instead of by employee contributions, which they feared would raise prices, lower wages, and hurt consumers.[3] Abraham Epstein and Isaac Rubinow, both prominent scholars of social policy, advocated nationally administered unemployment insurance financed in part by government contributions and in part by employer reserves.[4] Harry Hopkins, head of the Fed-

[2] Abraham Holtzman, *The Townsend Movement: A Political Study* (1963; reprint, New York: Octagon Books, 1975).

[3] Kenneth Casebeer, "The Workers' Unemployment Insurance Bill: American Social Wage, Labor Organization, and Legal Ideology," in *Labor Law in America*, ed. Christopher Tomlins and Andrew King (Baltimore: Johns Hopkins University Press, 1992), pp. 231–59.

[4] Jerry R. Cates, *Insuring Inequality: Administrative Leadership in Social Security* (Ann Arbor: University of Michigan Press, 1983), p. 23.

eral Emergency Relief Administration; various staff in executive agencies; and the American Association of Social Workers recommended that relief and social insurance of all kinds be merged, so that any citizen who was unemployed, elderly, or ill, regardless of need, would be eligible to receive payments from the national government out of general tax revenues.[5]

Though from very different sources, these proposals shared some common expectations about central features of permanent social policies. Their proponents desired programs that would be fairly universal in coverage, administered in large part by the national government, and financed through general revenues. In all of these regards, their proposals differed vastly from the initial plans of the Roosevelt administration.

Incorporating Social Insurance and Social Work

Roosevelt himself wished for a comprehensive and universal system of social insurance. In private musings to cabinet members, he argued for "cradle to the grave" (his own term, though it was later used to describe the Beveridge Plan in Great Britain) coverage for all citizens: "I see no reason why every child, from the day he is born, shouldn't be a member of the social security system. When he begins to grow up, he should know he will have old-age benefits direct from the insurance system to which he will belong all his life. If he is out of work, he gets a benefit. If he is sick or crippled, he gets a benefit. . . . And there is no reason why just the industrial workers should get the benefit of this. Everybody ought to be in on it."[6] In later years, Roosevelt conveyed to Secretary Perkins his feeling that "his own broad outlook . . . had been chiseled down to a conservative pattern in our plan."[7] Roosevelt's hopes for a seamless policy for all did not cohere, however, with his own specific policy preferences nor with the early decisions by officials in his administration to use both work-related and public assistance measures, incorporating different groups in each.

The president envisioned work-related social insurance as an alternative far preferable to long-term general relief, which he feared would have ill effects on recipients, place too heavy a toll on government revenues, and be subject to the vacillation of politics. He did acknowledge a necessity for some forms of public assistance, however, as long as programs were narrowly crafted to apply to particular groups of "deserving" recipients.[8]

---

[5] Frances Perkins, *The Roosevelt I Knew* (New York: Harper and Row, 1946), pp. 284–85.
[6] Ibid., pp. 282–83.
[7] Ibid., p. 284.
[8] Franklin D. Roosevelt, "Message to Congress . . . June 8, 1934," in Perkins, *Roosevelt I Knew*, p. 284; Irving Bernstein, *A Caring Society* (Boston: Houghton-Mifflin, 1985), p. 50; Altmeyer, *Formative Years*, p. 11; William E. Leuchtenburg, *Franklin D. Roosevelt and the New Deal* (New York: Harper and Row, 1963), p. 133; Mark Leff, "Taxing the 'Forgotten

Following the president's general inclinations but not the Hopkins or Lundeen style of combining benefits for all needy people into one program, Roosevelt's advisers quickly decided to use a "piecemeal approach," incorporating a variety of programs organized according to different principles and aimed at different groups within one comprehensive legislative package.[9] The earliest proposals sketched by Roosevelt administration officials included some programs that drew on the social insurance tradition, targeting wage earners, and others that reflected the maternalist tradition of social work and public assistance, addressing the concerns of those who lacked long-term labor-force experience.[10]

Social insurance advocates had worked quite separately from social work proponents in earlier decades, sometimes even with hostility for each other. In fact, when a Roosevelt administration official consulted with Edith Abbott, a professor of social work at the University of Chicago long associated with maternalist reform, she let him know that she had "little faith in social insurance, believing that it is very costly and will not take care of a large part of the people who are most dependent." [11] Nonetheless, the two approaches came into confluence in the Roosevelt administration, joined by officials who respected both approaches.

One of the most important participants in laying the groundwork for the legislation was Frances Perkins, who had a background in both reform traditions and personal relationships with experts in both fields. Throughout the teens, Perkins had worked in New York as a social reformer in the maternalist tradition. Later she became the state's industrial commissioner, and in serving under then-Governor Roosevelt, she had promoted studies of the feasibility of a state-wide plan for unemployment insurance. When Roosevelt asked her to serve as his secretary of labor, she told him of her hope to establish both old age insurance and unemployment insurance.[12] When he appointed her as the head of the CES, she found her opportunity,

Man': The Politics of Social Security Finance in the New Deal," *Journal of American History* 70 (September 1983): 359–81.

[9] This description appeared later in Committee on Economic Security, "The Report on Economic Security," in *The Report of the Committee on Economic Security of 1935 and Other Basic Documents relating to the Development of the Social Security Act*, 50th anniversary ed., ed. National Conference on Social Welfare (Washington, D.C.: National Conference on Social Welfare, 1985), p. 3.

[10] "Plan for Study of Economic Security," "Committee on Economic Security" file, Official File of the President (hereafter, OF) Box 1086, Franklin D. Roosevelt Library, Hyde Park, N.Y. (hereafter, FDR); Linda Gordon, *Pitied but Not Entitled* (New York: Free Press, 1994), chaps. 4 and 6.

[11] "Views of Miss Edith Abbott of the University of Chicago on a Feasible Program for Economic Security," August 25, 1934, p. 1, Records of the Committee on Economic Security (hereafter, CES), Correspondence regarding Proposals for the Economic Security Program, 1934–35, box 54, Records of the Social Security Administration. Record Group 47, (hereafter, RG 47), National Archives, Washington, D.C. (hereafter, NA).

[12] Perkins, *Roosevelt I Knew*, pp. 93, 103–6, 152.

and she advocated a plan that combined both social insurance and public assistance. As she explained in later years, "It was evident to us that any system of social insurance would not relieve the accumulated poverty. . . . It was never, I think, suggested by any reasonable person that relief should be abandoned in favor of unemployment and old-age insurance, but it was thought that there could be a blend of the two."[13]

Besides Perkins, Roosevelt was surrounded by others who were social insurance supporters and who had ties with the maternalist reform tradition. Roosevelt's consultants were partial to the form of social insurance associated with the "Wisconsin school" as opposed to the "Ohio" variant advanced by Epstein and Rubinow. The Wisconsin approach originated with University of Wisconsin economist John Commons, a social insurance expert whose large and devout following of graduate students became active reformers and helped make Wisconsin the vanguard of Progressivism during previous decades.[14] According to the Progressive ideal, government was to be structured to curb the power of special-interest groups and to promote the economic and social well-being of the individual citizen.[15] As a means toward those ends, Commons's students had designed the nation's first unemployment insurance law, enacted in Wisconsin in 1932.

Roosevelt also sought out the advice of Supreme Court Justice Louis Brandeis, whose own daughter Elizabeth was both ensconced in the social work tradition and an expert on social insurance, besides being married to Paul Raushenbush, author of the Wisconsin unemployment insurance law. Harvard Law School Professor Felix Frankfurter, himself a Brandeis protégé and a personal friend and valued adviser to Roosevelt, was also partial to the Wisconsin variety of social insurance.[16] In addition, he had bonds to the maternalist tradition, as he had been recruited by the National Consumers' League to formulate legal strategy for the case of protective labor laws for women in the 1908 decision, *Muller v. Oregon.*[17]

Perkins asked her second assistant secretary of labor, Arthur J. Altmeyer, to develop plans for the subjects to be studied by the CES and for the membership for the technical board charged with assisting the committee. Altmeyer was firmly rooted in the Wisconsin approach to social insurance: he

---

[13] Ibid., *Roosevelt I Knew*, p. 281.

[14] Russell B. Nye, *Midwestern Progressive Politics* (East Lansing: Michigan State University Press, 1959), pp. 190–209.

[15] Robert S. Maxwell, *LaFollette and the Rise of the Progressives in Wisconsin* (Madison: State Historical Society of Wisconsin, 1956), p. vii; see also chap. 9.

[16] See Bruce Allen Murphy, *The Brandeis/Frankfurter Connection* (New York: Doubleday, Anchor, 1983), pp. 165–77.

[17] Gordon, *Pitied but Not Entitled*, pp. 83–84, 155–56; correspondence between Edwin E. Witte and Felix Frankfurter, CES, Correspondence Regarding Proposals for the Economic Security Proposal, 1934–35, box 56, RG 47, NA; *Roosevelt and Frankfurter: Their Correspondence, 1928–1945*, annotated by Max Freedman (Boston: Little, Brown, 1967), pp. 222–25.

had been Commons's student at the University of Wisconsin and executive secretary of the Wisconsin Industrial Commission before coming to Washington. He was also friends with Katharine Lenroot, chief of the Children's Bureau in the Department of Labor, herself a former Commons student and the daughter of a Wisconsin state legislator. Already he had promised Lenroot that funds for an expansion of mothers' pensions and other programs for children would be included in the economic security bill.[18]

Perkins's and Altmeyer's respect for and ties to both the Wisconsin social insurance approach and the social work tradition of public assistance illuminate why the CES proceeded to develop social policy in a manner distinct from many of the other popular approaches being discussed in the 1930s. They made the early choices to promote a variety of types of programs geared for people who were differently situated, and they selected both a technical board of experts in those program areas to develop specific proposals and a large staff to conduct studies. For the post of executive director of CES, they appointed Edwin E. Witte, chairman of the Department of Economics at the University of Wisconsin, another Commons protégé who had helped design Wisconsin's unemployment compensation program. Altmeyer himself became the chair of the technical board.[19]

Thus the Roosevelt administration had already, by June 1934, started down a path toward developing two distinct types of programs: one geared primarily for wage earners and the other for "deserving" people not covered by the first approach. With only one-quarter of the female population participating in the work force at any given time in the mid-1930s compared with more than three-quarters of the male population, the programs were bound from the start to acquire a fairly gender-specific base of beneficiaries. Still, the specific qualifications for coverage and eligibility had yet to be established, and the character and status of each type was yet to be determined. The social insurance initiatives were new to the United States, however, and their future was highly questionable; by contrast, the categorical assistance–type programs for the "deserving poor" were considered a familiar and reputable alternative to general relief and the poorhouse, even if they come to seem conservative to many in the social work community by the 1930s.

Though there was little dissent in the administration over the general types of programs to be included in the basic framework for the legislation, there was no consensus on matters of jurisdiction for the administration of particular programs. How far and in what ways would New Deal social policy stretch prevailing assumptions about federalism? To what extent

[18] Altmeyer, *Formative Years*, p. 7; *Reminiscences of Katharine Lenroot*, OHC, pp. 33–34.
[19] Altmeyer, *Formative Years*, pp. 7–8. On the dominance of the Wisconsin school in the CES, see *Reminiscences of Eveline M. Burns*, OHC, pp. 23–24, 27–28, 33–35, 57.

would national government assume a new role as the locus of redistribution for American society? The answers to such questions are central to understanding how the new state created in the New Deal would incorporate citizens.

Federalism

Roosevelt was a pragmatist in matters of policymaking, ready to experiment in search of approaches that worked.[20] In calling for the development of an economic security plan, he proposed "maximum cooperation between the States and the Federal Government."[21] Although Roosevelt's words promised that national government would come to play some sort of permanent role in social policy, the intergovernmental arrangements and power balance for administering new policies was anything but clear.

Policymaking camps in the administration scrambled to influence the direction that the development of the Economic Security Bill would take, and some tried to bring the pressure of influential outsiders to bear on the president. Presidential advisers Tom Corcoran and Ben Cohen orchestrated a meeting between Supreme Court Justice Brandeis and Roosevelt. During the Progressive Era, Brandeis had emphasized the ability of the states to serve as "laboratories of democracy" for policy innovation and experimentation. His views still reflected the faith in decentralization that marked the prevalent strands of Progressive Era thought, aside from the more Hamiltonian twist promoted by thinkers such as Herbert Croly.[22] Writing to their mentor and former professor Felix Frankfurter after Roosevelt's meeting with Brandeis, Corcoran and Cohen reported that Brandeis "did not like the scheme in the Skipper's [Roosevelt's] mind because it left administration completely in the Federal Government as opposed to the States. The Skipper gave the impression that there was nothing as yet cut and dried about the scheme and that it was all in the making."[23] Roosevelt might have been undecided about jurisdictional matters, but the inner

---

[20] James MacGregor Burns, *Roosevelt: The Lion and the Fox* (New York: Harcourt, Brace and World, 1956), p. 244.

[21] Franklin D. Roosevelt, "Message to Congress Reviewing the Broad Objectives and Accomplishments of the Administration, June 8, 1934," in *Report of the Committee on Economic Security*, ed. National Conference on Social Welfare, pp. 138.

[22] Nye, *Midwestern Progressive Politics* p. 349; Otis L. Graham, Jr., *Toward a Planned Society from Roosevelt to Nixon* (New York: Oxford University Press, 1976), pp. 310–16. As Graham has noted, "The radicalism of Brandeis had always been at bottom the fierce localism of Jefferson, humanized by deep sympathies with the unfortunate." Otis L. Graham, Jr., *An Encore for Reform: The Old Progressives and the New Deal* (New York: Oxford University Press, 1967), p. 124.

[23] Evidently Roosevelt was pleased with the conversation. He wrote to Frankfurter, "I had a most satisfactory talk with Justice Brandeis before he left. He has and is a 'great soul.'" Both letters in *Roosevelt and Frankfurter*, pp. 222–25.

circle of CES officials were already convinced that the states should be primarily responsible for administering the new programs.

Perkins, Altmeyer, and Witte, coming from backgrounds in state-level social reform during the Progressive Era, were believers in the notion that states should serve as laboratories for experimenting with social and labor legislation.[24] As Perkins later explained:

> At that time the states' rights issue was as important in the North as it was in the South. I still am a person who feels that we should never take away from the states their responsibility for a great many of these operations in the social field. There should only be federal action at a point where it is the only way in which there can be cooperation between the states . . . We were still holding to that idea that the states must participate, the states must develop their own programs, and the federal government is merely holding the kitty, so to speak, in order to equalize the costs.[25]

The approach of these officials reflected the realities of struggling for reform at the state level in the period before the New Deal. They keenly felt the need to protect state-level initiatives from the reach of the Supreme Court, and they wanted to build on the policy foundations already established by reformers like themselves in the Progressive Era. Although only Wisconsin had an unemployment insurance law in place by 1934, about half of the states had enacted old age pensions, and forty-five had mothers' pensions laws on the books.[26] To extend and improve such programs, these CES leaders remained insistent that the economic security legislation should emphasize joint federal-state programs rather than strictly national ones.[27]

Immediately after being appointed director of CES, Witte corresponded with and visited several scholars, labor leaders, and elected officials to elicit their views on creating social policy. He reported, "Justice Brandeis is strongly of the opinion that all types of social insurance should be administered by the states" and "Prof. Frankfurter shares Justice Brandeis' views that the legislation proposed should contemplate state administration, with the federal government merely prescribing the broad general standards. He

---

[24] James T. Patterson, *The New Deal and the States* (Princeton: Princeton University Press, 1969), pp. 3–4; *The Reminiscences of Thomas H. Eliot*, OHC, p. 22; Arthur A. Ekirch, Jr., *Progressivism in America: A Study of the Era from T. R. to Woodrow Wilson* (New York: Watts, New Viewpoints, 1974), chap. 7.

[25] *Reminiscences of Frances Perkins*, OHC, vol. 2, pt. 4, p. 631.

[26] Committee on Economic Security, "Report on Economic Security," pp. 4–5; Ann Shola Orloff, "The Political Origins of America's Belated Welfare State," in *The Politics of Social Policy in the United States*, ed. Margaret Weir, Ann Shola Orloff, and Theda Skocpol (Princeton: Princeton University Press, 1988), pp. 37–80.

[27] See *Reminiscences of Arthur J. Altmeyer*, pp. 105, 187–88.

would draw the federal legislation in such a way as to permit considerable experimentation by the states."[28] Of those Witte interviewed, only New York's Mayor LaGuardia made a strong argument for national administration and standards. Witte reported, "He has no faith in state administration. . . . He believes that the states are dying units of government and would not build up a system of social insurance around them." LaGuardia added that if state administration were used, the national government would need to hold the states to "rigid standards, to insure particularly that the funds would be spent in the industrial areas where most needed."[29] LaGuardia's view was not surprising, coming from a mayor of a major city in the prereapportionment era, when state legislatures were notoriously unresponsive to urban needs. But the others Witte consulted reinforced CES leaders' predilections for modeling social policy on a fairly traditional model of federalism.

Besides the predispositions of CES officials and advisers and the influence of policy precedents, the Roosevelt administration had political reasons for favoring policy designs that left considerable autonomy to the states. After all, Congress continued to be dominated by southern Democrats who were particularly wary of excessive intervention by the national government in matters they felt should be reserved to state and local governments. Roosevelt was willing to yield to those demands to gain the necessary support for his proposals.[30]

Other important constituencies had also become distrustful of extensive federal government power in social policy, particularly after the administration of the FERA in the early New Deal. In Roosevelt's first months in office, he had advanced federally funded relief programs when local relief and private charities had proven inadequate; the first and most comprehensive had been the FERA. The FERA moneys were initially welcomed by local administrators and politicians, but before long the program began to evoke hostility toward the federal government because of the act's stipulation that localities could not interfere with its operations.[31] FERA left local

---

[28] "Memorandum on the Views relating to the Work of the Committee on Economic Security Expressed by Various Individuals Consulted," pp. 1–2, CES, Staff Reports, 1934–35, box 21, Witte file, RG 47, NA. For an interesting exchange between Witte and Frankfurter on this question, see Frankfurter file, CES, Correspondence regarding Proposals for the Economic Security Program, box 56, RG 47, NA.

[29] "Memorandum on the Views Relating to the Work of the Committee," p. 5.

[30] Elizabeth Sanders, "Business, Bureaucracy, and the Bourgeoisie: The New Deal Legacy," in *The Political Economy of Public Policy*, ed. Alan Stone and Edward J. Harpman (Beverly Hills, Calif.: Sage, 1982), pp. 115–40; Richard Franklin Bensel, *Sectionalism and American Political Development, 1880–1980* (Madison: University of Wisconsin Press, 1984), pp. 147–74.

[31] Blanche D. Coll, *Safety Net: Welfare and Social Security, 1929–1979* (New Brunswick: Rutgers University Press, 1995), pp. 21–33; Patterson, *New Deal and the States*, chap. 3; Gordon, *Pitied but Not Entitled*, pp. 188–91.

officials skeptical about social programs that permitted what they viewed as excessive federal control.

Several persons in the Roosevelt administration also felt restrained by the specter of Supreme Court scrutiny, particularly because there were few precedents for federal government activity in the realm of social welfare policy. They reasoned that policy designs that modeled the federal-state cooperation implicit in other already established grants-in-aid programs, such as the Morrill Act or Federal Highway Act, stood a better chance of passing the constitutionality test than strictly national programs.[32]

Finally, the administration's preference for leaving significant authority to the states was a defensive political tactic should all else fail. Thomas Eliot, the lawyer who drafted the administration's bill, recalled how Roosevelt candidly articulated this rationale: "You know, Huey Long may be the next President of the United States; and if that kind of a thing happened, we'd all be thankful if as much power is in the state governments as we can put there."[33] Roosevelt's words expressed both the fear of more radical, redistributive alternatives as Long's share-the-wealth agenda and the hope that the abilities of states to act as laboratories of democracy, as his own New York had during the Progressive Era, could be enhanced.

Despite the strong support by CES leaders for an economic security plan that gave ample authority to states and that included both social insurance and public assistance programs, substantial battles lay ahead over particular program designs and administrative arrangements. The politics of the formation of programs for the elderly resulted in a policy innovation well beyond the scope of what Perkins, Altmeyer, and Witte could have imagined, and the implications for citizenship and gender were vast.

The Formation of Policies for the Elderly in the CES

The Roosevelt administration moved quickly to advance its own version of social insurance for the elderly partly because it was anxious to preempt far more radical proposals. A widespread, multifaceted grass-roots social movement had emerged in the 1930s and was clamoring for highly redistributive government-sponsored pensions to make the lives of elderly Americans more secure. Huey Long's share-our-wealth plan, the Ham and Eggs agenda in California, and several other proposals mobilized the citi-

[32] "Extract from a Memorandum by Jane Perry Clark on Analysis of Types of Federal State Relationships in Relation to a Program of Economic Security," Jane Perry Clark file, CES, Staff Reports, 1934–35, box 17, RG 47, NA; Perkins, *Roosevelt I Knew*, pp. 286–87. See also V. O. Key, *The Administration of Federal Grants to States* (Chicago: Public Administration Service, 1937), pp. 1–31.

[33] *Reminiscences of Thomas H. Eliot*, p. 11.

zenry, but none had as much geographic reach or exerted as much influence on national institutions as the Townsend plan.[34] Supporters of the plan, which was named for initiator Francis Townsend, an elderly doctor in Long Beach, California, made their voices heard loud and clear to members of Congress. They insisted that the new taxes necessary to fund the generous pensions would be well compensated for by the stimulation of the economy which would result from the mandatory spending by elderly people.[35] By contrast, the CES proceeded to develop a two-tiered plan for the elderly, promoting federal grants-in-aid for old age assistance to garner public support, and soft-peddling a contributory social insurance program.

Although the policymaking traditions that shaped the CES's two programs had gendered roots, the battles over the formation of OAI and OAA in 1934–35 had more to do with the shape of American federalism than with ideas about gender roles. In further contrast to Progressive Era social policymaking, important male and female reformers were found on each side of the debate.

Scholars have labeled social insurance reform plans in the early twentieth century a "male vision," [36] but in fact the "driving force" [37] behind the New Deal program which became the centerpiece of America's welfare state was a woman, Barbara Nachtrieb Armstrong. An associate professor of law at the University of California, with no personal connections to the Wisconsin school, Armstrong was hired as the director of planning for the CES old age security staff.[38] She was assisted by J. Douglas Brown, an economist from Princeton University; Murray Latimer, chairman of the Railroad Retirement Board; and Otto Richter, an actuary. Latimer acted as the chairman of the subcommittee in representing the group on the Technical Board that advised the CES.

Armstrong came to Washington in 1934 with a refined analysis of U.S. economic security problems and a well-developed plan for social insurance firmly in her mind. She had, just two years before, published her treatise on the subject, *Insuring the Essentials: Minimum Wage plus Social Insurance, a Living Wage Program*. In keeping with the social insurance approach to

[34] Alan Brinkley, *Voices of Protest: Huey Long, Father Coughlin, and the Great Depression* (New York: Knopf, 1982); on the Ham and Eggs movement, see Frank A. Pinner, Paul Jacobs, and Philip Selznick, *Old Age and Political Behavior: A Case Study* (Berkeley: University of California Press, 1959), 4–7, 33–34.

[35] See Perkins, *Roosevelt I Knew*, p. 294; *Reminiscences of Eveline M. Burns*, pp. 51–52.

[36] Gordon, *Pitied but Not Entitled*, p. 146.

[37] *Reminiscences of Eveline M. Burns*, p. 52.

[38] Armstrong suspected that she had been recommended to Roosevelt by Gerald Swope, head of General Electric. Swope had read her book on social insurance and sent a complimentary letter about it to her publisher, and it was passed along to her. *Reminiscences of Barbara Nachtrieb Armstrong*, OHC, p. 30. Witte commented that she "was one of the small number of people who were considered for staff positions prior to my selection as executive director." Witte, *Development of the Social Security Act*, p. 30.

social provision, she set her sights on the prevention of poverty, a goal that had not been achieved by the poor laws, private charities, or public assistance programs inscribed with the norms of social work. She believed that the old age pension programs developing in the states contained eligibility stipulations resembling "poor relief": they "rob [the applicant] of the dignified position of an individual."[39]

Led by Armstrong, the Old Age Security Committee planned for contributory social insurance to be the primary program for aiding the elderly in the long term, upholding Roosevelt's desire for a plan in which benefits would be viewed as a right, not subject to shifting political winds.[40] The foursome also believed, though, that an expanded program of public assistance for the elderly would be essential for responding to existing need until the funds for the social insurance program became established.[41] Armstrong herself was particularly attuned to the situation of women who might not be covered by the social insurance plan and for whom noncontributory pensions would be essential. She stressed the need to provide assistance, for example, to widows of workers who had died before becoming eligible for pensions, to widows whose husbands had worked in lucrative, uninsured jobs but lacked adequate provision for their later years, and to men and women who lacked a sufficient work history to be eligible for assistance.[42] One of Armstrong's ambitions was to design old age insurance to include as many women as possible.

Old Age Insurance

Like male advocates of social insurance, Armstrong assumed that a core program of social provision should be organized around work-force participation, necessarily targeting primarily male breadwinners in family units.[43] Unlike her male counterparts, however, Armstrong was insistent that widows of male wage earners should be eligible for benefits in their own right. Her written reports for CES bear testimony to her attempts to establish survivors' insurance from the start.[44] Such efforts were opposed,

---

[39] Barbara Nachtrieb Armstrong, *Insuring the Essentials: Minimum Wage plus Social Insurance, a Living Wage Program* (New York: Macmillan, 1932), pp. xvii, 436.

[40] Barbara Nachtrieb Armstrong, "Memorandum on Section 5: Old Age Retirement," pp. 3–4, CES, Staff Reports, 1934–35, box 23, RG 47, NA; Bernstein, *Caring Society*, p. 50.

[41] "Summary of Discussion of the Old Age Security Committee," September 26, 1934, p. 1, CES, General Records of the General Director and Staff, 1934–35, box 1, RG 47, NA.

[42] Barbara Nachtrieb Armstrong, "Old Age Assistance and Old Age Pensions in the Various States," CES, Staff Reports, 1934–35, box 23, RG 47, NA.

[43] Armstrong, *Insuring the Essentials*, pp. 145–48.

[44] Barbara Nachtrieb Armstrong, "Possibilities of a Unified System of Insurance against Loss of Earnings," pp. 1–4, 8, CES, Staff Reports, 1934–35, box 17, RG 47, NA, and "Estimated Number of Workers Covered by Old Age Annuity System," CES, Staff Correspondence, 1934–35, box 12, RG 47, NA; J. Douglas Brown and Barbara Nachtrieb Armstrong, "Plan for Federal Compulsory Contributory Pension Insurance," CES, Staff Reports, 1934–

however, by the executive director. Said Armstrong, "Every time I'd put in a report that we ought to have survivors' insurance as well, Mr. Witte would take it out."[45] The CES regarded such benefits as desirable but not an immediate priority, and did not include the plans in the bill sent to Congress in January 1935.

Chairman Perkins did, however, expand the proposed coverage of OAI in one important regard that Armstrong's committee had assumed might be too challenging in both fiscal and administrative terms. Perkins insisted that domestic and agricultural workers be included among the beneficiaries of the contributory program.[46] Such a provision would affect workers in notoriously low-paying and difficult work and include more than 90 percent of African American women and a majority of African American men, as well as high proportions of other nonwhite men and women.[47]

The most significant and contentious battles in the creation of OAI was over the issue of national versus state-level administrative jurisdiction for the program. Although CES leaders had already made their preference for predominantly state-level programs clear early in the summer of 1934, the Old Age Security Committee headed by Armstrong convened in late summer and voiced unanimous support for a fully national system.[48] The members argued that the mobility of the population would cause a federal-state program administrative difficulties; for people might work in several states and retire in yet another. A federal system would assure quicker and fuller coverage of more of the population, and compliance would be superior because, Armstrong's subcommittee reasoned, "there is a definitely greater respect for federal requirements than for local requirements in matters of social control." The subcommittee acknowledged that a state system might be preferable for political reasons, but they countered that those favoring "states' rights" should be pleased if the federal government unburdened states of the duty of providing for much of their elderly population.[49]

35, box 17, RG 47, NA. See also J. Douglas Brown, *An American Philosophy of Social Security* (Princeton: Princeton University Press, 1972), p. 132.

[45] *Reminiscences of Barbara Nachtrieb Armstrong*, p. 98.

[46] Ibid., pp. 129–30.

[47] Department of Labor, Women's Bureau, *The Negro Woman Worker*, by Jean Collier Brown, Bulletin 165 (Washington, D.C.: GPO, 1938), pp. 2–3; Phyllis Palmer, "Outside the Law: Agricultural and Domestic Workers under the Fair Labor Standards Act," *Journal of Policy History* 7 (1995): 436, n. 13. In the West, a majority of Chicanos and Mexican Americans worked in agricultural and domestic work, and Asian American women made up a high proportion of domestics in some coastal cities.

[48] *Reminiscences of Eveline M. Burns*, pp. 52–55.

[49] Quotation in Armstrong, "Memorandum on Section 5," p. 1; "Summary of Discussion of the Old Age Security Committee of the Technical Board," September 26, 1934, CES, General Records of the Executive Director and Staff, 1934–35, box 1, RG 47, NA; *Reminiscences of Thomas H. Eliot*, p. 30; Altmeyer, *Formative Years*, p. 25.

When Armstrong announced that her subcommittee was planning to advance OAI on a national scale as the centerpiece of their plan for the elderly, controversy ensued. Thomas Eliot, general counsel for the CES and a recent graduate of Harvard Law School, objected that such a plan would be unconstitutional. Armstrong had to remind Eliot that she was herself a law professor, and she assured him that she had consulted on the subject with scholars who were considered renowned authorities on matters of constitutionality.[50]

Subsequently, Armstrong's group proceeded to gather verification of support for their position from such experts. Dudley O. McGovney, professor of constitutional law at the University of California, responded that in his opinion the Constitution did not present any obstacles to the creation of a tax on employers and employees nor to the appropriation of benefits from a national reserve fund, and he had reviewed the judicial precedents for each activity in detail.[51] Armstrong then traveled to Cambridge, Massachusetts, where she met with Harvard law professor Thomas Reed Powell, whose opinion on such matters was considered definitive. Eliot had been convinced that Powell would view a national OAI scheme as unconstitutional; in fact Powell insisted on the contrary and drafted a letter to clarify his understanding of the matter.[52] After consulting Professor Edwin S. Corwin at Princeton and Professor Douglas Maggs at Duke, the group working on old age security plans reiterated their position of support for a straight national plan instead of a state-federal plan, saying they were "convinced that only the former can be relied upon to provide adequate old age security."[53]

Meanwhile, CES leaders remained opposed to a national scheme for OAI. Frances Perkins continued to be uncomfortable with the proposition, and she charged Eliot with the responsibility of trying to come up with viable state-administered old age insurance plans, an effort that proved futile.[54] After Armstrong's committee presented definitive evidence in mid-November that a national plan would be the most feasible and that important legal scholars considered it to be constitutional, CES leaders suddenly hinted that old age insurance plans might be dropped entirely. In the presi-

[50] *Reminiscences of Barbara Nachtrieb Armstrong*, pp. 74–76.

[51] Memorandum, Dudley O. McGovney to Barbara Nachtrieb Armstrong, "Answer to Questions on Constitutional Chances of Three Schemes Outlined in Mr. Thomas H. Eliot's Memorandum," October 22, 1934, CES, Staff Correspondence, 1934–35; box 12; RG 47, NA.

[52] *Reminiscences of Barbara Nachtrieb Armstrong*, pp. 76, 93, 95.

[53] "Outline of Old Age Security Program Proposed by Staff," November 9, 1934, CES, General Records of the Executive Director and Staff, 1934–35, box 1, RG 47, NA; Brown, *American Philosophy of Social Security*, pp. 9–16.

[54] George Martin, *Madam Secretary: Frances Perkins* (Boston: Houghton Mifflin, 1976), p. 348; *Reminiscences of Thomas H. Eliot*, p. 29–30.

dent's speech at a conference on economic security on November 14, he read language drafted by Witte: "I do not know whether this is the time for any federal legislation on old age security."[55] Outraged, Armstrong's group retaliated by contacting friends in the press. An editorial in papers in the Scripps-Howard chain and a lead article in the *New York Times* criticized Roosevelt for abandoning old age insurance plans. Roosevelt, apparently dismayed by the negative coverage, henceforth expressed more genuine interest in the OAI program.[56] Witte was infuriated by the Armstrong group, which he suspected of instigating the reaction, and he continued to have misgivings about a national plan. Likewise, Frankfurter persisted in recommending that the CES "use our best statesmanship to make the states and regions do what they are capable of doing." Meanwhile, however, support for the national plan emerged from an unexpected quarter.[57]

In December, the old age security subcommittee of the Advisory Council to the CES, a group of prominent leaders of the business community, labor unions, and national organizations, gave its support to national arrangements for OAI. Standard Oil Company president Walter Teagle defended the plan against the objections of Molly Dewson, whose ties lay with the maternalist reform tradition and who was representing the NCL. Armstrong believed that Dewson's opposition was motivated by her loyalty to and friendship for Secretary Perkins. Dewson's position was defeated, and Teagle was joined by other industrialists in the full Advisory Board in support of the plan. Thereafter, Armstrong and Brown believed they had won on the feature of old age insurance most important to them: national administration and standards.[58]

Besides matters of coverage and administrative jurisdiction, the design of OAI also involved issues of financing and tax and benefit structures. Although CES leaders believed that some funds from general revenues would be required to support the program, Roosevelt took a firm stand in favor of traditional insurance principles. He insisted that the program be financed entirely by payroll taxes so that its character would be distinct from relief and so that it would gain long-term political support. Secretary of the Treasury Henry A. Morgenthau likewise demanded that fiscal conservatism guide the design. The plan that eventually emerged required both

[55] Letter and attached speech, Edwin Witte to Frances Perkins, November 10, 1934, p. 3, CES, Correspondence regarding Proposals for the Economic Security Program, 1934–35, box 55, RG 47, NA.

[56] Brown, *American Philosophy of Social Security*, pp. 16–17; *Reminiscences of Barbara Nachtrieb Armstrong*, pp. 68, 104–5.

[57] Letters, Witte to Frankfurter, November 19, 1934, and Frankfurter to Witte, November 27, 1934, both in CES, Correspondence regarding Proposals for the Economic Security Program, 1934–35, box 56, RG 47, NA.

[58] *Reminiscences of Barbara Nachtrieb Armstrong*, pp. 82–83, 156–57, 168; Brown, *American Philosophy of Social Security*, pp. 21–22.

employers and employees to contribute to retirement funds according to a regressive combination of a flat payroll tax rate and a ceiling on taxable wages.[59]

Benefits were to be administered according to a graduated, though mildly progressive, scheme.[60] Unlike the Townsend plan, which called for flat benefits financed by government revenues for all elderly people, OAI would distribute benefits that correlated to the previous earnings of recipients while they had participated in the work force. In describing the plan, CES officials emphasized especially the redistributive aspects of the benefit structure: "Insurance benefits should be so graduated relative to contributions that (a) persons of lower average income and (b) persons coming under the system relatively late in life should receive higher proportionate benefits. As a social mechanism aimed at the prevention of dependency, an old-age insurance system should be adjusted in some measure to the relative needs of various classes of beneficiaries."[61] But although low-income people would receive more in proportion to their wages and tax payments than high-income people, the redistributive dimension of the OAI structure was to be countered by the regressive tax structure and the wage-related benefits ladder.[62] To qualify for benefits, furthermore, workers would have to have a long-term, relatively full-time record in covered employment. Because only one-quarter of the female population was employed, and because women tended to enter and exit the work force more frequently than men owing to responsibilities for child rearing, benefits were bound to go mainly to men. The financing and benefits arrangements, therefore, amplified the stratification of a work force already divided in terms of gender while partially ameliorating the conditions of some at the bottom of the wage scale.

In sum, the proposal for OAI was in some regards conservative and oriented toward better-off male workers but, in other regards bold, sweeping, and innovative, at least by U.S. standards. The plan was exceptional in omitting survival benefits for widows and children. Already, fourteen other nations had enacted old age insurance plans complete with survivors' in-

---

[59] Leff, "Taxing the 'Forgotten Man,'" pp. 364–81; Witte, *Development of the Social Security Act*, pp. 149–50.

[60] Perkins, *Roosevelt I Knew*, p. 292.

[61] Social Security Board, *Social Security in America: The Factual Background of the Social Security Act as Summarized from Staff Reports to the Committee on Economic Security* (Washington, D.C.: GPO, 1937), p. 203, 197–214; see also CES, "Report of the Committee on Economic Security," pp. 43–55.

[62] Years afterward, Frances Perkins explained that a system of wage-related benefits had seemed preferable to a flat plan because the former would uphold the "work ethic": "The easiest way would be to pay the same amount to everyone. But that is contrary to the typical American attitude that a man who works hard, becomes highly skilled, and earns high wages 'deserves' more than one who had not become a skilled worker." Perkins, *Roosevelt I Knew*, p. 292; see also *Reminiscences of Eveline M. Burns*, p. 75.

surance, but the CES reported that though such a system was desirable, further investigation was needed to justify any such proposal.[63] On financing, the plan was regressive not only because, as Mark Leff has shown, it placed a heavy burden on the "forgotten man at the bottom of the economic pyramid" but, moreover, because it would extract the greatest sacrifice from the disproportionately female workers who earned the lowest wages.[64] To J. Douglas Brown and Barbara Armstrong, however, the proposal was radical because it established old age benefits as a matter of right on a nationwide basis. They were proud of that hard-won achievement and convinced that expanded coverage and a more generous benefit structure could follow in later years.[65]

Old Age Assistance

Given the widespread, immediate need among the elderly and the political imperative to respond to popular movements demanding expanded old age pensions, both Armstrong's committee and CES leaders agreed on the need to include noncontributory old age assistance in the bill going to Congress. As recalled by Frank Bane, who served as executive director of the Social Security Board from 1935 to 1938 and who had been director of the American Public Welfare Association at the time of the law's passage, "Old age assistance was the burr under the saddle for most of these programs at that time . . . because of two gentlemen . . . namely Townsend and Huey Long and the movements which they represented." [66] Because Congress was beseiged with demands for pensions for the elderly, CES members predicted that the program was sure to be popular. In fact Eliot, who actually drafted the final bill, sought to warm Congress to the entire economic security package by placing old age assistance in the prominent position of "Title I." [67]

In creating OAA, the program that would be of most significance for women, since they were largely excluded from OAI, the CES adopted a plan that reflected a preference for leaving considerable administrative authority to the states and which built on the foundations of the programs that already existed in twenty-eight states. Like the Dill-Connery Bill already before Congress, the program would be designed as a federal grant-in-aid to states. A central aim would be to assist states that had not yet done so to enact pension programs for the elderly poor and to raise benefit

[63] SSB, *Social Security in America*, pp. 183, 204.

[64] Leff, "Taxing the 'Forgotten Man,' " pp. 378, 381.

[65] Brown, *American Philosophy of Social Security*, pp. 20–21; *Reminiscences of Barbara Nachtrieb Armstrong*, p. 168.

[66] *Reminiscences of Frank Bane*, OHC, p. 25.

[67] *Reminiscences of Thomas H. Eliot*, p. 36.

levels in programs already in place. The Roosevelt administration hoped also to transfer the responsibility for relief back to the states by pushing them to carry a share of the responsibility for the needy. OAA would require national government to provide one-half of the benefits for those elderly whom the states determined to be eligible, matching up to a limit of fifteen dollars per month per person.[68]

CES officials did want to establish more generous standards for OAA programs already in existence and to assure nationwide application of such standards. First, their proposal dictated that for any state to gain matching funds, the program would have to be implemented statewide rather than only in certain localities, as was more typical in the existing system. Second, though the committee planned for states to retain a substantial measure of discretion with respect to eligibility, it did insist that state administrators of OAA provide "a minimum assistance grant which will afford a reasonable subsistence compatible with decency and health." The stipulation would force states to raise benefit levels: in 1934, states offered average grants of only $15 month. The CES's version of the bill also required that such benefits be granted to persons with incomes too low to provide such a "reasonable subsistence" and whose personal property was valued at less than $5,000, more generous than the $3,000 ceilings on combined property and income limits typical in existing laws.[69]

Maternalist reformers, though unenthused about OAI, did push for nationally uniform standards for the grants-in-aid program. Grace Abbott, who served on the Advisory Council, contacted Witte in December 1934 to complain about the residency requirement that was to be part of the OAA provision. The CES had proposed that matching grants be denied to states that imposed requirements of five years or more of residence in the state within the previous ten years. Abbott was concerned that the proposal might be construed as setting a minimum standard rather than a maximum, and she sought clarification. Further, she argued that residence in a particular state should not be required, only residence in the nation.[70] Witte assured her of the law's clarity of purpose on the first count, but he either failed to understand her second point about national rather than state citizenship or chose to ignore it. In Witte's mind, the plan amounted to a significant improvement on current state laws, where the majority of states required fifteen years of residence.[71]

On January 17, 1935, only six months after he had established the CES,

[68] CES, "Report of the Committee on Economic Security," pp. 26–28.

[69] SSB, *Social Security in America*, quotation on p. 195; see also pp. 191–95; Altmeyer, *Formative Years*, p. 128; Coll, *Safety Net*, p. 42.

[70] Letter, Grace Abbott to Edwin E. Witte, January 2, 1935, Abbott Papers, box 54, folder 2, Regenstein Library, University of Chicago (hereafter, UC).

[71] Letter, Edwin Witte to Grace Abbott, January 9, 1935, ibid.; Coll, *Safety Net*, p. 42.

President Roosevelt presented the report of his cabinet committee to Congress and urged swift action on the proposal. The bill was introduced in the Senate by Robert F. Wagner (D-N.Y.) and Pat Harrison (D-Miss.) and in the House by Robert L. Doughton, chairman of the House Ways and Means Committee (D-N.C.) and David J. Lewis (D-Md.).

The Economic Security Bill in Congress

In Congress, where the Economic Security Bill gradually came to be known as the "Social Security Act," the basic framework of the CES plan remained intact, but substantial changes occurred in the details of the legislation. Writing to Advisory Council president Dr. Frank Graham soon after Congress began to consider the bill, Edwin Witte described the challenges facing the legislation:

> There is a great deal of opposition to the Economic Security Bill from two groups, the conservatives and the radicals. Our program apparently is the "middle of the road" proposal which is drawing fire from reactionary business interests and extreme conservatives on the one hand, and on the other, from the Townsendites and the advocates of the Lundeen Bill. There is one group which thinks we do not have sufficient standards and a much larger group which condemns us because we do not allow sufficient freedom to the states. This latter sentiment is particularly pronounced among the Senators from the southern states.[72]

The battles over the Economic Security Bill in Congress, like those in the CES, had much to do with the future arrangements of federalism and seemingly little to do with gender politics. States' rights advocates, on the one hand, set out to scale back the reach of national government standards in both OAI and OAA. Advocates of more generous and redistributive plans, on the other hand, sought to expand the reach of the federal treasury. Representatives of the South spoke in both voices, promoting decentralized state-building as a means of maintaining regional autonomy and, at the same time, demanding progressive taxation and redistributive schemes to promote recovery in the region most ravaged by the depression.[73] Despite the various aims, the resolution of the conflicts would have significant implications for citizenship and gender.

The primary battles in Congress occurred on a couple of fronts. The

[72] Letter, Edwin E. Witte to Frank P. Graham, February 1, 1935, CES, Staff Correspondence, 1934–35, box 16, Witte file 1, RG 47, NA.

[73] Bensel, *Sectionalism and American Political Development*, pp. 152–53.

drive to reduce standards took place primarily in secretive, closed-door executive sessions of the committees charged with reporting the bill. Both committees that considered the bill, the House Ways and Means Committee and the Senate Finance Committee, were dominated by southerners.[74] The drive for more expansive national spending on social programs occurred especially on the floor of the House, where members seized every opportunity to have their populist rhetoric preserved for the record.

Committees held hearings on the bill from January into February. The Ways and Means Committee proceeded with mark-up on the bill first, reporting out a bill on April 5. The Finance Committee, meanwhile, waited until the House had completed action on the bill in April, then reported out its own bill on May 20.

Old Age Insurance

The Ways and Means Committee retained the national structure of the contributory program for the elderly, but sharply curtailed the program's coverage, eliminating approximately one-quarter of the work force which would otherwise have been included.[75] The scope of national rights of social citizenship thus became increasingly circumscribed by gender and race.

Although the CES, hopeful that the new legislation would reach employees "at the very bottom of the economic scale,"[76] had included agricultural, domestic, and "casual" or temporary workers in their plan, congressmen in the Ways and Means Committee appeared to be looking for a way to exclude such persons. According to University of Chicago economist Paul Douglas, not only southerners favored the exclusions; "There were Congressmen from other sections of the country where there were unpopular racial or cultural minorities who wanted to have their states left more or less free to treat them as they wished."[77] Early in the hearings, CES director Witte had suggested that perhaps different collection techniques, such as the stamp-book method used in Europe or annual reports and payments by employers, could be implemented for including such workers in OAI.[78] Subsequently, however, Secretary Morgenthau shocked fellow CES

---

[74] Witte, *Development of the Social Security Act*, p. 100.

[75] Letter, Edwin E. Witte to Harry L. Hopkins, February 26, 1935, p. 2, CES, General Records of the Executive Director and Staff, 1934–35, box 9, RG 47, NA.

[76] CES, "Report of the Committee on Economic Security," p. 49.

[77] Paul H. Douglas, *Social Security in the United States* (New York: Whittlesey House, 1936), pp. 100–101. Presumably, Douglas was making insinuations about westerners, who also favored the exclusion of such groups in New Deal legislation; see Palmer, "Outside the Law," pp. 416–40.

[78] Of those countries with compulsory contributory old-age insurance programs in 1933, the vast majority covered domestic and agricultural workers; see SSB, *Social Security in America*, p. 183.

members by announcing that he and his staff had decided that such categories of workers should be omitted from coverage under the work-related programs, citing the administrative difficulties of collecting payments from employers with so few employees.[79] Committee members acted on the treasury secretary's expert opinion and agreed to exclusion of such categories.

Thus the vast majority of African Americans, as well as disproportionate numbers of Latinos and Asian American men and women, lost the opportunity to be granted a social right of inclusion in a national program for the elderly. According to the Census, 89.6 percent of all agricultural workers were male. African American women were reported to be twice as likely as other women to work in the fields. Probably this figure underestimated their actual participation in agricultural work, however, because the census noted that female family members of sharecroppers, though typically expected to help with the harvest, were usually unpaid and therefore were not part of their official count. In domestic work, women accounted for 93.3 percent of all employees.[80]

The desperately low wages of such workers made saving for old age impossible. All men and women in agriculture earned extremely low wages, averaging $86 annually for men and $67 for women.[81] In 1934, the Young Women's Christian Association compiled data on household employment in the South and found the average weekly wage for African American domestics to be $6.17 a week, for average work weeks that were 66 hours long. In some areas, wages were much lower: during the administration of the National Industrial Recovery Act, the Joint Committee on National Recovery found the wages of African American domestics in thirty-three northern counties of Mississippi averaged less than $2 per week.[82]

Religious and nonprofit organizations prompted the exclusion of several other categories of workers which were disproportionately female. Numerous churches, particularly the Episcopal and Presbyterian, as well as organizations such as the National Hospital Association and various educational institutions argued that they depended on private donations for support and that paying taxes for employees would place an undue burden on them. The Ways and Means Committee was moved by their pleas and excluded such occupations as well.[83] Women employees accounted for 75.7 percent of all teachers, 74.6 percent of all religious workers, and 64.3 percent of all social and welfare workers.[84] Though some workers in

[79] Ibid., pp. 901–2; Perkins, *Roosevelt I Knew*, pp. 297–98.
[80] Bureau of the Census, *Census of the Population: 1940, Summary Report*, table 58 (Washington, D.C.: GPO, 1940), pp. 75–80.
[81] Ibid., table 72, pp. 120–22.
[82] Department of Labor, *Negro Woman Worker*.
[83] Witte, *Development of the Social Security Act*, pp. 154–55.
[84] Bureau of the Census, *Census of the Population: 1940, Summary Report*, table 58, pp. 75–80.

such organizations were already covered by public pensions or retirement funds, many of the most poorly paid teachers were employed in states that had no old age coverage, and most of the 300,000 nurses and practically all of the 45,000 women in social and religious work were without any such benefits.[85] Altogether, according to Alice Kessler-Harris, "Sixty percent of the excluded workers were female—in a labor force where less than 30 percent of women were employed." [86]

In the course of deliberations, the Ways and Means Committee briefly revived the concern for survivors earlier demonstrated by Armstrong and abandoned by the CES. Thomas Eliot remembered the committee asking, "But what about the poor widow, after the man who has been receiving benefits dies?" [87] Seemingly anxious to include survivors' benefits, the committee "ordered an adjournment for four days while [House legislative counsel, Middleton] Beaman and I wrote a new clause." The committee quickly lost interest, however, when, a few days later, Eliot and Beaman showed them a complicated model draft for survivors' benefits. The entire proposal was instantly dropped.[88]

In sum, the program that Armstrong and Brown had worked so hard to establish as the source of national, standardized rights of citizenship for elderly Americans had come to be, through the negligence of the CES and the actions of the Ways and Means Committee, geared primarily to men, particularly white ones. Both the House and Senate committees made further changes in the financing arrangements for the program, but its administrative design and coverage were left intact throughout further deliberations.[89] Meanwhile, much greater attention was given to the program to which the women ineligible for OAI would need to turn, old age assistance.

Old Age Assistance

As debate over the Economic Security Bill intensified in Washington, newspapers in the South expressed the fears of the region that federal standards in the law would challenge local societal norms thus far protected by

[85] Department of Labor, Women's Bureau, "Old Age Security Legislation from the Viewpoint of Women," speech by Mary Anderson before District of Columbia League of Women Voters, December 1935, microfilm 16:0133, p. 14, LMDC.

[86] Alice Kessler-Harris, "Designing Women and Old Fools: The Construction of the Social Security Amendments of 1939," in *U.S. History as Women's History*, ed. Linda K. Kerber, Alice Kessler-Harris, and Kathryn Kish Sklar (Chapel Hill: University of North Carolina Press, 1995), p. 92.

[87] Thomas Eliot, "Social Security: The First Half-Century, a Discussion," in *Social Security: The First Half-Century* (Albuquerque: University of New Mexico Press, 1988), p. 35.

[88] *Reminiscences of Thomas H. Eliot*, pp. 52–53.

[89] These changes, aimed to make the program entirely self-supporting, were urged by the administration, particularly by Roosevelt himself and by Secretary Morgenthau. Witte, *Development of the Social Security Act*, pp. 150–51; Leff, "Taxing the 'Forgotten Man.'"

state laws. An editorial in the Charleston *News and Courier* lamented, "With our local policies dictated by Washington we shall not long have the civilization to which we are accustomed."[90] More pointedly, the Jackson *Daily News* explained, "The average Mississippian can't imagine himself chipping in to pay pensions for able-bodied Negroes to sit around in idleness on front galleries."[91] Indeed, in the South the "civilization to which we are accustomed" meant a society organized by a strict racial hierarchy, given legal sanction through Jim Crow laws and institutionalized through the sharecropping and tenant-farming system. Southern congressmen responded to these anxieties by pressing states' rights in the mark-up of the OAA portion of the bill. Having already excluded so many women and minority men from the purely national program for the elderly, they proceeded to eradicate national standards in the grant-in-aid program for the elderly.

Representative Howard W. Smith (D-Va.) suggested various changes to OAA to restrain federal government power. First, he took issue with the requirement that states must grant sufficient old age assistance benefits to provide, when added to a recipient's income, "a reasonable subsistence compatible with decency and health." He explained, "My objection . . . would be answered by a provision in the bill which took away from some person in Washington the power to say when the State of Virginia could participate; in other words, for someone in Washington to say what was a reasonable and decent subsistence down in the Blue Ridge Mountains of Virginia."[92] Second, Smith argued that states should be able to determine eligibility criteria themselves, specifically in regard to social provision for African Americans:

MR. SMITH: . . . Of our 116,000 [persons over age 65 in Virginia] practically 25 percent are of one class that will probably qualify 100 percent. I am interested . . . [in] a provision in this law that permits the State to govern itself on that proposition.

MR. JENKINS: . . . Would the gentleman state what class he means by that?

MR. SMITH: Of course, in the South we have a great many colored people, and they are largely of the laboring class.[93]

---

[90] George Brown Tindall, *The Emergence of the New South, 1913–1945* (Baton Rouge: Louisiana State University Press, 1967), p. 491.

[91] Ibid.

[92] House Ways and Means Committee, *Hearings on the Economic Security Act, H.R. 4120*, 74th Cong., 1st sess., February 6, 1935, p. 975.

[93] Ibid., p. 976.

As Witte reported, many southern members "feared that someone in Washington would dictate how much of a pension they should pay to the negroes."[94]

Later, in executive session, the Ways and Means Committee took measures to reassert state authority over the policy. First, the committee struck from the bill the standard of "reasonable subsistence," leaving states free to offer pensions as small as they wished and still be eligible to receive matching funds from the national government. As well, conditions for approval of state plans by the national government were rewritten and stated negatively, leaving states free to impose any variety of eligibility criteria not forbidden by the federal statute. For example, the bill was altered to allow states to impose property restrictions on assistance recipients rather than determine need simply on the basis of income.

Finally, language on the selection of personnel was softened to prevent federal administrators from imposing the merit system on state agencies.[95] Since their first victory in the Pendleton Act of 1883, reformers had struggled to replace the old spoils system of staffing government jobs with one based on the merit principle and fair, open, competitive examinations.[96] In most of the country and in urban machine politics, however, jobs in government agencies were still filled through political appointments in an entrenched system of patronage; the Ways and Means Committee acted to preserve that tradition. As explained by Paul Douglas:

> It was argued that the states should be free to administer these laws in virtually any way they wished and should not be compelled to follow standards laid down by a central government, which could not know the local situation as they did. One reason was, undoubtedly, the fact that the standards of personnel which would be set by the federal government would be higher than those to which the vast majority of states, with the honorable exception of states like New York, Massachusetts, and Wisconsin, would conform. In other words, there was every probability that the local political machines would not be allowed to dominate these state services if the federal administrative bodies were given control over the standards to be followed locally in selecting the personnel.[97]

In the more candid words of Representative Fred Vinson (D-Ky.), which resonated with disdain for FERA and its manner of implementation, "No damned social workers are going to come into our state and tell our people

[94] Letter, Edwin E. Witte to Raymond Moley, March 6, 1935, CES, Staff Correspondence, 1934–35, box 15, Witte file 1, RG 47, NA.
[95] Ibid.; Witte, *Development of the Social Security Act*, pp. 144–45.
[96] Patricia Wallace Ingraham, *The Foundation of Merit: Public Service in American Democracy* (Baltimore: Johns Hopkins University Press, 1995), p. 26.
[97] Douglas, *Social Security in the United States*, pp. 106–7.

who to hire."[98] Instead, the committee added a clause to the bill which denied to the Social Security Board authority over practices related to the "selection, tenure of office, and compensation of personnel."[99]

In the Senate Finance Committee, the attack on Title I became even more vociferous. Senator Harry F. Byrd (D-Va.) led the charge for states' rights, insisting that the original bill threatened the states by granting "dictatorial power" to national administrators in Washington. The committee proceeded to eliminate all remaining references to the "decency and health" clause throughout the bill, amplifying the changes already made in the House Ways and Means Committee. Again, as observed by Witte, it was: "very evident that at least some southern senators feared that this measure might serve as an entering wedge for federal interference with the handling of the Negro question in the South. The southern members did not want to give authority to anyone in Washington to deny aid to any state because it discriminated against Negroes in the administration of old age assistance."[100] In sum, the congressional committees had altered the bill so that it gave far more discretion to the states than even the strongest proponents of federalism in the Roosevelt administration had desired. The states gained the ability to receive matching grants no matter how low their benefit levels and regardless of the qualifications they imposed on applicants for assistance. The weakening of federal controls for old age assistance would have extensive implications in terms of both gender and race, given that already the coverage of the two programs for the elderly appeared to be quite sex and race specific.

The Road Not Taken

Congressional committees had quietly acted to curtail the scope and reach of national government in the Economic Security Act, but other members of Congress made noisy appeals for a more expansive role, demanding that national funds be appropriated in a generous and redistributive fashion. The efforts for more expansive old age benefits were centered in the House, typically the body more likely to articulate demands emanating from the grass roots. Popular movements, particularly the Townsend crusade, had considerable influence on what in John Kingdon's terms could be called an alternative "stream"[101] of policy development for elderly Americans. Several representatives from western states, where the

---

[98] Martin, *Madam Secretary*, p. 354.

[99] Public Law 271, 74th Cong., 1st sess. (August 14, 1935), *Social Security Act of 1935*, H.R. 7260, title III, sec. 303(a)1 and title IV, sec. 402(a)5.

[100] Witte, *Development of the Social Security Act*, pp. 143–44.

[101] The metaphor is borrowed from John Kingdon, *Agendas, Alternatives, and Public Policy*, 2d ed. (New York: HarperCollins, 1995).

Townsend movement was particularly strong, served as advocates for the plan.[102] Besides the Townsendites, many southern representatives from impoverished districts were outspoken in demanding more generosity from the national government.

Supporters of the Townsend movement deluged Congress with letters and a petition bearing the names of twenty million supporters, and several state legislatures passed resolutions urging Congress to enact the Townsend Plan.[103] Several congressmen pressured Roosevelt to lift the $15 maximum federal grant limit and to offer instead grants of at least $50, if not $100 or $200 per month.[104] The Roosevelt administration remained staunchly opposed to such proposals, but they did receive a thorough hearing on the House floor.

Amid the lively debate over plans for the public assistance for the elderly, the future of U.S. federalism was at stake, and it was not clear which path would be chosen. On the right of the political spectrum, Republican opponents of any such legislation typically called the bill an attempt at "socialism" which would foster the "sovietization of America" by placing excessive power in the federal government.[105] In the center, supporters of the administration's bill insisted that the federal government had to take some action to ensure income security; they also derided "radical" alternatives, namely, the Lundeen and Townsend plans, as outrageously expensive and unworkable. Several southern Democratic House leaders were in this group, advancing the administration's bill as amended in committee as the best means of delivering social provision while maintaining local discretion. Representative Doughton, for instance, emphasized that the Economic Security Bill would "enhance very greatly the security of the American worker"[106] while preserving American institutions, namely, federalism:

> The proposed bill goes further in granting full discretion and authority to the States than any similar Federal-aid legislation within recent years. . . . If the Federal government were to go further and take over the entire problem of old-age pensions, as is advocated by some, it would be contrary to our fundamental political institutions and would place upon the National Government a tremendous financial burden without the protection of local vigilance which will prevail if local taxpayers are required to bear part of the cost.[107]

---

[102] Committee on Old Age Security of the Twentieth Century Fund, Inc., *The Townsend Crusade* (New York: Twentieth Century Fund, 1936), pp. 5–15.

[103] Letter, Witte to Moley, March 6, 1935, p. 3.

[104] Letter, Franklin D. Roosevelt to Felix Frankfurter, February 9, 1935, President's Personal File (hereafter, PPF) 140, FDR.

[105] According to Altmeyer, the Republicans were most worried about old age insurance. Altmeyer, *Formative Years*, pp. 37–38.

[106] *Congressional Record*, 74th Cong., 1st sess., April 11, 1935, vol. 79, pt. 5:5468.

[107] Ibid., 5469–70.

Other southerners, however, joined with westerners to resist the bill on populist grounds. They emphasized the dire need of their districts for more generous, redistributive grants-in-aid, and they argued that a bill designed according to the arrangements of federalism would preserve and heighten inequalities between American citizens.

These critics of the administration's bill charged that the matching-grant formula would treat needy people differently based on the relative wealth of the region in which they lived, helping rich states to become richer while offering little to poorer states. The character of citizenship would be determined largely by the health of a state's economy, dividing Americans in the experience of citizenship rather than granting equal inclusion in the polity to all. Charged Representative William Colmer (D-Miss.), "I was alarmed and amazed to discover that there was a possibility—nay, more than that, a strong likelihood—that another imaginary line would be drawn like a veritable Mason and Dixon's line that would divide this great country of ours into two sections. One section into which these unfortunate dependent persons in need of the provisions of this bill would be benefited, while in the other these benefits would be lacking." [108] Congressman John Robsion (R-Ky.) concurred and made a pitch for national rights of social citizenship: "Those who need aid most will receive the least, or none at all. The U.S. should treat all of its old and needy citizens alike." [109] And Congressman John McClellan, (D-Ark.) joined in: "State boundary lines should not be regarded. . . . We should amend this bill. . . so that the national responsibility, here recognized, to this class of our citizens shall be discharged equitably and without discrimination against any American citizen regardless of his state citizenship." [110] Though they proposed nearly fifty amendments and even replacements to the Economic Security Bill, these proponents of national social citizenship had little on their side in Congress save the power of rhetoric. Their own fellow southerners had already given their support to the administration's bill, and though the administration would have preferred more uniform national standards in public assistance than the Ways and Means Committee would tolerate, still Roosevelt and CES leaders were far more amenable to such compromise than to more redistributive plans.[111]

Throughout the legislation's journey through Congress, Roosevelt administration leaders remained very pessimistic about the bill's chances of passage. Already, in March, Witte summoned the assistance of the network

---

[108] Ibid., April 15, 1935, 5706.

[109] Ibid., 5693.

[110] Ibid., 5706; see also comments of Representative John Miller (D-Ark.), p. 5785.

[111] Letters, Witte to Mary B. Gilson, April 11, 1935, and Witte to Raymond Moley, May 10, 1935; both in CES, Staff Correspondence, 1934–35, box 15, Witte file 1, RG 47, NA.

Table 2. Old Age Insurance and Old Age Assistance, compared

	OAI	OAA
Level of governmental administration	National	Joint national-state
Contributory v. noncontributory	Contributory	Noncontributory
Financing arrangement	Tax on employers, held by national government	Grant-in-aid, 1 : 1 ratio
Eligibility determined by	National standards	States
Merit system	Yes	No

of women's reform organizations to urge passage of the bill. Grace Abbott, acting on behalf of the American Public Welfare Association, drafted a letter of support for the bill addressed to the president and Congress, collected the names of prominent signatories in a variety of organizations, and sent press releases to major newspapers for publicity.[112] Despite the intensity and fury of the debate, the actual opposition to the legislation in the final votes was relatively minor. In the House, Congresswoman Isabella Greenway (D-Ariz.) offered an amendment for national government to provide fifty dollars per person per month in old age assistance grants to the states on a nonmatching basis, but it was defeated after Roosevelt refused to lend his support. A revised version of the Townsend plan was defeated 206–56, the Lundeen Bill suffered a loss of 204–52, and several other proposals to liberalize the administration's bill were defeated as well. Finally, on April 19, the House passed the bill in a landslide vote of 371 to 33.[113] Redistributive plans garnered much less support in the Senate than in the House. An amendment sponsored by Senator William Borah (R-Idaho), which would have established a minimum benefit of thirty dollars for OAA and dropped the requirement that states match funds from the national government, was defeated 60–18.[114] The Senate passed the administration's bill (Table 2) on June 19 with a vote of 77 to 6. After a lengthy conference, the bill was passed again by both chambers and signed into law by President Roosevelt on August 14, 1935.[115]

In sum, arguments made in Congress for expanding guaranteed national

[112] Letter, from thirty-two signatories, "to the President and Congress of the U.S.," March 13, 1935; also John B. Andrews to Grace Abbott, March 22, 1935; also "Two Groups Press for Wagner Bill," *New York Times*, March 22, 1935; all in Abbott Papers, box 54, folder 4, Abbott Correspondence, CES, Staff Correspondence, 1934–35, box 12, RG 47, NA.

[113] Douglas, *Social Security in the United States*, pp. 108–9; Altmeyer, *Formative Years*, pp. 37–38; Witte, *Development of the Social Security Act*, pp. 98–99.

[114] Douglas, *Social Security in the United States*, pp. 109–10, 116–17.

[115] Bernstein, *Caring Society*, pp. 69–70.

social citizenship for elderly Americans were largely ineffectual. Congress acted instead to further exaggerate the distinctions in an already divided plan for social policy. The national program of OAI became geared even more exclusively toward white men than it had been in the plans of the CES. The OAA program, which would cover the women and minority men excluded from OAI, was altered to be particularly subject to the differential political economies of the states.

From the Viewpoint of Women

Only months after the passage of the Social Security Act, Mary Anderson in the Women's Bureau pointed to the different treatment of men and women in the new law:

> On the surface it may seem that the subject of the social security program is not one that calls for consideration by sex, but that it applies alike to men and women. However, on penetrating below the phraseology of the law one soon discovers a number of factors reflecting considerable differences between men and women in regard to the general outlook and effects of the social security program, upon which the Nation is now embarking. In other words the whole story shapes up rather differently from the viewpoint of women as compared with men.[116]

In a number of speeches and radio addresses, Anderson drew on the analysis of the Women's Bureau and contended that women, compared to men, would gain little from the package of social programs.

Anderson criticized the tax and benefit features of OAI, pointing out that because employed women earned much lower wages than men, the payroll tax would create more of a burden for women than men, and women's average benefits would be much smaller than men's:[117] "We can not help but be struck by the lack of real justice in the situation. Women like men may work hard all their lives in offices, stores, and factories, putting into their jobs as much time, energy, and often just as much skill as do men, yet not only must they accept lower pay during their working life but smaller benefits during their old age. We wonder why a woman is always expected to be able to subsist on less than a man is."[118] Women workers, just like men, bore financial responsibility for the support of family members, but

---

[116] Department of Labor, Women's Bureau, "Women Workers and the Social Security Program," address by Mary Anderson before the Indianapolis Council of Women, January 7, 1936, p. 2, Department of Labor, Women's Bureau, microfilm 16:0155, 0271, LMDC.

[117] Department of Labor, Women's Bureau, "Old Age Security," pp. 9, 15.

[118] Ibid., p. 16.

with their lower wages, such expenditures made saving for old age extremely burdensome.

But the biggest problem with OAI, Anderson emphasized, was that so few women would receive coverage under the law. Because three-quarters of all adult women were not employed in the paid work force in the 1930s, and because women tended to participate in the paid work force only intermittently, in order to balance wage earning with domestic responsibilities, most would be ineligible for the program. By electing to award OAI only for paid work, the CES had overlooked the value of the nonpaid work of raising children and maintaining the domestic sphere:

> There are those [women] who have never worked for a livelihood but have always been dependent upon others, a father, husband, son, or daughter. Women in this class far outnumber men, they stand as proof that women as a whole do not have equal opportunity with men to save for themselves and to build up the necessary funds against old-age destitution. It is true that many of these women—those who are wives of breadwinners, or those who are mothers, for example, have made important economic contributions to their families and to society in the form of services.[119]

The omission of most women in the contributory program was sure to prove problematic, Anderson warned. After all, wives were not legally guaranteed a definite share of their living husbands' income except in the case that a husband was found guilty of nonsupport, and even though widows would be granted a share of their deceased husbands' estates, destitution would continue to lie in store for many. Since so few women participated in the work force long term, they lacked the "equal opportunity with men to save for their own futures"; but those same criteria paradoxically made them ineligible for OAI.[120]

A majority of women, left out of OAI, would be subject instead to benefits that would vary from state to state and from region to region and standards that would depend on the politics of the state or locality. Thus, though the benefits of the average women covered by the contributory program would be low, Anderson argued that such a woman would still be better off than those who had to rely on OAA:

> She knows that the regular monthly benefit will automatically begin, dating from her 65th birthday. She will not have to establish her claim to these benefits as will the indigent old woman to the old-age assistance under the Federal-State system. Nor will the former woman have the disadvantage as

---

[119] Ibid., p. 7.
[120] Ibid., passim. Paul Douglas concurred; Douglas, *Social Security in the United States* 2d ed. (1939), p. 170.

will the latter of a required number of years of residence in a particular State. The former does not have to face the humiliation of having her relatives, whether willing or unwilling, required by law to come to her rescue, if possible, to the same extent as does the penniless old woman. . . . The [former] woman . . . does not face the stigma of charity . . . as does the old person in want who does have to prove her poverty before obtaining assistance.[121]

Though neither system would greatly enhance the lives of elderly women, Anderson, like Armstrong and Brown, was convinced that women would be better off in the program in which benefits were guaranteed nationally as a matter of right than in one that varied with state and local administrative norms.

How had the Social Security Act been rendered so gender biased? Policymakers had not acted deliberately to elevate men in the polity while maintaining control over women.[122] In fact, public officials who were particularly concerned about women, namely Armstrong and Perkins, had been actively involved in creating both policies. Ultimately, two dynamics of policymaking had prevailed to inadvertently marginalize women.

Policymakers had shaped both programs in keeping with the gendered hierarchy of society, assigning different status to "independent" and "dependent" persons. In creating OAI, policymakers in the CES and congressional committees had concentrated on full-time participants in the paid labor force, the "forgotten men" whom Roosevelt intended to include in New Deal policy. Though the subject of survivors' benefits came up at various stages in the process, time and again it was tabled by officials preoccupied with the classic subject of liberalism, the "independent" citizenworker. Like other privileges of liberal citizenship, benefits in the program would be considered "as a right" for those who qualified for coverage. Old age assistance, by contrast, was planned for those who were "dependent upon the public for support," the language of "rights," notably absent.[123]

Simultaneously, policymakers creating the two programs had acted to shape federalism anew. Whereas OAI was developed, successfully, as a hallmark of national social citizenship for those included in its benefits, OAA provided a means of reaffirming and even strengthening the power of individual states in defining citizenship. Administration policymakers, whose perspectives had been shaped by the intellectual traditions of the Progressive Era, had taken the initiative to make states active agents in the program. Then congressional committees, anxious to preserve states' rights

---

[121] Department of Labor, "Old Age Security Legislation," pp. 11–12.

[122] See, by contrast, Mimi Abramovitz, *Regulating the Lives of Women: Social Welfare Policy from Colonial Times to the Present* (Boston: South End Press, 1989).

[123] For the use of such language, see CES, "Report of the Committee on Economic Security," pp. 5, 25, 26.

and local autonomy in defining the social order, had made authority for the program far more thoroughly decentralized.

Thus, under the programs for the elderly in the Social Security Act of 1935, social citizenship in the national state was linked to independence as defined by wage earning—unless the wage earners happened to be toilers in excluded occupations. The mostly white, male wage earners were granted standing before the national government, yielding a right to benefits in old age. Other citizens were left as subjects of the states, dependent on public assistance to sustain them in a needy old age.

But the story of the development of the two programs for the elderly did not end with the passage of the Social Security Act. The large portions of the population excluded from OAI would enormously complicate Roosevelt's hopes that it, rather than OAA, would become the dominant program. The political forces that had propelled the issue of aid for the elderly into the national spotlight had not been satisfied by the administration's package, and they continued gathering momentum and provoking legislators, especially at the state level. The early years of implementation of the two programs continue the story of how the New Deal state reconstructed citizenship.

CHAPTER FOUR

The Development and Implementation of Old Age Insurance and Old Age Assistance

MR. McCORMACK. Of course, this annuity is a matter of right.
MR. ALTMEYER. Yes.
MR. McCORMACK. A man 65 years of age who is on the rolls receives it without regard to his income?
MR. ALTMEYER. Yes, sir.
MR. McCORMACK. And if he dies, his widow then secures what she is entitled to, what is provided for her, as a matter of right.
MR. ALTMEYER. Yes, sir.

> —*Hearings Relative to the Social Security Act Amendments,*
> House of Representatives, 1939

It is my hope that when we come to passing legislation dealing with human need we can forget the section of the country from which we come . . . when it comes to old-age pensions we should realize that we are dealing with citizens of the United States. Their relief ought to be upon two bases: First, citizenship; and second, need. We in the South, the North, the East, and the West recognize today that this is one great country, not split up into 48 subdivisions in matter of human need. Let us legislate upon this basis.

> —Rep. W. F. Norrell, Arkansas, *Congressional Record,* June 1939

Policymakers had barely discussed the situation of elderly women during the creation of the Social Security Act, yet during the early years of the law's implementation, women figured prominently among the beneficiaries in what became a burgeoning Old Age Assistance program. States acted quickly to take advantage of the matching federal funds available for the program. In several states, particularly in the West, the same cross-gendered, cross-class popular movements that had pressured Congress in 1935 turned their energies toward state legislatures, prompting the establishment of especially generous pensions and lax eligibility requirements. Elderly women in those states began to receive benefits on a fairly equitable basis with men.

Meanwhile, the distribution of Old Age Insurance benefits was not even scheduled to begin until 1942, though the collection of payroll taxes commenced in 1937. The program quickly came under attack by leaders in the Republican Party and the business community. They disparaged the policy's financing arrangement, which permitted the federal treasury to hold high levels of government reserves from contributions to the program. In the 1936 presidential campaign, Republican candidate Alf Landon charged that OAI was "a cruel hoax" and "a fraud on the working man." [1] Some critics advocated changing to a "pay-as-you-go" system in which lower payroll taxes would be supplemented in future decades by funds from general revenues, an approach Roosevelt had opposed. [2]

National administrators grew alarmed as the public assistance program for the elderly threatened to undermine the establishment of the contributory program, and the place of gender relations in the social welfare apparatus figured prominently in both their analysis of the problem and their proposed solution. This chapter examines the institutional and political factors that shaped the transformation of the two programs during the late 1930s and early 1940s. Changes in the policies and their administrative development once again reorganized older Americans under the auspices of two qualitatively different sovereignties. This time, however, some women who fit a model of good citizenship that had nothing to do with work-force participation were brought into the realm of a fully national social policy. At the same time, the distinctions between the national and state-level realms of social citizenship were strongly reinforced.

The Early Development of Social Security Act Programs for the Elderly, 1935–1939

The Social Security Act established an independent, three-member board appointed by the president to oversee the administration of the programs included in the legislation. In 1936, Arthur Altmeyer became chairman of the Social Security Board (SSB), a position he was to hold for decades to come. Under his leadership, the SSB quickly gained a reputation for competent professionalism and became a major political actor in steering the

---

[1] Letter, Mike Cowles to Charles Poletti, November 20, 1935, Felix Frankfurter Papers, FDR; letter, John S. Winant to Franklin D. Roosevelt, September 28, 1936, "Social Security" file, President's Secretary's File (hereafter, PSF) 165, FDR; Arthur J. Altmeyer, *The Formative Years of Social Security* (Madison: University of Wisconsin, 1968), p. 88.

[2] Frances Perkins, *The Roosevelt I Knew* (New York: Harper and Row, 1964), pp. 293–94; Edwin E. Witte, "Organized Labor and Social Security," in *Labor and the New Deal*, ed. Milton Derber and Edwin Young (Madison: University of Wisconsin Press, 1961), p. 257; Mark H. Leff, "Taxing the 'Forgotten Man': The Politics of Social Security Finance in the New Deal," *Journal of American History* 70 (September 1983): 3366–71.

subsequent development of the law.[3] The first challenge for the SSB involved managing the wildfire development of OAA.

The Rapid Development of OAA

The political attractiveness of redistributive pension schemes for the elderly continued to grow after the passage of the Social Security Act and drove the development of OAA programs at the state level.[4] While the Townsend movement persisted in making demands on national government, the activities of the more than seven thousand Townsend clubs created a fervor for generous OAA programs by the states. The American Public Welfare Association reported that during 1938 alone, 745 bills concerning assistance for the elderly were introduced in state legislatures, calling for more liberal and redistributive versions of old age pensions.[5] States proceeded to implement OAA with remarkable haste, all but Virginia having programs in place by the end of 1937. Several states adopted higher, more generous standards than the Social Security Act required, erasing need requirements and raising benefits rates.[6]

The proportion of the elderly population receiving assistance differed greatly from state to state. As Figure 2 shows, the highest rates of beneficiaries per thousand aged persons occurred mostly in states in the Southwest and Rocky Mountain regions of the West. In those states, poverty was high, the Townsend movement enjoyed some of its greatest strength, and state governments were particularly responsive to popular demands owing to institutionalized procedures such as the referendum, ballot initiative, and direct primary.[7] In December 1937, nearly 60 percent of persons over sixty-five years old in Oklahoma were in receipt of grants, as well as 49 percent in Utah, 45 percent in Colorado, and 41 percent in Texas. Though southern states were among the very poorest in the union, most states in the former confederacy adopted the program slowly. The delayed development of

[3] Brian Balogh, "Securing Support: The Emergence of the Social Security Board as a Political Actor, 1935–1939," in *Federal Social Policy*, ed. Donald T. Critchlow and Ellis W. Hawley (University Park: Pennsylvania State University Press, 1988), pp. 55–78; Arthur M. Schlesinger, Jr., *The Coming of the New Deal* (Boston: Houghton-Mifflin, 1959), pp. 312–15.
[4] Frank A. Pinner, Paul Jacobs, and Philip Selznik, *Old Age and Political Behavior: A Case Study* (Berkeley: University of California Press, 1959), chap. 1; Abraham Holtzman, *The Townsend Movement: A Political Study* (1963; reprint, New York: Octagon Books, 1975).
[5] Altmeyer, *Formative Years*, pp. 9–10; Jerry Cates, *Insuring Inequality: Administrative Leadership in Social Security, 1935–1954* (Ann Arbor: University of Michigan Press, 1983), chap. 2; Marietta Stevenson, "Recent Trends in Public Welfare Legislation," *Social Service Review* 3 (1939): 442.
[6] Stevenson, "Recent Trends in Public Welfare Legislation."
[7] SSB, *Third Annual Report* (Washington, D.C.: GPO, 1938), p. 81; see also Paul H. Douglas, *Social Security in the U.S.*, 2d ed. (New York: Whittlesey House, 1939), pp. 359–60. On the regional strength of Townsend clubs, see Holtzman, *Townsend Movement*, pp. 52–53.

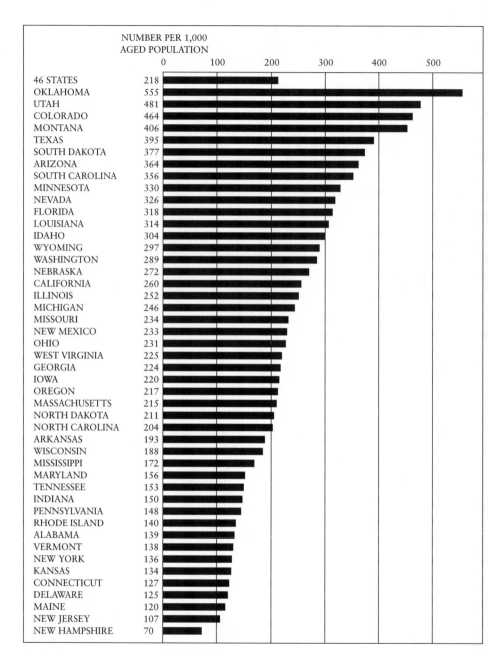

NUMBER PER 1,000
AGED POPULATION

		0	100	200	300	400	500
46 STATES	218						
OKLAHOMA	555						
UTAH	481						
COLORADO	464						
MONTANA	406						
TEXAS	395						
SOUTH DAKOTA	377						
ARIZONA	364						
SOUTH CAROLINA	356						
MINNESOTA	330						
NEVADA	326						
FLORIDA	318						
LOUISIANA	314						
IDAHO	304						
WYOMING	297						
WASHINGTON	289						
NEBRASKA	272						
CALIFORNIA	260						
ILLINOIS	252						
MICHIGAN	246						
MISSOURI	234						
NEW MEXICO	233						
OHIO	231						
WEST VIRGINIA	225						
GEORGIA	224						
IOWA	220						
OREGON	217						
MASSACHUSETTS	215						
NORTH DAKOTA	211						
NORTH CAROLINA	204						
ARKANSAS	193						
WISCONSIN	188						
MISSISSIPPI	172						
MARYLAND	156						
TENNESSEE	153						
INDIANA	150						
PENNSYLVANIA	148						
RHODE ISLAND	140						
ALABAMA	139						
VERMONT	138						
NEW YORK	136						
KANSAS	134						
CONNECTICUT	127						
DELAWARE	125						
MAINE	120						
NEW JERSEY	107						
NEW HAMPSHIRE	70						

Figure 2. OAA recipients per 1,000 population aged 65 and over in states with plans approved by the Social Security Board, June 1938. From Social Security Board, *Third Annual Report of the Social Security Board* (Washington, D.C.: GPO, 1938), p. 81.

OAA in the South reflected the lack of institutional precedents in the area, the continued resistance by public officials to disturbing the low-wage labor system, and the lack of political power for African Americans owing to the Jim Crow system and such impediments to voting as literacy tests and poll taxes. Louisiana, however, ranked twelfth in distribution of benefits in June 1938, an exception explained by the influence of Huey Long and populist politics.[8]

Similarly, the level of OAA payments varied dramatically from state to state, as shown by Figure 3.[9] Benefit levels were highest where public pressure had resulted in the enactment of a minimum state guaranteed cash income for all aged people. In California, where a minimum income of $35 per month was guaranteed, OAA benefits had averaged $32.33 in June 1938; Massachusetts, making a guarantee of $30 per month, paid average OAA benefits of $27.80, and Colorado, guaranteeing $45 per month, offered average benefits of $26.79.[10] The massive increase in state appropriations for assistance programs, especially OAA, presented these states with a fiscal dilemma, and most responded by imposing new sales taxes on consumer goods.[11] The lowest benefit levels were in the South. Benefits of less than $11 per month were offered in Arkansas, Georgia, North Carolina, Louisiana, Alabama, South Carolina, and Delaware; Mississippi paid the very lowest average benefits of $4.79 per month.[12]

Many states took the initiative to liberalize eligibility rules above standards required by national administrators and in advance of the enforcement of national restrictions. Some enacted residence requirements more flexible than the five-year minimum permissible under the act, and others opted to liberalize eligibility requirements regarding maximum admissible property and income. Though the national age requirement was not scheduled to go into effect until 1940, all states had granted aid to people sixty-five or older by 1939.[13]

By the late 1930s, OAA was a program that varied substantially from state to state but tended toward generosity and broad coverage and, notably, tended to treat women on a fairly equitable basis with men. Because

---

[8] Douglas, *Social Security in the U.S.*, pp. 358–64.

[9] SSB, *Third Annual Report*, p. 82; Douglas, *Social Security in the U.S.*, p. 370.

[10] Douglas, *Social Security in the U.S.*, pp. 369–72. With a strong Townsend movement, Massachusetts was an exception among states in the East. See Martha Derthick, *The Influence of Federal Grants* (Cambridge: Harvard University Press, 1970), pp. 54–56; also Holtzman, *Townsend Movement*, pp. 111, 208.

[11] James T. Patterson, *The New Deal and the States: Federalism in Transition* (Princeton: Princeton University Press, 1969), pp. 93–95; George Brown Tindall, *The Emergence of the New South, 1913–1945* (Baton Rouge: Louisiana State University Press, 1967), p. 490; John Braeman, Robert H. Bremner, and David Brody, eds., *The New Deal: The State and Local Levels* (Columbus: Ohio State University Press, 1975), 2:184, 286.

[12] Douglas, *Social Security in the U.S.*, pp. 369–72.

[13] Stevenson, "Recent Trends in Public Welfare Legislation," pp. 442–44.

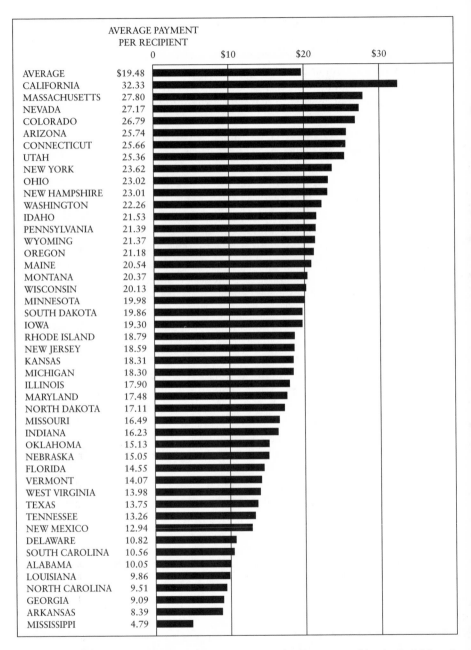

	AVERAGE PAYMENT PER RECIPIENT			
	0	$10	$20	$30
AVERAGE	$19.48			
CALIFORNIA	32.33			
MASSACHUSETTS	27.80			
NEVADA	27.17			
COLORADO	26.79			
ARIZONA	25.74			
CONNECTICUT	25.66			
UTAH	25.36			
NEW YORK	23.62			
OHIO	23.02			
NEW HAMPSHIRE	23.01			
WASHINGTON	22.26			
IDAHO	21.53			
PENNSYLVANIA	21.39			
WYOMING	21.37			
OREGON	21.18			
MAINE	20.54			
MONTANA	20.37			
WISCONSIN	20.13			
MINNESOTA	19.98			
SOUTH DAKOTA	19.86			
IOWA	19.30			
RHODE ISLAND	18.79			
NEW JERSEY	18.59			
KANSAS	18.31			
MICHIGAN	18.30			
ILLINOIS	17.90			
MARYLAND	17.48			
NORTH DAKOTA	17.11			
MISSOURI	16.49			
INDIANA	16.23			
OKLAHOMA	15.13			
NEBRASKA	15.05			
FLORIDA	14.55			
VERMONT	14.07			
WEST VIRGINIA	13.98			
TEXAS	13.75			
TENNESSEE	13.26			
NEW MEXICO	12.94			
DELAWARE	10.82			
SOUTH CAROLINA	10.56			
ALABAMA	10.05			
LOUISIANA	9.86			
NORTH CAROLINA	9.51			
GEORGIA	9.09			
ARKANSAS	8.39			
MISSISSIPPI	4.79			

Figure 3. Average OAA payment per recipient in states with plans approved by the Social Security Board, June 1938. From Social Security Board, *Third Annual Report of the Social Security Board* (Washington, D.C.: GPO, 1938), p. 82.

OAA was meant for the elderly poor rather than for retired, long-term breadwinners, it was bound to apply to both men and women. And because OAI was not yet in effect, popular movements focused their attention on improving OAA benefits, and their activism was to the equal advantage of men and women. In fact, in its first few years the assistance program for the elderly rapidly became the most widespread program in the history of U.S. social policy to incorporate women on a basis relatively equal to men.[14]

Formally, OAA was granted to nearly equal proportions of men and women, and informally, an even higher proportion of women than men benefited from the program. According to the aggregate data collected by the SSB for 1937–1938, men, who were 50.1 percent of the population over sixty-five, constituted 50.6 percent of those receiving OAA and women, 49.4 percent.[15] The SSB staff recognized, however, that the data did not reflect the fact that in the case of married couples, men were more often considered the head of household and were thus recorded as the sole recipients of benefits even though they shared the funds with their wives.[16] Male beneficiaries, moreover, were far more likely to be married; female beneficiaries, to be widowed. From 1937 to 1938, as shown by Figure 4, only 28.1 percent of the men but 59.7 percent of the women beneficiaries were widows, whereas 57.9 percent of the men and only 30.8 percent of the women beneficiaries were married.[17] Subsequently, a large number of married women who shared grants with their husbands, as many as 78,878, were not represented in the aggregate data. The inclusion of those women reveals that women constituted a 55.7 percent majority of OAA beneficiaries, with men only 44.3 percent.[18]

Furthermore, despite public assistance agencies' custom of regarding husbands as the primary recipients of aid, the implementation of OAA revealed a new willingness of officials to allocate benefits more equitably. Some states awarded joint grants to married couples: among couples receiving OAA between 1939 and 1940, one-third of the wives were granted

---

[14] Although pensions for Civil War veterans had been both generous and remarkably widespread early in the century, women received coverage only as dependent survivors of male veterans rather than through more universal criteria. Theda Skocpol estimates that in 1910, 18 percent of the U.S. population sixty-five and over received such benefits, but a far greater portion of aged men were covered than women: 28.5 percent versus 8 percent; see Theda Skocpol, *Protecting Soldiers and Mothers: The Political Origins of Social Policy in the United States* (Cambridge: Harvard University Press, 1992), pp. 1, 102, 107–11, 129, 132.

[15] SSB, "Sex, Marital Status, and Living Arrangements of 1 Million Recipients of Old-Age Assistance," *Social Security Bulletin* 2 (February 1939): 20–22.

[16] Memorandum, M. D. Ring to Mr. Lakeman, June 14, 1937, SSB, Central File, Master File, 1935–47, box 236, file 641, RG 47, NA.

[17] SSB, "Sex, Marital Status, and Living Arrangements," pp. 20–22.

[18] SSB, "Variations in Assistance Payments and Social Characteristics of Recipients Accepted for Old-Age Assistance," by Ellen J. Newman, *Social Security Bulletin* 4 (October 1941): 30–31.

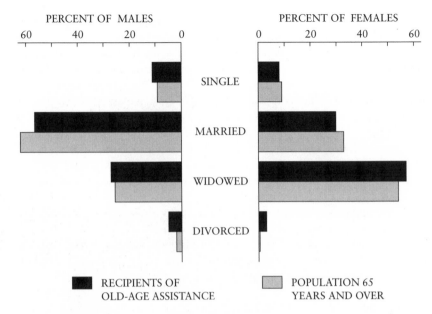

Figure 4. Percentage distribution of males and females according to marital status, for OAA recipients accepted during the fiscal year 1937–38 and for the population 65 years and over, in all states. From Social Security Board, *Social Security Bulletin* 2 (February 1939): 21.

benefits in their own names. Commenting on the novelty of such allocation patterns, a study in the *Social Security Bulletin* noted that many women were thus receiving money in their own names for the first time in their lives.[19]

The relatively equal status of women and men in OAA was further underscored by the similarity in benefit levels to each group. Given local discretion in setting benefit levels according to client needs and resources, benefits could potentially vary widely, but average benefit levels were only slightly lower for women than for men: for 1937–39, men on OAA received an average of $18 per month; women, $17.[20] Among elderly people living alone, women recipients received average benefits of $21, slightly higher than the $20 average for men. In states that administered joint grants to married couples, benefits typically amounted to nearly twice the level of average individual grants.[21]

[19] Ibid.

[20] Ibid., p. 30.

[21] Memorandum, Wilbur J. Cohen to A. J. Altmeyer, December 17, 1938, SSB, Chairman's Files, Subject Files, 1935–40, box 93, file 622, RG 47, NA; letter, A. J. Altmeyer to M. A. Linton, November 23, 1937, SSB, Central File, Master File, 1935–47, box 236, file 632.36, RG 47, NA.

By contrast, the administration of OAA was uneven in terms of race. In most states outside the South, African Americans did benefit fairly equally with whites from the liberalization of OAA. In some states in the Northeast and Midwest, average benefits to African Americans were higher than those for whites, presumably because need was greater.[22] In the South, however, African Americans were underrepresented on public assistance, and their average benefit levels were consistently lower than those for whites.[23] In Texas, for example, white beneficiaries received average monthly grants of $14.94 versus $11.88 for blacks. The lowest grants occurred in the cotton-producing counties: in Alabama in 1939, the average OAA grant in cotton counties was $7.16 in contrast to $11.42 in non-cotton counties.[24] In the Southwest, the SSB encountered resistance by local authorities in granting OAA to Mexicans and to Indians who were living on reservations.[25]

In sum, the eligibility criteria and early implementation of OAA resulted in relatively equitable treatment of beneficiaries in terms of gender, and in states where popular movements pushed for liberalization of benefits, women gained from generous grants and standards similar to men's. This outcome shows that in the presence of powerful and effective social movements, liberalizing tendencies can be carried out even under a program that leaves great autonomy to individual states, and those changes can benefit women and men equally in a program under which both sexes are subject to similar eligibility criteria. Yet the discretion permitted to individual states enabled southern ones to curtail the reach of the assistance program, and African Americans, regardless of gender, bore the brunt of the inadequate coverage and benefit levels in the region.

The SSB Tries to Stem the Tide

SSB bureaucrats, charged with running a national agency, quickly acquired priorities different from those of the leaders in the Committee on Economic Security, who had so prized the states' role as laboratories for policy experimentation. SSB officials were exasperated by their own lack of control over the unwieldy state-run OAA program. They took a dim view

---

[22] Jill Quadagno, *The Transformation of Old Age Security* (Chicago: University of Chicago Press, 1988), p. 135.

[23] SSB, "Race, Nativity, Citizenship, Age, and Residence of 1,000,000 Recipients of Old-Age Assistance," *Social Security Bulletin* 2 (June 1939): 23–25.

[24] Quadagno, *Transformation of Old Age Security*, pp. 133, 132–37.

[25] "Arizona," April 6, 1936, SSB, Chairman's Files, Subject Files, 1935–40, box 93, file entitled "Reports on States"; all contents of file entitled "600: Arizona," SSB, Chairman's Files, State Files, 1935–40, box 106; "Arizona," January 30, 1940, SSB, Records of the Executive Director, Subject Files, 1935–40, box 298; all in RG 47, NA.

of states with expansive, generous OAA plans, fearing they might drain national coffers. These agency personnel believed the financing mechanism for the contributory program promised a more fiscally secure approach to long-term security for the elderly, but they worried that if the trends of the late 1930s continued, the program would never go into effect.[26] In the Bureau of Public Assistance (BPA), the SSB agency charged with overseeing the administration of the public assistance programs, the social workers despised the matching-grant design of OAA because it reinforced inequalities between the states.

Jane Hoey, a former social worker and administrator from New York City who had been appointed director of the BPA, was among the first to alert the SSB to the dangers of current trends. She feared that the intended distinctions between OAA and OAI would dissolve by the time OAI benefits went into effect. After all, the pension movements in the states advocated guaranteed, "flat" or fixed pensions to all elderly persons, regardless of need. The problem, in Hoey's mind, was that such developments jeopardized the ability of the national government to assist the most destitute elderly in many low-income states. As long as national monies were diverted to better-off states with generous OAA plans, funds would remain unavailable to help the poorer states to better assist their most needy elderly.[27]

Acting on such concerns, the SSB began a long struggle to restrain what it perceived to be the excesses of OAA in some states, to raise OAA benefit levels in other states, and most important, to fortify old age insurance. First, Hoey and the team of social workers in the BPA insisted on using their profession's family-budgeting techniques to assess applicant need, and they promoted the use of means testing. Thomas Eliot, counsel to the SSB, warned that the 1935 statute did not specify that OAA grants were explicitly for "needy" persons. Nonetheless, the board yielded to the social workers' demands and began requiring states to figure benefits on an individual basis by subtracting each applicant's available income and property (resources) from his or her living expenses (requirements). The SSB pushed states to use investigative social work procedures that would permit officials to be particularly strict in taking account of all property and income of each potential beneficiary or spouse. The board also indicated disapproval of state plans that guaranteed identical benefits to all elderly people below a certain income level, even though Eliot admitted that the agency's authority in such issues was questionable. Such alterations, Hoey believed,

[26] Balogh, "Securing Support," pp. 63–65.

[27] Memorandum, Jane M. Hoey and H. P. Seidemann to John J. Corson, February 6, 1937, SSB, Records of the Executive Director, Subject Files, 1935–40, box 274, file 620, RG 47, NA; Blanche D. Coll, *Safety Net: Welfare and Social Security, 1929–1979* (New Brunswick: Rutgers University Press, 1995), pp. 62–63, 91–92; Cates, *Insuring Inequality*, p. 147.

would make OAA seem less like a right, distinguishing its identity from OAI, and would enable administrators to concentrate on providing for the neediest.[28]

Second, Chairman Altmeyer and fellow SSB members commenced a public relations war to promote OAI. Though Altmeyer, like his fellow reformers from Wisconsin, had not been a vocal proponent of OAI as designed under Barbara Armstrong in 1935, as chief of the SSB he became a staunch defender of the contributory program. He sought to advance OAI as a "matter of right" for recipients, to allow them to retain their dignity in old age. By contrast, he portrayed OAA as demeaning because it required subjecting oneself to "distasteful and demoralizing" scrutiny by social workers.[29] The discourse became increasingly gender specific as Altmeyer justified OAI benefits as superior to OAA because they were tied to participation in the paid work force and thus epitomized the (implicitly male) virtues of "individual initiative," independence, and self-sufficiency: "Because, by and large, Americans believe that each man ought, insofar as possible, to do *his* part for his *own* security, social insurance has a strong appeal. Since these benefits . . . are in proportion to the individual worker's past earnings and are payable as a matter of right, they may truly be said to represent self-earned security." [30] The public assistance program for the elderly which had emerged from a Progressive Era tradition of social provision for the "deserving poor," was being stigmatized, through the policy decisions and rhetoric of the SSB, as part of an effort to elevate OAI.[31] The SSB was attempting to elevate a program geared for men at the expense of a program that served men and women equitably.

Meanwhile, however, in studies conducted by its own research staff, the SSB began to confront more fundamental obstacles to the establishment of the contributory program. No amount of rhetoric or disparagement of the public assistance program could correct for the fact that OAI excluded nearly half the working population and totally omitted the three-quarters of the female population who did not participate in the paid work force. Research reports made it obvious, furthermore, that working women, owing to their occupations and status, would gain little from OAI.

[28] *Reminiscences of Jane Hoey*, OHC, pp. 22–25; Cates, *Insuring Inequality*, pp. 106–17; Coll, *Safety Net*, pp. 84–91.

[29] Altmeyer as quoted in Cates, *Insuring Inequality*, p. 29; see also Balogh, "Securing Support," pp. 63–68.

[30] Altmeyer as quoted in Cates, *Insuring Inequality*, p. 31.

[31] On this tradition of social welfare benefits as a reward for socially necessary work, see Ann Shola Orloff, "Gender in Early U.S. Social Policy," *Journal of Policy History* 3 (1991): 249–81. The tradition was carried on and advocated in the New Deal by public officials such as those in the Children's Bureau and Women's Bureau and was reflected in the wide congressional and public support for programs such as OAA and ADC; see Otis L. Graham, Jr., *An Encore for Reform: The Old Progressives and the New Deal* (New York: Oxford University Press, 1967).

Though African American women were 3.5 percent of the labor force, only 1.1 percent of them were covered by OAI. Occupational segregation actually gave white working women a coverage advantage over other groups: they were 26.1 percent of all covered workers but only 20.8 percent of the labor force.[32] With the high turnover among women in the labor market, however, such figures vastly overstated women's actual coverage. Without steady, long-term work-force participation, women would not be eligible for future benefits.[33] The low median wages of women as well as nonwhite men covered by OAI meant, furthermore, that their future OAI benefits would be paltry, as benefits would be proportional to wages. Though women made up 27.4 percent of all persons for whom OAI wage reports were submitted in 1937, they received but 16.2 percent of total reported wages. White men paying into the OAI system had annual average wages of $1,091; white women, $552; black men, $457; and black women, $256.[34]

Such data showed that while the SSB and BPA were struggling to save the fledgling and besieged OAI program and to quell the upsurge in OAA, their efforts were effectively missing the mark. The exclusion and marginalization of so many people under OAI was beginning to constitute a significant obstacle to administrators trying to establish the contributory program as the primary program and to render the assistance program merely a residual safety net. In effect, a program oriented toward independent wage earners was foundering because the structure of prevailing social and economic relationships meant that large segments of the population, especially women and nonwhite men, remained poor or dependent on others. The private systems of relationships through which such groups were maintained in a "dependent" status—marriage and domestic responsibilities for women and sharecropping or domestic service for nonwhite men and women—proved inadequate to provide sufficient care for them in old age; thus they accounted for a large share of the population most in need of

[32] SSB, "Wage Reports for Workers Covered by Federal Old-Age Insurance in 1937," by John J. Corson, *Social Security Bulletin* 2 (March 1939): 3–9. Corson's report, appearing one year before the 1940 census, used out-of-date figures for the proportion of each group in the work force generally but still made accurate overall judgments about the underrepresentation of blacks, especially women. To add clarity, 1940 census figures have been used here, though of course policymakers were not yet privy to the new data. See SSB, "Employment and Wages under Old-Age and Survivors Insurance, 1940," by Merrill G. Murray and Mason C. Doan, *Social Security Bulletin* 5 (May 1942): 6.
[33] Martha H. Swain, *Ellen Woodward: New Deal Advocate for Women* (Jackson: University Press of Mississippi, 1995), p. 147.
[34] SSB, "Age and Sex Differentials in Taxable Wages Reported for 1937," by Max J. Wasserman and Katherine D. Wood, *Social Security Bulletin* 2 (June 1939): 13–14; SSB, "Employees and Their Wages under Old-Age and Survivors Insurance, 1937–1939," by John J. Corson, *Social Security Bulletin* 4 (April 1941): 6.

noncontributory pensions. Policymakers were confronted with the dilemma of having to deal with a gender system and patterns of racial stratification that assigned "dependence" to particular groups in society and, at the same time, trying to make as many people as possible fit into a program deliberately rooted in the notion that coverage must be tied to participation and "independent" status in the paid work force.

The 1939 Amendments to the Social Security Act

In April 1937, the Supreme Court, so feared by the CES in 1935, handed down a landmark decision that signaled a change of course. With the *National Labor Relations Board v. Jones and Laughlin Steel Corp.* decision, the Court approved the expanded reach of national governing power that was the hallmark of the most innovative New Deal legislation.[35] Then in May, the Court confirmed the constitutionality of the OAI title of the Social Security Act.[36] Emboldened by the news, the SSB altered its strategy from merely promoting an inadequate OAI program to planning sweeping changes in the basic structure of policy.[37] Through the 1939 Amendments to the Social Security Act, bureaucrats and policymakers intervened to save and fortify the contributory program, deflate public pressure in the pensions movement, and stifle liberalizing trends in OAA. As national administrators sought to make the contributory program for the elderly more established and permanent, the place of women in the social welfare apparatus figured prominently in their plan to resolve the problem.

Recommendations of the Advisory Council on Social Security

The initial momentum for alterations to the 1935 law came from Congress. Already in February 1937, complaints about the financing of the OAI program had prompted the Senate Finance Committee, at the initiative of Republicans, to recommend the formation of an advisory committee to study the subject. The SSB and a subcommittee of the Finance Committee met to select an advisory council that would include several representatives of labor, industry, and public organizations, including three female social reformers. The council was to be chaired by Professor Douglas J. Brown, who had assisted Armstrong in formulating OAI for the

---

[35] 301 U.S. 1 (1937).
[36] *Helvering v. Davis*, 301 U.S. 619 (1937).
[37] J. Douglas Brown, *An American Philosophy of Social Security* (Princeton: Princeton University Press, 1972), p. 133.

CES.[38] "Extreme radicals"—that is, the Townsendites and other advocates of more redistributive plans—were purposefully excluded.[39]

Before the Advisory Council on Social Security met, Altmeyer, on behalf of the SSB, took several months to consider options for amending the OAI program. In September 1937, he wrote to President Roosevelt to lay out his plan. Altmeyer reviewed the various sources of opposition to OAI, then suggested, "I think it is possible not only to offset these attacks on the Social Security Act, but really to utilize them to advance a socially desirable program. . ."[40] Altmeyer planned to seize the opportunity provided by conservative critics of OAI in order to actually liberalize the program, making it more expansive and generous than the 1935 law had allowed.

When the Advisory Council convened in November 1937, it approved Altmeyer's plan. The council suggested that the full-government-reserve plan, under attack from all sides, be abandoned in favor of a pay-as-you-go financing system assisted by government revenues.[41] It recommended that benefits commence earlier than planned, in 1940 instead of 1942. The council made, as well, several recommendations aimed at increasing the size and scope of OAI benefits in order to reduce the need for OAA. As a means of increasing average benefits, the council proposed changing the benefit formula to relate to previous average monthly wages before retirement rather than to average cumulative wages.[42] The group recommended the extension of coverage to domestic and agricultural workers and employees in nonprofit religious, charitable, and educational institutions.[43] The council devoted most of its attention, however, to the proposal it considered most significant: the inclusion of benefits for family members of covered persons.

[38] 1937–38 Advisory Council on Social Security, "Final Report," and Robert M. Ball, "The 1939 Amendments to the Social Security Act and What Followed," both in *The Report of the Committee on Economic Security of 1935 and Other Basic Documents relating to the Development of the Social Security Act*, 50th anniversary ed., ed. National Conference on Social Welfare (Washington, D.C.: National Conference on Social Welfare, 1985), pp. 175–77 and 161–72, respectively.

[39] Witte, "Organized Labor and Social Security," p. 257.

[40] Memorandum, Mr. Altmeyer to the President, September 11, 1937, "SSB, July-December 1937," OF, 1710, box 1, FDR.

[41] Altmeyer, *Formative Years*, pp. 91–92; 1937–38 Advisory Council, "Final Report," pp. 180–81.

[42] The primary benefit amount was to equal 40 percent of the first $50 of a person's average monthly wage just before retirement, plus 10 percent of the next $200, plus an increment based on the years of covered employment. This alteration was intended to make benefits more generous for everyone, as most people would retire when they were earning their highest income; yet it would preserve the mildly progressive, graduated character of benefits, so that white men, whose earnings had typically been highest, would receive the highest benefits. SSB, "Social Insurance and Public Assistance Payments," by Elva Marquard, *Social Security Bulletin* 6 (December 1943): 17; SSB, "Employees and Their Wages, 1937–1939," p. 6.

[43] 1937–38 Advisory Council, "Final Report," p. 180.

In a set of measures that would involve national government in supporting gender relations in the private sphere and would seemingly compromise
some of the prized individualistic principles of the SSB, the Advisory Council urged that OAI benefits be extended to wives, aged sixty-five and over,
of living beneficiaries, as well as to widows and children of deceased beneficiaries. Such recommendations appear to have been an abrupt and paradoxical reversal of the principles on which the program rested. After all,
the SSB had been trying to establish a great divide between the bases for inclusion in the public assistance and contributory programs, stressing that
the former was for needy, "dependent" persons, the latter for "independent" wage earners who had established an "earned right" to benefits. The
Advisory Council itself advanced that same view: "The council believes
that such a method [OAI] of encouragement of self-help and self-reliance
in securing protection in old age is essentially in harmony with individual
incentive within democratic society. It is highly desirable in preserving
American institutions to remove from as many individuals as possible, in
the years to come, the necessity for dependency relief and to substitute instead protection . . . in the productive processes of the country." [44] In light
of this dichotomy, the addition of wives and widows to the contributory
program might have been viewed as weakening OAI's legitimacy: for such
persons would be explicitly included as "dependents" of men rather than
as self-sufficient wage earners. The council's proposal would transform
OAI from a program built on insurance principles to one based on income
transfers. [45]

But although a few members of the Advisory Council questioned the rationale for the scheme, most did not consider the inclusion of the principle
of "family protection" to be contrary to the ideas underlying the policy. In
a study of the proceedings of the Advisory Council, Alice Kessler-Harris
found that council members generally spoke of the reforms as enlarging the
rights of male breadwinners rather than extending a social right to women
previously excluded from the system. Such benefits would strengthen men's
capacity to perform their assigned role in the gender system, in effect enabling them to provide for their families, even after their own deaths. [46]
Among those articulating such ideology in promotional speeches for the
plan was Molly Dewson, who in 1937 had been appointed to the SSB. She

[44] Ibid., p. 185.

[45] Richard V. Burkhauser and Karen C. Holden, "Introduction," in *A Challenge to Social
Security: The Changing Roles of Women and Men in American Society*, ed. Burkhauser and
Holden (New York: Academic Press, 1982), pp. 4–8.

[46] Alice Kessler-Harris, "Designing Women and Old Fools: The Construction of the Social
Security Amendments of 1939," in *U.S. History as Women's History: New Feminist Essays*,
ed. Linda K. Kerber, Alice Kessler-Harris, Kathryn Kish Sklar (Chapel Hill: University of
North Carolina Press, 1995), pp. 94–100.

argued, "Men who can afford it always consider it their first duty to provide insurance protection for their wives and children. Survivors' benefits extend the same kind of protection to families who need it most and can afford it least." [47] Douglas Brown also stressed that the wife's benefit would be "considered a dependent's allowance . . . and not a true benefit" and would be "payable to her husband on her behalf." [48] In its summary of recommendations, in fact, the Advisory Council listed the provisions pertaining to survivors and wives under the section on the expansion of benefits rather than in the section on increased coverage, reflecting members' understanding that the alteration was intended to improve the overall level of benefits for primary beneficiaries as (male) heads of households, rather than to include women in a promise of social citizenship. [49]

Following the SSB's recommendations, the Advisory Council proposed that familial benefits be correlated directly to the benefit levels of primary beneficiaries. The wage-oriented structure of taxes and benefits for wage earners would remain intact, with the benefits for wives and widows arranged in a lower-tier but similarly graduated fashion corresponding to their husbands' former earnings. Retired workers whose wives were sixty-five or older were to receive "supplementary allowances" amounting to an extra 50 percent of the benefit for their wives. Widows were to receive benefits equal to three-quarters of the benefits their husbands would have received. [50]

While incorporating married women into the contributory program on a noncontributory basis, the council proposed, in yet another paradoxical decision, to disqualify those same women from receiving benefits based on their own participation in the paid work force. The system would be organized such that a married woman would be eligible for either a wife's allowance or a benefit based on her own previous earnings, whichever would be larger. Given the differential in average wages between men and women, women's earned benefits would typically be smaller than 50 percent of their husbands'. In opting for the wives' allowance, however, they would gain nothing from the payroll taxes they themselves had paid into the system. No provisions were to be made for spousal or survivors' benefits for husbands, denying working women the opportunity to provide for their husbands in retirement or death. In full, such arrangements implicitly elevated

---

[47] Mary Dewson, "Fifty Years' Progress toward Social Security," address before the State Convention of Affiliated Young Democrats, New York City, May 21, 1938, Dewson Papers, box 9, FDR.

[48] Brown, *American Philosophy of Social Security*, 1972, p. 135.

[49] 1937–38 Advisory Council, "Final Report," pp. 179–80.

[50] Ibid., pp. 89–90; SSB, "Economic and Social Status of Beneficiaries of Old-Age and Survivors Insurance," by Edna C. Wentworth, *Social Security Bulletin* 6 (July 1943): 13–14. For a detailed treatment of these discussions, see Kessler-Harris, "Designing Women and Old Fools," pp. 87–106.

men's roles and devalued women's roles in the paid work force, reinforced the ascribed gender role of "breadwinner" for men and "dependent wife" for women, and denied women the opportunity to be rewarded for both their paid and unpaid roles.[51]

In sum, in seeking to promote and broaden a policy for the elderly which was staunchly defended as belonging to "independent" citizens, the Advisory Council chose the ironic strategy of utilizing women's "dependence" on men. The legitimacy of that choice would permit a seamless incorporation of a much wider portion of the population into OAI, proving a masterful strategy for broadening the popular base for the program.

The Advisory Council submitted its recommendations in the form of a final report on December 10, 1938, and subsequently the SSB presented to the president a set of proposals for amending not only OAI but the public assistance titles in the Social Security Act as well. The SSB wanted to reform OAA both to rein in excesses in certain states and to foster minimum national standards in both benefit levels and administrative procedures. On January 16, 1939, Roosevelt transmitted the recommendations to Congress with a hearty endorsement for their enactment.[52]

The administration's proposals reached a Congress ready to act to appease elderly Americans. The Townsend movement had just made its greatest political impact in the 1938 congressional elections. Many Republicans running for Congress had sought to win the support of Townsendites by attacking the Social Security Act and campaigning for more generous pension plans for the elderly. More than 90 such Republicans were elected in 1938, diminishing the Democratic majority in the House from 328 to 226. The Democratic leadership, anxious to respond to public sentiment on their own terms, prepared to act swiftly to amend the Social Security Act.[53]

Expanding OAI to Wives and Survivors

Although there had been no public outcry demanding the inclusion of wives and widows in OAI, and despite the seeming contradictions implicit in including noncontributing beneficiaries in the contributory program, Congress greeted the administration's plan with remarkable nonchalance. Testifying in congressional hearings on the bill, spokesmen for the administration made their intentions clear: such alterations were simply a means of improving the overall benefit structure of OAI. The fact that the changes would reinforce a widely accepted and idealized form of gender relations in public policy simply offered an additional rationale for the dramatic

---

[51] 1937–38 Advisory Council, "Final Report," pp. 189; Kessler-Harris, "Designing Women and Old Fools," pp. 100–101.

[52] Altmeyer, *Formative Years*, pp. 96–99.

[53] Holtzman, *Townsend Movement*, pp. 103–4.

change. As Brown told the House Ways and Means Committee, "The method we have employed to date was largely the protection of the individual, but . . . at the base of American civilization is the concept of the family and . . . the perpetuation of that concept is highly important."[54]

Almost none of those who testified before Congress reacted with alarm to the proposed inclusion of survivors and wives in the policy. An exception was Abraham Epstein, a long-time proponent of pensions for the elderly and director of the American Association for Old Age Security, who expressed concern that such plans would direct redistribution in an upward direction, with dire consequences for poorer Americans: "But I want also to call your attention to the fact that in doing so you will be throwing out millions of dollars on people who are not social problems, and at the same time you will be stingy with those who will be social problems. For instance, under this act the next year we will pay pensions to people that are of the Rockefeller type just because they are insured and we will pay annuities to their wives, their widows, and to their children, and so forth."[55] Epstein admonished the Roosevelt administration for reacting to "charlatans," meaning the Townsendites, and trying to rush ill-conceived amendments through Congress.[56] He recommended instead that wives and survivors should be cared for under improved public assistance programs, fortified through more generous and redistributive measures to equalize conditions between states and improve overall standards. Congressional committees were unmoved however, and they proceeded to specify the conditions under which such benefits would be administered.

Regardless of the intent of the Advisory Council to simply enhance the rights of male beneficiaries, Congress inscribed the benefits for wives and widows in statutory law as entitlements, as matters of right for women themselves. To qualify, however, women would have to fit several criteria. A wife of an insured man would be "*entitled* to a wife's insurance benefit" as long as she was at least sixty-five, living with her husband at the time of application, and not divorced.[57] The exemption of divorced women meant that 789,000 women at the time would be flatly excluded from benefits. Although national government would administer the policy, individual states would affect women's chances of being considered eligible for the benefits because states would retain the power to determine whether and when

[54] House Committee on Ways and Means, *Hearings relative to the Social Security Act Amendments of 1939*, 76th Cong., 1st sess., February 1939, p. 1217.

[55] Senate Committee on Finance, *Hearings on Amendments to the Social Security Act of 1935*, 76th Cong., 1st sess., June 1939, pp. 1058–1059.

[56] For their part, the Townsendites criticized the policy as well. Senator Sheridan Downey from California, a Townsend plan proponent, decried the strategy of including wives and widows in OAI as "chicanery," claiming that it was intended to give Americans the mistaken notion that OASI would be a generous policy. Ibid., p. 471.

[57] Public Law 379, 76th Cong., 1st sess., August 10, 1939, *Social Security Act Amendments of 1939*, title II, sec. 202(b)(1). Emphasis mine.

common-law marriages would be recognized and the duration of manda-tory waiting periods after a divorce before a new marriage could be recognized.[58] Widows, similarly, would be "entitled" to benefits as long as they had not remarried, were at least sixty-five, and were living with their husbands at the time of death. In the case of either wives' or widows' benefits, the dual-entitlement provision stipulated that if a woman were eligible for a primary benefit based on her own earnings, her spousal benefit would be reduced by the amount of her "earned" benefits.[59]

In some regards, such requirements inscribed conventional gender roles and relations into law. The amendments sanctified the traditional family model. Single, divorced, and unmarried women remained beyond the bounds of inclusion, and married women were required to sacrifice any benefits they might have received from their own participation in the paid work force.[60] Yet, remarkably, the provisions included a vast number of women in national social citizenship, entitling them to benefits as a right. Women who fit the mold of "dependent wives" would thus be rewarded as beneficiaries of a national program whereby their security no longer hung solely on either the good fortune, hard work, generosity, and longevity of their husbands or the local eligibility criteria for old age assistance. Granted, women covered by the program would be maintained at a level relative to and lower than the class status of their husbands, but still, the new arrangements did promise a more certain future.

Both chambers of Congress proceeded unflinchingly to enact these dramatic alterations into law, transforming OAI into Old Age and Survivors' Insurance. To save the contributory program, Congress affirmed a violation of OAI's own principles by granting benefits to a class of people who had not contributed to the program through labor and payroll taxes and whose care had previously been considered the responsibility of mechanisms in private social and economic life. This action amounted to an acknowledgement that a system based solely on individual benefits to individual contributors would fail to provide security for the majority of family groupings and leave the ranks of public assistance beneficiaries continuing to swell. Policymakers readily chose the alternative of including married women in national social citizenship in their old age.

[58] Mimi Abramovitz, *Regulating the Lives of Women: Social Welfare Policy from Colonial Times to the Present* (Boston: South End Press, 1989), pp. 262–63; SSB, "Relationship as a Problem in Old-Age and Survivors Insurance," by Michael Fooner and Robert Francis, *Social Security Bulletin* 4 (August 1941): 24–32.

[59] Public Law 379, title II, sec. 202(b)(2), (d)(2), and (e)(2).

[60] Martha Derthick, *Policymaking for Social Security* (Washington, D.C.: Brookings, 1979), pp. 261–62; Barbara Bergmann, "The Housewife and Social Security Reform: A Feminist Perspective," in *Challenge to Social Security*, ed. Burkhauser and Holden, pp. 229–33; Abramovitz, *Regulating the Lives of Women*, pp. 252–66, Kessler-Harris, "Designing Women and Old Fools," pp. 87–106; Gwendolyn Mink, *The Wages of Motherhood: Inequality in the Welfare State, 1917–1942* (Ithaca: Cornell University Press, 1995), p. 136.

Limiting Old Age and Survivors' Insurance

Once Congress had calmly agreed to bring an entire class of non-wage earners under the auspices of a program originally based on individual earnings, legislators compounded the irony of their actions by limiting the ability of many low-wage workers to gain benefits under OASI. Policymakers proved more willing to extend benefits to women who had not worked for pay than to cover groups of wage earners who were disproportionately nonwhite, poor, and female.

During the hearings before the Ways and Means Committee, organizations such as the General Welfare Federation of America and the National Negro Congress expressed strong support for the Advisory Council's recommendation that domestic and agricultural employees be included in the contributory program.[61] Mary Anderson, director of the Women's Bureau, made a public appeal emphasizing the difficult working conditions of domestic workers and pleading for their inclusion.[62] As in 1935, the committee, in executive session, once again rejected the recommendation, on the grounds of administrative difficulties.[63] In fact, they broadened further the definition of agricultural workers exempt from the law, excluding employees engaged in the first processing of food as well.[64] Explained Committee Chairman Robert L. Doughton to Altmeyer, "Doctor, when the first farmer with manure on his shoes comes to me and asks to be covered, I will be willing to consider it."[65] The SSB and President Roosevelt actually had already received many letters from both agricultural and domestic workers requesting inclusion.[66] Furthermore, expansion of coverage to such workers would have helped to fortify OAI and diminish the future need for OAA, as well as appease groups that were wary of government-held reserves. But once again, the committee blocked changes that would threaten state and local autonomy in defining the conditions of such workers.[67]

[61] House Committee on Ways and Means, *Hearings relative to the Social Security Act Amendments of 1939*, pp. 128–30, 1542; 1937–38 Advisory Council, "Final Report," p. 6.

[62] Department of Labor, Women's Bureau, "Social Security for Household Employees," radio talk by Mary Anderson, Station WJSV, Washington, D.C., May 13, 1939, 9:45 A.M., microfilm 16:0745, LMDC.

[63] Comments by Ways and Means Committee Chair Doughton, *Congressional Record*, 76th Cong., 1st sess., 1939, vol. 84, pt. 6:6692.

[64] Witte, "Organized Labor and Social Security," p. 257; Public Law 379, title II, sec. 209(l).

[65] Altmeyer, *Formative Years*, p. 103.

[66] SSB, Records of the Executive Director, Subject Files, 1935–40, box 133, file 011.1, RG 47, NA.

[67] Quadagno, *Transformation of Old Age Security*, p. 146. During subsequent floor debates, the omission of domestic workers was never discussed except when Representative Frank Havenner (D-Calif.) lamented the exclusion of college students who worked in the kitchens of sororities or fraternities. The more commonplace situation of primarily nonwhite women went without comment. *Congressional Record*, 76th Cong., 1st sess., pp. 6933–34.

Congressional committees chose to comply with SSB recommendations when it came to restricting access to benefits in the contributory program by denying funds to workers who had been employed in covered occupations on an intermittent or low-wage basis, despite the fact that they had made contributions to the system. The provisions, which would help assure the solvency of the program, mandated that to be "fully insured," and thus to receive benefits at the time of death or retirement, a worker would be required to have worked at least one eligible quarter—a period of three months during which she earned at least fifty dollars in covered employment—for every two calendar quarters during her working lifetime. Once a person had worked for forty such quarters (a total of ten years), she would be considered "permanently fully insured." Alternatively, the families of male workers could be considered eligible for benefits if the worker was "currently insured," meaning that he had received at least fifty dollars during six of the last twelve quarters before death.[68] Such alterations would help finance the inclusion in OASI of beneficiaries, wives, and widows, who did not necessarily contribute to the system at all. Furthermore, benefits were to be figured according to a formula that took into account the "number of years in which $200 or more of wages were paid to such individual."[69] Thus, employees with very low wages or inconstant records of covered employment, particularly women and nonwhite and poor people, would be at risk of being ineligible for benefits or eligible for only the most minimal benefits.

Although SSB leaders played down the importance of these changes, the implications of dropping many workers who had paid OAI taxes from coverage did not go unnoticed.[70] Edwin E. Witte, who had returned to his faculty position at the University of Wisconsin after serving as director of the CES, highlighted the implications of the proposed changes for working women as he testified before the Senate Finance Committee:

> I call your attention particularly to the inequity of these provisions in relation to women employees. Women employees customarily are married after having been in employment for 5 or 10 years. They pay taxes, of course, under this plan, but if they are the young women of today, the women who are becoming married in these years, unless they can show the required years of earnings

---

[68] Compare the restrictions pertaining to benefits and eligibility in the 1935 law, Public Law 271, 74th Cong., 1st sess., August 14, 1935, *Social Security Act of 1935, H.R. 7260*, title II, secs. 202, 210(c), with the more restrictive terms of the 1939 amendments, Public Law 379, title II, sec. 209(e), (f), (g), and (h). See also SSB, "Workers with Annual Taxable Wages of Less Than $200 in 1937–1939," by Wayne F. Caskey, *Social Security Bulletin* 4 (October 1941): 17.

[69] Public Law 379, title II, sec. 209(e)(2).

[70] Ball, for instance, casts the 1939 amendments in a redistributive light in "1939 Amendments and What Followed," pp. 166–67.

in covered employment, they get neither a retirement allowance in their own right, nor any lump-sum payment.[71]

Committee member Senator Robert M. La Follette (R.-Wis.) upbraided Chairman Altmeyer for inequities stemming from the new restrictions, noting, "It was conceivable that a worker could fail to have earned the minimum required amount of wages by only one cent and be ineligible for benefits."[72] The restrictive amendments became law nonetheless, and without further attention. Criticizing such changes in later years, Witte charged, "Millions of people who were subject to the old-age and survivors' insurance taxes were cut off from all prospect of benefits."[73]

The combination of broadening and narrowing amendments to the OAI program in 1939 allowed proponents of the program to raise the level of benefits that would be paid to the first generation of beneficiaries by limiting eligibility for those benefits to the better-off, full-time, long-term workers and their families. Congress also made the program more attractive for beneficiaries by adopting a freeze on payroll taxes for employers and employees and by changing to a "pay-as-you-go" financing system to satisfy concerns about accumulating large government reserves.[74] Wives and survivors who had not paid into the system were thus included at the expense of nonwhite, poor, and female workers. For those left out, the fate of proposed changes in the public assistance program for the elderly would be of utmost importance.

Efforts to Improve OAA

Drawing on its experience with OAA in the first years of implementation, the SSB proposed to restrain excessive tendencies in some states and also to raise national standards to improve the program in states where benefits were most meager. On the first count, the board wanted to establish in law the approach toward assessing need for assistance which the BPA had been promoting under Hoey's leadership, stipulating that states deduct income and resources from assistance requirements for the elderly. The object was to deter states such as Oklahoma, California, and Colorado from distributing particularly generous grants through "guaranteed income" and "flat" plans. Fearing that supporters of more generous pensions might sense "ambiguity in the existing law," however, the SSB did not

---

[71] Senate Committee on Finance, *Hearings on Amendments to the Social Security Amendments of 1935*, p. 247.
[72] Altmeyer, *Formative Years*, pp. 107–8.
[73] Witte, "Organized Labor and Social Security," p. 259.
[74] Altmeyer, *Formative Years*, pp. 103, 106.

make a formal recommendation to Congress; instead, Altmeyer proposed the alteration in an executive session of the Ways and Means Committee.[75] The committee agreed, adding to Title I the clause requiring that each state plan for OAA must "provide that the State agency shall, in determining need, take into consideration any other income and resources of an individual claiming old-age assistance."[76] Where the 1935 statute had read that benefits could be offered to "each individual who at the time of such expenditure is sixty-five years of age or older and is not an inmate of a public institution," the word "needy" was added as a necessary qualifier before "individual."[77] The new language remained in the bill through final passage, inscribing the public assistance program henceforth with means testing, a characteristic greatly at odds with the rights-based orientation of OAI.

The Ways and Means Committee proved unamenable to the SSB's proposals meant to liberalize OAA in states where benefits and coverage were particularly low. As in 1935, the committee refused to approve the SSB's recommendation for merit-system hiring in state agencies administering the program.[78] Neither was the committee interested in the provision the SSB regarded as most important: a change from the matching-grant formula for public assistance to a "variable-grant" arrangement in which the federal contribution would vary in accordance with the ability of each state to pay benefits. The SSB had conducted extensive research on the impact of such arrangements and was convinced that the matching-grant system tended to exacerbate inequalities between states and that variable-grant arrangements, by contrast, would help to elevate living standards in the poorest areas.[79] The Ways and Means Committee balked at the proposal, showing itself more willing to approve restraints on liberal and wealthy states known for being generous than to support efforts to lift standards in states that were poorer or more conservative.[80]

During the floor debates in the House, however, numerous representatives, responding to popular pressures, devoted impassioned rhetoric to the cause of national minimum benefit levels. Representative William Colmer (D-Miss.) proposed an amendment calling for guaranteed minimum payments to the elderly arranged through variable federal grants based on state

[75] Ibid., p. 105.

[76] Public Law 379, title I, sec. 101(7).

[77] Compare Public Law 271, title I, sec. 3(a)(1), with the same section in Public Law 379.

[78] Letter, Wilbur J. Cohen to A. W. Wilcox, August 29, 1938, SSB, Chairman's Files, Subject Files, 1935–40, box 93, file 622, RG 47, NA.

[79] See Records of the Executive Director, Subject Files, 1935–40, box 274, file 622, and Chairman's Files, Subject Files, 1935–40, box 93, file 622.31, both in SSB, RG 47, NA.

[80] Altmeyer, *Formative Years*, p. 105.

per capita income.[81] Another proposed amendment, advanced by Representative Byron Harrison (D-Miss.), would have required the federal government to contribute to OAA grants of up to $40 by paying four-fifths of the first $20 and half of the second $20 contributed by states.[82] In debating such amendments, members seized the opportunity to lambast the OAA program for rewarding better-off states and penalizing poorer states, as a few samples from the record illustrate:

> So the States that have not the financial resources to meet the contribution made by the Government are actually in the position of contributing to the States that have sufficient resources to meet this old-age assistance obligation.
>
> —Rep. Will Taylor (R-Tenn.)[83]

> The law we have today requiring the State to match dollar for dollar is nothing in the world but a farce, because the agricultural States and the poorer States of this Union are unable financially to put up on a dollar–for–dollar basis.
>
> —Rep. A. L. Ford (D-Miss.)[84]

Some Representatives addressed the issue of citizenship, arguing that all members of the United States who are in need should be treated alike, regardless of their state of residence:

> We should not put our stamp of approval on a bill . . . and make it contingent on what some State is willing to do. . . . In my judgement the Federal payment should be equal to all persons in the United States.
>
> —Rep. Quentin Burdick (D-N.D.)[85]

Most ardent supporters of variable or guaranteed grants, as suggested by these quotations, hailed from the ten poorest states in the union, primarily from the South. As in 1935, the southern delegation demanded generous, redistributive funds from the federal government at the same time that it insisted on freedom from intervention in state and local affairs.[86]

---

[81] *Congressional Record*, 76th Cong., 1st sess., p. 6684.

[82] Memorandum, Anne E. Geddes to Wilbur Cohen, June 7, 1939, "Estimates on the Harrison Proposal," Chairman's Files, Subject Files, 1935–40, box 93, file 622.31, SSB, RG 47, NA.

[83] *Congressional Record*, 76th Cong., 1st sess., p. 6682.

[84] Ibid., p. 6902.

[85] Ibid., p. 6849.

[86] On tensions within the southern delegations, see Richard Bensel, *Sectionalism and American Political Development, 1880–1980* (Madison: University of Wisconsin Press, 1984), p. 105; and Elizabeth Sanders, "Business, Bureaucracy, and the Bourgeoisie: The New Deal Legacy," in *The Political Economy of Public Policy*, ed. Alan Stone and Edward J. Harpman (Beverly Hills: Sage, 1982): 115–140.

In response to the surge of support for variable grants, the Ways and Means Committee reconvened in an informal caucus to reconsider their adoption. In a reversal of the previous stance, Chairman Doughton asked Altmeyer to inform the president that the committee intended to support such a proposal unless he voiced any objections.[87] True to his fiscal conservatism, however, Roosevelt responded immediately, insisting "this ought not to be done unless they provide the additional revenue." [88] As pressures for more generous payments from the national government continued, Roosevelt again signaled disapproval, warning, "There is great danger for if they do this now they will finally have the [national] Govt. [sic] paying it all." [89] Subsequently, Democratic Party leaders exerted discipline on their ranks, and all amendments for variable grants were defeated. The full House coalesced to pass the recommendations of the Ways and Means Committee in an overwhelming vote of 364 to 2.[90]

The matter of variable grants surfaced yet again, however, in the Senate Finance Committee. Senator Tom Connally (D-Tex.) proposed an amendment for a grant formula whereby the national government would contribute two-thirds of the first $15 for each beneficiary and half of additional funds provided by the states up to a $40 benefit per person. The Finance Committee defeated the amendment, but Connally introduced it again on the Senate floor. There, proponents pointed out that whereas current law permitted federal matching funds of $15 per recipient per month, allowing for $30 in benefits, low contributions from many states meant that the OAA benefit averaged only $19.55 and was often considerably lower. Connally insisted that OAA benefits should be a function of national citizenship: "We are saying to the State, 'We will only pay to your needy what you pay them.' Do not we owe any duty to the needy man himself? . . . If the Federal government owes the citizen an obligation, it owes it to him directly." [91] The Senate adopted the Connally amendment and passed the bill by a 57–8 margin.[92]

A conference committee then set to work to resolve the differences between the bills; it remained deadlocked for weeks over the Connally

---

[87] Memorandum, Altmeyer to the president, June 2, 1939, "Proposed Liberalization by Ways and Means Committee of Old Age Assistance," OF 1710, box 2, FDR.

[88] Memorandum, F.D.R. to General Watson, June 2, 1939, ibid.

[89] Memorandum, F.D.R. to Representative Doughton, June 8, 1939, OF 1710, box 2, FDR. James MacGregor Burns, in a conversation with the author in spring 1993, explained that Roosevelt's reaction fit his general inclinations. Roosevelt was quite willing to entertain new administrative roles for national government, as evidenced by his views on the economic security plan in June 1934, or regulatory roles as seen in his position on labor standards, but unwilling to commit general national government revenues for long-term spending plans.

[90] Altmeyer, *Formative Years*, p. 106.

[91] *Congressional Record*, 76th Cong., 1st Sess., p. 8852.

[92] Altmeyer, *Formative Years*, p. 111.

amendment. Altmeyer, trying to resolve the situation, presented the conferees with an alternative amendment that would have continued the 50–50 matching-grant formula but would also have mandated that the national government donate a minimum monthly grant of $7.50 per recipient even if the state put up less than that amount.[93] When President Roosevelt learned of Altmeyer's suggestion, however, he retorted, "Not one nickel more, not one solitary nickel. Once you get off the 50–50 matching basis, the sky's the limit, and before you know it, we'll be paying the whole bill. . . . What you are talking about are lopsided grants and I'm opposed to them."[94] The president's opposition reflected his steadfast distaste for permanent involvement by the national government in public assistance. Nonetheless, Altmeyer was disappointed, as well as embarrassed to have misinterpreted, several months earlier, what he thought was tacit approval from Roosevelt for at least mildly redistributive grants. Without the president's support, Senate conferees were forced to drop the Connally amendment, leaving OAA to vary in benefits from state to state and subject to severe underfunding in some states. The only victory for the SSB in terms of promoting more standardized OAA procedures nationwide was that the Finance Committee had included in their bill mild language mandating the adoption of merit systems by state agencies implementing public assistance, and the conference committee retained the measure. The bill returned to both houses of Congress for final passage and was signed into law by President Roosevelt on August 10, 1939.[95]

In sum, the 1939 Amendments to the Social Security Act changed the terms of coverage in the two programs for the elderly and sharpened the differentiation between their administrative styles. The changes represented a victory for administrators who were determined to strengthen the contributory program and to deflate pressures for expansive old age pensions financed solely by general government revenues. The SSB and congressional allies of popular movements had failed in their mutual goal, however, of securing at least minimum national standards for OAA for the elderly people in the poorest states. Roosevelt's own fiscal conservatism had thwarted the persistent efforts of both groups to make inclusion in the public assistance program more commensurate with national social citizenship. The amendments reconfigured the divisions drawn by the 1935 law, bringing many married white women under the contributory program while increasing the numbers of nonwhite men and women and poor, single, or divorced women who would be left to a public assistance pro-

[93] Ibid., pp. 104–5, 111–12.
[94] Ibid., p. 112.
[95] Ibid., pp. 112–13.

gram still variegated by federalism and newly endowed with mandatory means testing.

The Early 1940s: Divergence in the Status of the Elderly

Members of the SSB had hoped that the 1939 amendments would, in time, cause the ranks of OAA to decline and OASI to become established as the predominant social program for elderly Americans. Throughout the 1940s, however, popular movements continued to press the states for "flat" pension plans, OAA rolls remained high, and benefits became more generous in states able to match the federal government up to the new forty-dollar maximum. Regardless of the addition of wives and widows to the OASI roster, still in 1950 more Americans were receiving OAA checks than OASI benefits (2.8 million compared with 2.1 million).[96] In dollar amounts, average OAI and OAA payments were comparable in the early 1940s: in December 1942, average OAA grants were $23.43, 41¢ higher than average primary insurance benefits through OASI.[97] The generous average benefit levels under OAA compared with OASI, however, obscured more fundamental differences emerging in the character of the two programs as their distinct designs and administrative arrangements affected their development in the course of implementation.

Old Age and Survivors Insurance

When OASI benefits commenced in 1940, the chief hallmark of the program, as noted by the SSB, was its national uniformity: "Benefits in every part of the country are awarded under one law, one policy, one set of rules and regulations."[98] Recipients would enjoy the advantages of clear, impartial, and routinized procedures administered by a single tier of government. Moreover, OASI was to be considered a "right," so beneficiaries avoided the invasive means testing used to determine eligibility for public assistance.

This right of social citizenship had become delineated, however, in ways that stratified society by gender, race, earning status, and marital status. Men were the majority of primary beneficiaries, and women continued to be represented disproportionately on the OAA rolls. An in-depth study of

[96] Derthick, *Policymaking for Social Security*, p. 273.
[97] SSB, "Social Insurance and Public Assistance Payments," p. 16.
[98] SSB, "The Comparability of Public Assistance Payments and Social Insurance Benefits," by Jacob Fisher, *Social Security Bulletin* 7 (December 1944): 11.

two cities in 1941 and 1942 found that men constituted 84 percent of all primary beneficiaries of OASI in Philadelphia and 86 percent in St. Louis. Under OAA, by contrast, only 45 percent of the Philadelphia beneficiaries and 43 percent of those in St. Louis were men. Less than 5 percent of the primary beneficiaries of OASI were black, but African Americans were approximately one-quarter of OAA beneficiaries.[99] Families benefiting from OASI and OAA differed sharply in their access to income from other sources. In Philadelphia, only 2 percent of families receiving OASI benefits lacked other income, compared with 76 percent of families receiving OAA benefits; in St. Louis, 3 percent on OASI had no other income, compared with 41 percent on OAA.[100]

Studies in the 1940s quickly revealed the implications of the amendments in terms of gender and race in the work force. A report issued by the SSB in 1941 found that nearly one-quarter of the covered work force had such low total earnings in 1937 and 1939 that they might fail to qualify for coverage. The low-wage groups were disproportionately black and female: 42 percent of African Americans but only 22 percent of whites earned less than $200 annually, and 30 percent of women in contrast to 20 percent of men.[101] Another report highlighted the uneven likelihood of being considered "fully insured" on OASI among different groups of workers, by comparing the number of quarters of the year employees had worked. In 1940, 66 percent of covered white men had taxable wages in four quarters, compared with 61 percent of white women, 55 percent of black men, and 47 percent of black women.[102] Both reports noted that though some of the workers whose OASI status was threatened worked only intermittently, many others worked year-round but were employed for part of the year in noncovered occupations, such as domestic work and agriculture.

Wives of men covered by the contributory program had to have married their husbands according to conventional norms; otherwise, they quickly became subject to the vagaries of the states. Although OASI was run by national rules in other respects, individual states determined, with great variance, the legal requirements for waiting periods before remarriage after a divorce, and when a common-law marriage could be recognized as legitimate. For example, in Massachusetts and Michigan, marriages that occurred earlier than two years after a divorce could be declared invalid,

[99] Ibid., pp. 9–14.
[100] Ibid., pp. 13–14.
[101] SSB, "Workers with Annual Taxable Wages," pp. 19–20.
[102] SSB, "Employment and Wages, 1940," p. 8. For similar data with a focus on disparity in OASI coverage by race, see SSB, "Characteristics and Taxable Wages of Negro Workers, 13 Selected Southern States, 1938," by Charles L. Franklin, *Social Security Bulletin* 4 (March 1941): 21–31.

meaning that a woman widowed by her second husband might be considered ineligible for OASI benefits if she had, in the eyes of the law, remarried too quickly.[103]

Thus, through OASI, mostly white male workers and their wives or widows acquired status as national citizens. Regardless of where they lived in the United States, despite how many times they moved, whether or not they had relatives, beneficiaries received measures of security in a realm where standardized procedures were the norm and benefits were considered a right. Those relatively few women and nonwhites whose status in the work force did assure them of OASI coverage were treated, moreover, with the gender-blind and race-blind qualities of nondiscretionary policy implementation. Citizenship defined by the states, by contrast, assumed a very different character.

Old Age Assistance

For people ineligible for OASI, access to OAA after 1939 became more difficult to attain, and inclusion in the program become more stigmatized. Without a variable-grant formula, the program continued to develop in a manner that reflected the vicissitudes of federalism. As noted in the *Social Security Bulletin*, "Assistance payments . . . are based on individual need, and vary widely. Among families within a given jurisdiction they will vary to the extent that requirements and resources vary. Among jurisdictions, payments are influenced by variations in the recognition and measurement of requirements and resources, in the content and cost of living, in the availability of funds, and in willingness to appropriate money for public assistance." [104] Thus, for OAA recipients, the experience of social citizenship was defined according to the subnational boundaries of American federalism.

The fact that average benefits for OAA, nationwide, were comparable in the early 1940s to average OASI primary benefits obscured the tremendous variation in OAA benefits from state to state. In 1940, OAA payments ranged from a low of $7.87 on average per month in Arkansas to a high of $37.87 in California.[105] As Map 1 shows, states with the highest OAA expenditures lay west of the Mississippi River, where the Townsend organization continued to be strong. Southern states still had low benefits, but such diverse states as Vermont, Michigan, and some northern plains states had only slightly higher ones. The variation in average grants in the Four

---

[103] SSB, "Relationship as a Problem," p. 27.
[104] SSB, "Comparability," p. 11.
[105] SSB, "Social Insurance and Public Assistance Payments," pp. 20–21.

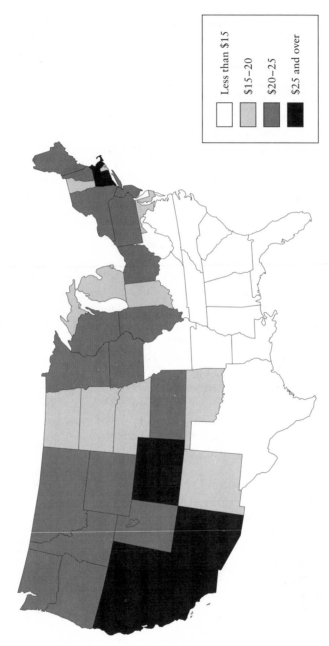

Map 1. Average OAA benefits by state, 1940. From "Classification of Average Old-Age Assistance Payments by States, December 1940," by Wilbur J. Cohen, file 641, in Central File, Master File, 1935–37, box 236, RG 47, NA.

Less than $15

$15–20

$20–25

$25 and over

Table 3. State averages for OAA and OASI, 1940

Average	Number of states	
	OAA	OASI
Total	51	51
$ 5.00– 9.99	7	—
$10.00–14.99	9	0
$15.00–19.99	11	8
$20.00–24.99	16	43
$25.00–29.99	6	0
$30.00–34.99	1	0
$35.00–39.99	1	0

Source: SSB, "Social Insurance and Public Assistance Payments," by Elva Marquard, Social Security Bulletin 6 (December 1943): 21.

Corners region linking New Mexico, Colorado, Arizona, and Utah exemplify how dramatically social policy could vary with political geography.[106]

The comparability of average OASI and OAA payments also masked the greater disparity in OAA benefits than in OAI benefits. Because OASI primary benefits were arranged on a scale proportional to former wages, they varied not only from one individual to the next but also in relation to the per capita income of each state and region, as wages were much lower in poorer areas. Still, OASI benefits tended to be much more uniform than OAA benefits, as seen in Table 3. Average primary OASI benefits by state ranged only from $18.58 to $24.57 in 1940; average OAA benefits, by contrast, were scattered widely between a low of $7.87 and a high $37.87. Western states were more likely to have OAA benefits that were much more generous than OASI benefits. In California, OAA payments averaged 162 percent above average OAI benefits; Colorado had the next highest ratio of 138 percent. More states, however, had lower OAA benefits. Kentucky, at the extreme end, offered public assistance benefits to the elderly that were $11.56 below average OAI payments in the state.

OAA was also imbued with variable state-to-state eligibility criteria unified only by the general invasiveness to which they subjected applicants. As of 1948, nineteen states made legal U.S. citizenship a requirement. Some states imposed moral requirements, disqualifying tramps or beggars or those who had been convicted of a crime.

The new requirement that recipients be determined to be "needy" was

---

[106] "Classification of Average Old-Age Assistance Payments by States, December 1940," by Wilbur J. Cohen; SSB, Central File, Master File, 1935–1947, box 236, file 641, RG 47, NA; Holtzman, Townsend Movement, pp. 191–98.

imposed with a particularly high degree of both variation and scrutiny of personal lives. In a 1942 experiment, 4 public assistance agencies in each of the 48 states were presented with a hypothetical but typical case of an application for OAA and were asked to determine whether, according to their own rules and regulations, the applicant would be determined to be "needy" and thus eligible. Of the 125 agencies in 44 states which responded to the query, 57 determined that the applicant would be ineligible for aid, and the remaining 68 concluded that the applicant was "needy" and thus eligible. Eastern states were more likely to declare the applicant ineligible; western states, "needy"; states in other regions were split. Determinations of need varied greatly within states, as well, given that only 5 states stipulated a particular dollar amount that determined need; most used vague definitions such as "insufficient income or other resources to provide reasonable subsistence compatible with decency and health." [107] States also employed a wide variety of criteria in measuring income and other resources. Many, particularly in the East, counted assistance from relatives as a resource, and some states even considered the existence of relatives, who *might* be able to provide support, as sufficient grounds for disqualification.[108]

In the absence of definitive criteria, personnel had to use their discretion. In the words of the office manager at the public assistance office in Pike County, Ohio: "There are no strict rules; we just use our own judgement." [109] This use of personal discernment was accompanied by the absence of clear professional norms for agency staff.

Professional administrative standards remained the exception rather than the rule through the 1940s. Although the 1939 amendments had required states to establish their own merit systems, the SSB had no authority over the hiring and firing of personnel.[110] States continued to enjoy autonomy in developing their own practices of recruiting and appointing administrative staff through competitive examinations, prohibition of discrimination, and some limits on political activity, in addition to creating a systematic classification of jobs. A wide array of merit systems emerged, varying not only between states but among localities as well. Discretion by local officials and an absence of professional norms combined in many areas to perpetuate racial bias. Despite the SSB's attempts to eliminate prac-

---

[107] Eveline M. Burns, *The American Social Security System* (Boston: Houghton Mifflin, 1949), quotation, p. 300; see also pp. 298–304; and David C. Adie, "Our Social Geography," *Survey* 76 (September 1940): 259–61.

[108] Burns, *American Social Security System*, p. 302.

[109] Report, A. G. Thomas to Francis A. Staten, "County Reports of Administration of Public Assistance Programs," February 2, 1939, p. 6, SSB, Records of the Executive Director, Subject Files, 1935–40, box 274, file 620.6, RG 47, NA.

[110] SSB, "Merit System Objectives and Realities," by Albert H. Aronson, *Social Security Bulletin* 13 (April 1950): 4.

tices that could foster discrimination toward minority groups, average OAA benefits were reported to be lower for nonwhite recipients than for white ones in eleven of seventeen states in 1944.[111]

For those in the ranks of OAA, especially elderly women and nonwhite men, the quality of their social citizenship was unified only by the fact that they were increasingly subject to copious investigation and scrutiny by state officials. Subject to provincial rule coupled with means testing and other invasive bureaucratic procedures, they were denizens of a sovereignty far from the national liberal realm governing rights-bearing persons.

Fragmenting Gender

Some scholars have criticized the manner in which women were incorporated into OASI, charging that the policy reinforces traditional gender norms by rewarding women more for being unpaid housewives than for participation in the paid work force and that it provides less well in general for women than for men in old age.[112] There is validity to such charges, but focusing on them obscures the significance of the inclusion of a majority of women in 1939 in a nationally administered program previously reserved for mostly male wage earners. In an era when a majority of families were composed of male breadwinners and female homemakers, the policy change meant that married women gained significant rights of nationally guaranteed social citizenship and thus fuller incorporation in the polity. At the same time, a myopic focus on how OASI institutionalizes and rewards the male breadwinner family model simultaneously conceals the effects of the 1939 amendments and the implementation of OAA for the disproportionate share of elderly women still excluded from the contributory program. The differential coverage and forms of implementation fragmented gender, facilitating a divergence in the fates of white middle- and working-class married women and those who were black, poor, single, or divorced.

The establishment of divisive criteria for eligibility in social programs for the elderly was hardly unique to the United States.[113] Nearly all countries

[111] SSB, "Equality of Rights to Social Security," *Social Security Bulletin* 10 (November 1947): 21.

[112] See, e.g., Burkhauser and Holden, "Introduction"; Jane Sherburne, "Women and Social Security: Seizing the Moment for Change," *The Georgetown Law Journal* 70 (August 1982): 1563–1604; Mary E. Becker, "Obscuring the Struggle: Sex Discrimination, Social Security, and Stone, Seidman, Sunstein, & Tushnet's *Constitutional Law*," *Columbia Law Review* 89 (March 1989): 264–89; and Barbara A. Mikulski and Ellyn L. Brown, "Case Studies in the Treatment of Women under Social Security Law: The Need for Reform," *Harvard Women's Law Journal* 6 (Spring 1983): 29–49.

[113] For comparative studies of social policies for the elderly which are attentive to gender, see essays in *The Sociology of Social Security*, ed. Michael Adler et al., esp. Stephan Leifbried

with contributory programs in place by 1933 adhered to capitalist norms by limiting benefits to certain categories of workers.[114] Traditional gender relations, meaning marriages with male breadwinners and female home-makers, were rewarded in the policies of fourteen European nations, often by redistributing from single individuals to single-earner couples. Old age assistance programs, already established in thirteen countries, were generally means tested. France and Great Britain, like the United States, already had two-tiered approaches to social provision for the elderly in the sense that each had established both a contributory and a public assistance program.[115]

What made the U.S. approach unique was the assignment of the two types of programs to the authority of two distinct realms of government.[116] The structure of federalism, combined with the cleavages in the Social Security Act and the 1939 amendments, facilitated the development of two distinct forms of citizenship, each under the auspices of a different sovereignty. Hence, as social citizens, persons would experience qualitatively different relationships vis-à-vis the state, in turn reinforcing distinctions in status between groups in society. Such political and administrative separations fostered tensions that festered over the next couple of decades, alienating citizens from one another.

---

and Ilona Ostner, "The Particularism of West German Welfare Capitalism: The Case of Women's Social Security," pp. 164–82, and Sheila Shaver, "Gender, Class, and the Welfare State: The Case of Income Security in Australia," pp. 145–63; and Ann Shola Orloff, *The Politics of Pensions: A Comparative Analysis of Britain, Canada, and the United States, 1880–1940* (Madison: University of Wisconsin Press, 1993). Certainly, countries varied in the extent to which they tried to make programs for the elderly adhere to "strict market principles" as opposed to emphasizing social protection; see John Myles, *Old Age in the Welfare State: The Political Economy of Public Pensions* (Lawrence: University of Kansas Press, 1989); and Gaston Rimlinger, *Welfare Policy and Industrialization in Europe, America, and Russia* (New York: Wiley, 1971), chap. 9.

[114] SSB, *Social Security in America: The Factual Background as Summarized from Staff Reports to the Committee on Economic Security* (Washington, D.C.: GPO, 1937), p. 183.

[115] Ibid., p. 182. Canada, like the United States, used federal/provincial administration for old age assistance but contrasts with the United States in critical dimensions of social policy for the elderly. First, in the 1930s, Canada lacked a comparable contributory program, so it could not be characterized as having a two-tiered approach. Second, though the provinces and especially Quebec had some control over old age assistance, in fact the programs were handled primarily at the national level. On differences in U.S. and Canadian federalism, see Robert T. Kudrle and Theodore R. Marmor, "The Development of Welfare States in North America," in *The Development of Welfare States in Europe and America*, ed. Peter Flora and Arnold Heidenheimer (New Brunswick, N.J.: Transaction Books, 1981), pp. 81–121.

[116] Granted, the gaining of social rights on the basis of paid work instead of caring, as under the contributory programs with spousal benefits, connotes different and gender-specific grounds from which citizenship is derived, as discussed in Ruth Lister, "Women, Economic Dependency, and Citizenship," *Journal of Social Policy* 19 (October 1990): 460; but more than basing social citizenship on different rationales for different groups, American policies actually created different forms of citizenship by placing administrative authority under different sovereignties.

CHAPTER FIVE

The Formation of Unemployment Insurance and Aid to Dependent Children

The present bill before the House of Representatives is one that provides for and attempts to take care of every victim of social and economic security from the time of birth until death. This humane legislation begins with *the queen and angel of the home, the mother.* Since God could not be everywhere, he created mothers to take His place. . . .

Mr. Chairman, the mother may be the queen of the home, but *the father is the breadwinner, the provider,* who keeps the home intact. The home is the foundation of all society. Upon it the superstructure of all government must rise. Destroy the home and you destroy the most sacred human institution devised by mankind.

—Representative William I. Sirovich (D-N.Y.),
Congressional Record, April 16, 1935

The Social Security Act of 1935 included two major programs aimed to assist non-elderly Americans who were deprived of economic security. Based on their assumption that people typically lived in two-parent families supported by male breadwinners, policymakers considered how public policies could assist families in particular circumstances when those arrangements failed to function properly. They planned both Unemployment Insurance to compensate full-time workers for lost wages when they became unemployed and Aid to Dependent Children to provide for mothers and their children when they became deprived of the support of a breadwinner.[1]

President Roosevelt and officials in the Committee on Economic Security considered their comprehensive proposal for social provision an apt opportunity to further and enhance the development of mothers' pensions. The earlier programs, primarily for widows and children, still enjoyed a fair measure of respect.[2] Administration officials believed that ADC, combined

---

[1] ADC was the precursor to Aid to Families with Dependent Children.

[2] Winifred Bell, *Aid to Dependent Children* (New York: Cambridge University Press, 1965), pp. 18–19; Ann Shola Orloff, "Gender in Early U.S. Social Policy," *Journal of Policy History* 3 (1991): 249–81.

with the public assistance program for the elderly, would help carry through the legislative process the program that they considered the most important and the most politically contentious in the entire legislative package: unemployment insurance.[3]

Until the Great Depression, unemployment was widely understood in the United States as a symptom of personal failure rather than the manifestation of a broad economic problem that should be addressed by public policy. The skyrocketing unemployment rates of the 1930s caused popular sentiments to begin to shift, but state governments had only barely begun to consider unemployment compensation programs seriously in response to pressure from active groups of reform-minded intellectuals.[4] Remarkably, the CES made unemployment insurance the cornerstone of the Social Security Act,[5] devoting far more time and resources to its development than to other parts of the bill.[6]

The policy choices in the design of UI and ADC would bear significant implications for the experience of social citizenship. The basic decisions about policy type—social insurance for the unemployed and public assistance for expanded mothers' pensions—were made early and remained intact throughout the legislative process. Still to be determined, however, was the manner in which the programs would fit into the changing shape of U.S. federalism.

The Formation of Policies for the Non-elderly in the CES

The tenor of discussions in the CES pertaining to plans for UI could not have been more different that those for ADC. The formation of UI involved CES leaders, well-known social reformers, and diverse camps within the administration and Advisory Council in a series of stormy battles over administrative design, particularly the appropriate roles of national and state governments. The creation of ADC, by contrast, was dominated exclusively by a pair of women reformers in the Children's Bureau. Unlike the

---

[3] Edwin E. Witte, *The Development of the Social Security Act* (Madison: University of Wisconsin Press, 1962), p. 111.

[4] On the factors that led to successful enactment of unemployment compensation at the state level—namely, alliances between reformers, organized labor, and a cohesive party organization—see Edwin Amenta et al., "The Political Origins of Unemployment Insurance in Five American States," *Studies in American Political Development* 2 (1987): 137–82.

[5] Frances Fox Piven and Richard A. Cloward, *Regulating the Poor* (New York: Random House, Vintage Books, 1971), pp. 61–66; George Martin, *Madam Secretary* (Boston: Houghton Mifflin, 1976), p. 341; Bruce Allen Murphy, *The Brandeis/Frankfurter Connection* (New York: Doubleday, 1983), pp. 165–78.

[6] Edward D. Berkowitz, *America's Welfare State* (Baltimore: Johns Hopkins University Press, 1991), pp. 28–29.

raging controversy over UI, the formation of ADC was characterized by an easy consensus as officials agreed to retain a high degree of state responsibility and local discretion for the program, even as they hoped to foster nationwide development.

Unemployment Insurance

When Great Britain became the first major European country to enact unemployment compensation in 1911, U.S. reformers, such as those in the American Association for Labor Legislation, grew interested in similar measures. The AFL, however, announced its opposition to unemployment policies, citing its traditional allegiance to an ethic of voluntarism to preserve its autonomy from the state. By the 1930s, some state-level federations of organized labor did support the development of unemployment compensation, and they established alliances with reformers and political parties to push for the enactment of legislation. Still, the decentralized system of federalism functioned as a deterrent to the development of UI, as opponents pointed out that states enacting such policies and employer taxes would place businessmen within their boundaries at a disadvantage in competing against those from states without such policies. By 1934, only Wisconsin had enacted a state-level unemployment compensation law.[7]

Despite the lack of precedents for unemployment compensation at the state level, though, the terms of disagreement over the design of such programs had become well established before President Roosevelt ever announced his intention to advance comprehensive legislation for economic security. Economists in Wisconsin, many important businessmen, and John Andrews, founder of the AALL, all championed the development of "plant reserves" for individual businesses at the state level. That approach, adopted in Wisconsin in 1932, required each business to make contributions into its own separate reserve account, which would in turn be used to provide benefits for persons unemployed by that particular business. To discourage businesses from laying off workers, firms with high unemployment would be taxed at a higher rate. Another group advocated a

---

[7] Edward J. Harpham, "Federalism, Keynesianism, and the Transformation of the Unemployment Insurance System in the United States," in *Nationalizing Social Security in Europe and America*, ed. Douglas E. Ashford and E. W. Kelley (Greenwich, Conn.: JAI, 1986), pp. 156–57; Amenta et al., "Political Origins of Unemployment Insurance"; Theda Skocpol, *Protecting Soldiers and Mothers: The Political Origins of Social Policy in the United States* (Cambridge: Harvard University Press, 1992), pp. 153–310; Theda Skocpol and Gretchen Ritter, "Gender and the Origins of Modern Social Policies in Britain and the U.S.," *Studies in American Political Development* 5 (spring 1991): 36–93. Eight states followed Wisconsin's lead in 1935; SSB, *Social Security in America: The Factual Background of the Social Security Act as Summarized from Staff Reports to the Committee on Economic Security* (Washington, D.C.: GPO, 1937), p. 6.

"pooled-funds" plan under consideration in Ohio, in which businesses would pool their contributions in one large fund to be used for unemployed persons from any firm. Various social workers, reformers, and intellectuals—notably Abraham Epstein, founder of the American Association for Social Security, and Isaac Rubinow—considered that approach to be superior because of its ability to spread risks widely and to provide uniform benefits.[8]

Soon after Roosevelt was inaugurated, Andrews, Paul Raushenbush, and his wife, Elizabeth Brandeis, began to work with Senator Robert Wagner to draft a legislative proposal that would encourage other states to adopt unemployment insurance plans of their own and at the same time preserve Wisconsin's law. They devised the "tax-offset" scheme, an arrangement that would impose a uniform national payroll tax on all employers as a means of reducing interstate competition but would then return the contributions from a particular state to that state's government if it had established an unemployment insurance law of its own. States would retain the freedom to adopt either individual plant reserves or pooled funds. In January 1934, Elizabeth Brandeis, with the assistance of her father, Louis Brandeis, called a meeting of administration officials at her home in Washington to promote the plan. After an enthusiastic response, a bill was drafted and introduced in Congress as the "Wagner-Lewis Bill." Because the bill did not dictate the type of law to be adopted, it forged a temporary peace among proponents of various plans, and all spoke out in favor of it, though some more enthusiastically than others, in congressional hearings in March 1934.[9]

By May, however, Roosevelt had decided to promote a comprehensive economic security plan instead, so he dropped his support for Wagner-Lewis. Immediately the divisions reappeared, as advocates for different types of plans hoped to influence the legislation.

Bryce Stewart, staff leader for the Unemployment Compensation Committee of the CES Technical Board, issued a report in September that urged the adoption of a fully national plan for unemployment insurance. The document insisted that such a plan would be preferable to any schemes involving individual state administration because it would be more efficient and impartial.[10] The Technical Board took the same position but urged that

[8] Daniel Nelson, *Unemployment Insurance: The American Experience, 1915–1935* (Madison: University of Wisconsin Press, 1969), pp. 192–95.

[9] Ibid., pp. 197–204; House Ways and Means Committee, *Hearings on the Wagner-Lewis Bill before the Ways and Means Committee, House of Representatives*, 73d Cong., 2d sess., March 21–March 30, 1934.

[10] Witte, *Development of the Social Security Act*, pp. 112–13; Letter, Thomas Eliot to Edwin Witte, November 5, 1934, CES, Correspondence regarding Proposals for the Economic Security Program, 1934–35, box 56, RG 47, NA.

constitutional concerns must first be addressed.[11] Weeks of controversy ensued, during which, in Witte's words, staff and board members "wrestled with this subject."

In time, proponents of a national system conceded slightly by offering a third alternative called the "subsidy plan." The proposal would, like the Wagner-Lewis scheme, rely on federal-state cooperation, but by contrast, states would have to comply with standards set by the national government in administering the program. All unemployment reserve funds, furthermore, would be held by federal reserve banks or the U.S. Treasury, an arrangement that Roosevelt advocated as a means of stabilizing the economy as a whole.[12]

Barbara Nachtrieb Armstrong, who had initially been hired as a consultant on both old age insurance and unemployment insurance, quickly became known as an advocate for national administration and national standards in the design of an unemployment compensation plan. She argued that because unemployment varied between states as much as 60 percent, national pooling of funds made much more sense than retaining states as units for reserves, because it would spread costs.[13] Soon after Armstrong's preference became clear, however, the CES director, Edwin Witte, informed her that her duties would be limited to the study of old age security.[14] When she continued to press for adoption of the subsidy plan at the very least, Ben Cohen took her out to lunch and relayed to her a message from his mentor, Felix Frankfurter, that she was to drop the matter. He explained that Frankfurter wanted her to understand that "the Brandeis family is involved in this unemployment insurance organizational matter and that his relations with the Brandeis family are such that nothing that you could say about the relative desirability of any alternative method would induce him to take issue with the Brandeis family."[15] In fact, key leaders of the CES also seemed sympathetic to the plan that rested on individual state authority.

At the helm of the CES, Frances Perkins favored the tax-offset plan. Besides her general inclinations toward promoting the states as primary actors in government, Perkins had doubts about whether a national law would be held constitutional and wanted to steer a cautious course in order to make at least some progress. She reasoned, "If the federal aspects

[11] "Preliminary Report of the Technical Board to the Committee on Economic Security," CES, General Records of the Executive Director and Staff, 1934–35, box 1, RG 47, NA.

[12] Frances Perkins, *The Roosevelt I Knew* (New York: Harper and Row, 1946), pp. 286–87.

[13] Witte, *Development of the Social Security Act*, pp. 116–17; Barbara Nachtrieb Armstrong, "Advantages of a Federal Subsidy Plan," November 7, 1934, CES, Staff Correspondence, 1934–35, box 17, RG 47, NA.

[14] *Reminiscences of Barbara Nachtrieb Armstrong*, OHC, pp. 36–40.

[15] Ibid., p. 58.

of the law were declared unconstitutional, in the federal-state system we would at least have state laws which could be upheld legally under the 'police power' of the states. Though state laws might not be uniform, they would be giving unemployed persons some income during a period of unemployment, and that would be an advance."[16] Furthermore, she doubted that Congress would pass a law favoring a purely national system.[17] Altmeyer and Witte, of course, both hailed from Wisconsin themselves and were interested in preserving the only state unemployment compensation law already implemented.[18] More important, Witte repeatedly offered Roosevelt's assumed preferences as his primary rationale for favoring the tax-offset plan.[19] Other CES members, however—namely, Harry Hopkins, Henry Wallace, and Henry Morgenthau, Jr.—were partial to national government administration.[20]

Witte and Perkins planned a speech for Roosevelt to deliver to the National Conference on Economic Security on November 14. Witte included language adhering to the traditional logic of federalism, stating, "For the administration of benefits, the states are the most logical units. At this stage, while unemployment insurance is still untried in this country and there is such a great diversity of opinion on many details, there is room for experimentation."[21] As the directive for joint federal-state action was dispersed through the news wires, Perkins and Witte believed that their efforts to advance the plan that relied most heavily on the individual states had triumphed.[22]

Forces for a national scheme for unemployment compensation continued, however, to press their case. First, at the conference, a group of "unemployment insurance experts" met and cast a symbolic vote of thirteen to three in favor of a straight national plan.[23] Next, the Advisory Council, chosen to represent the public's interest in the policymaking process, pre-

[16] Perkins, *Roosevelt I Knew*, p. 291.

[17] Ibid.

[18] *Reminiscences of Arthur J. Altmeyer*, OHC, p. 7; *Reminiscences of Frank Bane*, OHC, p. 39.

[19] Witte, *Development of the Social Security Act*, pp. 18, 111; *Reminiscences of Barbara Nachtrieb Armstrong*, pp. 51–54; Edwin E. Witte, "Balance of Power: Federal and State Governments Share in the Suggested Unemployment Compensation Programs," CES, Staff Reports, 1934–35, box 21, Witte file, RG 47, NA.

[20] Witte, *Development of the Social Security Act*, p. 112; Perkins, *Roosevelt I Knew*, p. 291; *Reminiscences of Arthur J. Altmeyer*, pp. 7–8.

[21] Letter and attachments, Edwin Witte to Frances Perkins, November 10, 1934, CES, Correspondence regarding Proposals for the Economic Security Program, 1934–35, box 55, RG 47, NA.

[22] Witte, *Development of the Social Security Act*, pp. 118–21.

[23] "Minutes of Meeting on Unemployment Insurance Experts," November 15, 1934, CES, Staff Reports, 1934–35, box 24, RG 47, NA.

sented more obstacles to the tax-offset supporters. Perkins told the Advisory Council at the start of its November 15 meeting that the president and his advisers favored a national-state system and that they should assume the issue was already decided.[24] Behind the scenes, however, Stewart of the CES staff had already successfully lobbied business interests on the Advisory Council to support the subsidy plan.[25] Eveline Burns, an economist at Columbia University and a member of the CES staff who also advocated national approaches, had conspired with Armstrong and privately influenced Frank Graham, president of the Advisory Council, to come out in favor of the subsidy plan. In addition, vice-president of the council, Paul Kellogg, editor of *Survey*, argued publicly for tough national standards.[26] Ultimately a majority of the Advisory Council, including the representatives of business and labor, voted nine to seven for the subsidy plan, with six members abstaining.[27]

But the appeals of experts and the Advisory Council would have little effect on the CES other than to slow their proceedings by a few weeks. Advocates of the tax-offset scheme exerted a final push to confirm the superiority of their plan.[28] Finally, one day during Christmas week, Perkins forced a decision. As she told it later, "I issued an ultimatum that the Committee would meet at eight o-clock at my house, that all telephone service would be discontinued at my house for the evening, and that we would sit all night, if necessary, until we had decided the thorny question once and for all."[29] By two o'clock in the morning the CES had finally decided in favor of the tax-offset plan, ignoring the majority opinion of the Advisory Council. They proposed a 3 percent payroll tax on employers and left all other such matters, such as the choice between pooled funds and plant reserves, benefit levels, and eligibility criteria, to be decided by the states.[30]

Yet even the unemployment insurance plan offering the least authority to the national government still retained a high degree of centralized power and offered the states significant incentives to develop their own plans. All

[24] *Reminiscences of Arthur J. Altmeyer*, p. 12.

[25] Witte, *Development of the Social Security Act*, pp. 50–66.

[26] Martin, *Madam Secretary*, pp. 350–52.

[27] Witte, *Development of the Social Security Act*, p. 118.

[28] Letter, John R. Commons to John B. Andrews, November 19, 1934, CES, Correspondence regarding Proposals for the Economic Security Program, 1934–35, box 55; Paul Raushenbush, "Fundamental Questions of Policy on Unemployment Insurance," December 3, 1934, CES, Staff Reports, 1934–35, box 24; Tom Corcoran, "Why the Wagner-Lewis Principle Should Not Be Opposed," CES, Staff Reports, 1934–35, box 17; all in RG 47, NA.

[29] Perkins, *Roosevelt I Knew*, p. 292.

[30] Arthur J. Altmeyer, *The Formative Years of Social Security* (Madison: University of Wisconsin Press, 1968), pp. 20–21; Witte, *Development of the Social Security Act*, pp. 125–27; Perkins, *Roosevelt I Knew*, pp. 290–92; Irving Bernstein, *A Caring Society* (Boston: Houghton Mifflin, 1985), p. 56.

employers would be required to pay a tax for covered employees, but those funds would be accessible to a state only if it passed a law acceptable to national administrators. Even then, the national government would hold the purse: employers would deposit such moneys in a new Unemployment Trust Fund with the Secretary of the Treasury or a federal reserve bank. States that failed to act would only be losing out themselves on contributions already made by employers within their boundaries.[31] CES had thus agreed to a plan for unemployment compensation which left more authority to the states than the old age insurance plan but which also would involve far more national government control than the public assistance plans.

From a comparative point of view, the fierce debate over UI was exceptional not only because of its relentless focus on matters of federalism, but also because policymakers neglected so entirely to raise issues about the consequences of unemployment for family members of those who lost their jobs. Policymakers knew that European countries typically included in their programs of unemployment compensation dependents' allowances for spouses and children.[32] Parties to the dispute as diverse in their viewpoints as Stewart and Raushenbush did agree, however, that unemployment compensation in the United States should bear no resemblance at all to means-tested relief measures. Staff reports explained that "dependents' allowances" would effectively introduce the concept of need into the program, blemishing the pure connection between contributions and benefits.[33] No one in the CES raised such considerations, though Harry Hopkins tried to promote a unified system of relief and social insurance, which was immediately rejected by Roosevelt for too closely resembling "the dole" system he so despised.[34] Armstrong submitted a proposal for a comprehensive version of social insurance which posed the question of whether housewives should be covered in a system of unemployment insurance.[35] Instead policymakers across the spectrum on issues of intergovernmental relations united to create programs wherein eligibility would be tied to participation and earnings in the paid work force.

Thus, unlike either the British system, which defined wives and children as "dependents" and eligible for allowances, or the Belgian system, where

[31] Public Law 271, 74th Cong., 1st sess. (August 14, 1935), *Social Security Act of 1935*, titles III and IX.

[32] SSB, *Social Security in America*, p. 119.

[33] Ibid.

[34] Martin, *Madam Secretary*, p. 345; Perkins, *Roosevelt I Knew*, p. 284.

[35] Barbara Nachtrieb Armstrong, "Possibilities of a Unified System of Insurance against Loss of Earnings," CES, Staff Reports, 1934–35, box 17, RG 47, NA. Homer Folks of the State Charities Aid Association raised such concerns, but as a member of the Advisory Committee on Child Welfare, his comments were ineffective; see letter, Homer Folks to Katharine Lenroot, November 7, 1934, Abbott Papers, box 54, folder 1d, UC.

benefit levels were structured according to sex and marital status and unemployed married women were excluded entirely, U.S. policymakers side-
stepped explicit attention to family structure and gender roles.[36] By the
same token, policymakers also avoided the inclusion of maternity benefits
for women despite the fact that several European and Latin American
countries already had such programs in place.[37] Rather, the plan proposed
by the CES viewed beneficiaries—at least ostensibly—with the gaze of classical liberalism: as abstract, independent individuals, devoid of a specific
gender role.

Yet, at the same time, policymakers operated on the assumption that the
primary function of unemployment insurance was to replace the wages of
male breadwinners, who were understood to earn a "family wage."[38] Experts had already recommended the omission from coverage of part-time
workers, namely women:

> There are some, particularly women, who wish to be employed for only a few
> hours per day or per week. Such persons as these are only casual or inciden-
> tal members of the real labor supply and do not need or deserve the same pro-
> tection as those who are fully dependent upon industry for employment. It
> would be well, therefore, . . . [that] those who are normally involved in in-
> dustry for at least half of the standard working hours should come under un-
> employment insurance, but this should not be the case for those who have
> more than one leg in the home.[39]

The committee followed suit by recommending discretionary guidelines for
the states which would have implications for women and nonwhite workers in particular. In its official report to the president, the CES suggested
that states adopt "provisions to protect funds against heavy drains by particular classes of employees," namely the "casual workers" and those in
"seasonal industries." The report read: "Unemployment compensation is
best adapted to employees who normally have some degree of security in
their employment. Such workers, we feel, should be given some protection

---

[36] SSB, *Social Security in America*, pp. 24–26, 33, 40.

[37] Maternity benefits were mentioned in the "Report of the Committee on Economic Security" as one aspect of the health insurance program which failed to materialize; see CES, "Report of the Committee on Economic Security," in *The Report of the Committee on Economic
Security of 1935 and Other Basic Documents relating to the Development of the Social Security Act*, 50th anniversary ed., National Conference on Social Welfare (Washington, D.C.:
National Conference on Social Welfare, 1985), pp. 41–42. On maternity benefits in other
countries by the early 1930s, see Barbara Nachtrieb Armstrong, *Insuring the Essentials* (New
York: Macmillan, 1932), pp. 345, 350.

[38] Perkins, *Roosevelt I Knew*, pp. 284–85; Witte, *Development of the Social Security Act*,
p. 114; Bernstein, *Caring Society*, p. 55.

[39] Paul H. Douglas, *Standards of Unemployment Insurance* (Chicago: University of Chicago Press, 1933), p. 50.

against exhaustion of the funds by others who work only intermittently." [40]
With this recommendation, the CES implicitly suggested that the concerns
of full-time male breadwinners were to be given priority for UI benefits,
inasmuch as it was they who were most likely to have had long-term,
constant jobs.[41] In other matters of eligibility, the CES would defer to the
states.

Aid to Dependent Children

The idea that the national government could help to promote the development and enhancement of social programs had originated in the Children's Bureau. Founded in 1912 to investigate and report on matters pertaining to the welfare of children, the bureau had conducted numerous
studies regarding such subjects as child labor and maternal and infant
health, making bureau officials well aware of the inadequacy of local relief
in meeting need among children.[42] They believed that national government
could play an important role in modernizing social programs. In a plea for
national assistance in 1932, Edith Abbott (sister of Bureau Chief Grace Abbott and also a social reformer) wrote: "The plain facts that Washington
must face are that the United States can get money, and the local governments are everywhere bankrupt and incompetent. The politicians and not
the people are responsible for the fact that we have an old-fashioned taxation system that makes it impossible through the maze of state constitutions, city charters and statutory limitations on the raising of poor funds to
get money swiftly for local emergency needs." [43] As the Children's Bureau
had already demonstrated in administering the Sheppard-Towner Act, the
first American social program in which federal moneys were provided to
the states on a matching basis, national funds could be used not only to
raise the level of benefits but also to pressure state governments to improve
standards of service and care by developing professional administrative
practices.[44] The bureau had thus played a significant role in establishing the
legitimacy of the grant-in-aid approach to social policy.

Early in the depression, Bureau Chief Grace Abbott had suggested that

[40] CES, "Report of the Committee on Economic Security," p. 21.

[41] Diana M. Pearce, "Toil and Trouble: Women Workers and Unemployment Compensation," *Signs* 10 (1985): 441.

[42] Grace Abbott, "Recent Trends in Mothers' Aid," *Social Service Review* 8 (1934): 191–
210.

[43] Edith Abbott, "The Fallacy of Local Relief," *New Republic*, November 9, 1932, pp. 348–
50.

[44] "Views of Miss Edith Abbott of the University of Chicago on a Feasible Program for Economic Security," August 25, 1934, CES, Correspondence regarding Proposals for the Economic Security Program, 1934–35, box 54, RG 47, NA; Letter, Grace Abbott to Edwin Em-
bree, October 12, 1929, Abbott Papers, box 36, folder 15, UC.

mothers' pensions provided a ready program through which national government could assist needy families, especially if the policy was expanded to reach more children.[45] Then in the last year of Hoover's administration, Katharine Lenroot, acting chief of the bureau, had attempted to obtain an appropriation of one hundred thousand dollars to assist states in encouraging counties to develop a set of services for children. The proposal had been rejected, but after Roosevelt became president and Perkins was appointed secretary of labor, the climate had changed. Lenroot told her old friend Altmeyer, who was appointed assistant secretary, of her previous effort to obtain federal aid for children. He replied, "Oh, don't be silly. We'll get you much more money than that through the economic security program."[46]

After the formation of the CES in the summer of 1934, Witte contacted Lenroot, who had become chief of the Children's Bureau after Abbott returned to her position as professor of social work at the University of Chicago, and Martha Eliot, the chief medical officer for the bureau. Witte told them that President Roosevelt and Secretary Perkins wanted the committee to consider the security needs of children and that they, in consultation with Abbott, were to design proposals for such programs. Lenroot seized the opportunity to advance the inclusion of two initiatives for children in the legislation: federal grants to states to expand and strengthen mothers' pensions and an educational program to promote child and maternal health, similar to the expired Sheppard-Towner policy.[47]

The program that became ADC was designed primarily by Lenroot and Abbott, and they created it with remarkably little deliberation. As they understood it, the program should offer federal moneys to match state and local funds in a grant-in-aid program; federal funds would be contingent on "satisfactory plans of administration and standards of aid" in state programs.[48] Witte had informed Lenroot and Eliot that all proposals should feature a central role for individual state activity. Unlike the resistance with which other officials, charged with developing unemployment and old age insurance, met such guidelines, women associated with the Children's Bureau did not question the approach. In fact, federal grants-in-aid to state units exemplified their ideal of the appropriate model for social programs.[49]

[45] Grace Abbott, "Recent Trends in Mothers' Aid," p. 210; Lela B. Costin, *Two Sisters for Social Justice* (Urbana: University of Illinois Press, 1983), p. 208.

[46] *Reminiscences of Katherine Lenroot*, OHC, pp. 33–34, 86.

[47] Letter, Katharine Lenroot to Grace Abbott, August 17, 1934, Abbott Papers, box 54, folder 1a, UC; *Reminiscences of Katharine Lenroot*, pp. 33–34.

[48] Memorandum, Katharine Lenroot to Mrs. Hopkins, June 28, 1934, box 479, file 0-5-4-10-0, RG 102, NA.

[49] Letter, Katharine Lenroot to Grace Abbott, August 17, 1934, Abbott Papers, box 54, folder 1a, UC.

For although the Children's Bureau officials had been advocates of national government power relative to others in the Hoover administration, which they criticized for its emphasis on localism,[50] compared with many other New Deal social policymakers they were protective of traditional federalism. The Abbotts and Lenroot retained a measure of the Progressive Era attitude of distrust for national intervention in social policies, fearful that local initiative might be displaced. They were still attached to the notion that national policies should function primarily to encourage, rather than to organize or replace, state and local initiatives.[51]

The manner in which Grace Abbott and Lenroot designed ADC epitomized their ambivalence about the role of national government in relation to the states. They wanted to use national government power to expand the development and implementation of mothers' pensions. Lenroot reasoned that the "spotty" implementation of mothers' pensions was attributable to the fact that only seventeen state governments actually supported mothers' pensions financially; the other twenty-nine left the entire responsibility to local governments, which were generally unable to shoulder the burden.[52] She and Abbott believed that the grants-in-aid formula would induce state governments to appropriate funds to increase the coverage and level of benefits in the program. To ensure statewide program coverage, Abbott insisted that states should not be allowed to receive any grants-in-aid unless the program was implemented in all political subdivisions.[53]

The two officials also wanted to raise the standards of state laws,[54] and toward that end they drafted a law aimed at stimulating coherent administrative practices and less restrictive residence requirements than under mothers' pensions.[55] States would be required to centralize the administration of the law, and the agencies assigned with implementation would be charged with following methods recommended by a national agency and would have to submit regular reports to that agency.[56] Mothers' pensions

---

[50] Edith Abbott, "The Fallacy of Local Relief."

[51] Katharine Lenroot, "Preliminary and Confidential Suggestions for Development of a Children's Program as Part of a Federal Security Program," p. 1, Abbott Papers, box 61, folder 3, UC.

[52] Katharine Lenroot, "Special Measures for Children's Security," Abbott Papers, box 61, folder 3, UC; *Reminiscences of Katharine Lenroot*, p. 92.

[53] Katharine Lenroot to Grace Abbott, January 10, 1935, Abbott Papers, box 61, folder 4, UC; SSB, *Social Security in America*, pp. 288–89.

[54] Letter, Lenroot to Grace Abbott, October 13, 1934, Abbott Papers, box 61, folder 3, UC; Katharine Lenroot, "Aid to Dependent Children," in SSB, *Social Security in America*, p. 248.

[55] *Reminiscences of Katherine Lenroot*, pp. 25, 33; Lenroot, "Preliminary and Confidential Suggestions," p. 3.

[56] Lenroot, "Preliminary and Confidential Suggestions," p. 2; Public Law 271, title IV, sec. 402 (a); Eveline M. Burns, *Toward Social Security* (New York: McGraw-Hill, 1936), pp. 111–12.

laws of twenty-one states made eligibility contingent on state residence for two to five years, and in thirty-five states they required residence in the same county or town for at least one or two years. Abbott and Lenroot proposed that national funds not be made available to states with residence requirements greater than one year or any local residence requirements whatsoever.[57]

Although Abbott and Lenroot hoped to use national government power to liberalize and expand mothers' pensions, the way they structured funding for the program showed their tendency to retain ample responsibility for the states and even for the localities. Lenroot suggested a matching-grant system wherein one-third of the funds would come from each level of government: federal, state, and local.[58] Whereas CES proposed fifty million dollars from the national government for the first year of the OAA program, the Children's Bureau officials recommended only half that amount, twenty-five million dollars, for the first year of ADC. In fact, when Lenroot first asked Abbott for her advice on requesting one-and-a-half million dollars for the entire package of child welfare services in the Social Security Act, Abbott responded that the amount was too much and that Lenroot should only request one million. In part, the low figure reflected the fact that bureau officials had struggled for years to obtain equally modest appropriations from Congress for the Sheppard-Towner program, only to have it rescinded entirely.[59] More fundamentally, the approach exemplified Abbott and Lenroot's view of the role of national government. As Lenroot said, "We were still thinking very much in terms of state responsibility. . . . We were very much imbued with the idea that the federal grant should be a stimulating, helping, somewhat equalizing factor for the most needy states, but should not take the place of state and local financial responsibility for services to children."[60] She believed that through a grants-in-aid program, the federal government could achieve a larger goal of promoting the development and professionalization of state-level welfare departments, thus strengthening the ability of the states to act effectively in administering other social programs.[61]

The emphasis that Children's Bureau officials placed on state and local administration of programs fused with their attitudes about proper delivery of services. In contrast to other reformers and social workers who

[57] SSB, *Social Security in America*, table 49, pp. 235–36; testimony of Katharine Lenroot, House Ways and Means Committee, *Hearings on the Economic Security Act*, H.R. 4120, 74th Cong., 1st sess., January 26, 1935, p. 267.
[58] CES, "Report of the Committee on Economic Security," pp. 26–27, 36–37.
[59] Linda Gordon, *Pitied but Not Entitled: Single Mothers and the History of Welfare, 1890–1935* (New York: Free Press, 1994), p. 257.
[60] *Reminiscences of Katherine Lenroot*, p. 99.
[61] Lenroot, "Preliminary and Confidential Suggestions," p. 2.

viewed the determination of eligibility as the central task of public administrators, Abbott and Lenroot considered the provision of benefits as subordinate to the maternalist goal of educating poor women in child rearing and domestic skills. Funding for fatherless children should be accompanied, they thought, by child welfare services. Local officials, they reasoned, would best understand the situation of women in their own proximity and would be most adept at handling such responsibilities.[62]

Ultimately, the program put forth by Abbott and Lenroot represented, more than any other feature of the Economic Security Bill, a traditional application of preexisting principles of federal-state relations and epitomized incrementalism in policymaking. By attempting only to expand the application of the mothers' pensions, Lenroot and Abbott offered a proposal for child security that was much more narrow than many public officials and social workers would have preferred. Some feminist women reformers had argued since the 1920s that benefits for children should be granted regardless of family composition, as in the family allowances of some European countries.[63] A variety of proposals that would have applied to all needy children appeared in the Lundeen Bill and in the plans of Hopkins and Federal Emergency Relief Administration staff, the Advisory Committee on Public Employment and Relief, the National Association of Social Workers, and the American Public Welfare Association.[64] Those alternatives, however, each placed aid to children in the context of noncategorical assistance to all needy persons, a notion that had no place in the framework recommended by Roosevelt or in the goals of the bureau.

The Children's Bureau officials, following the rationale on which mothers' pensions had been established, believed strongly in using carefully defined categorical assistance programs to separate mothers and children, who were among the "worthy poor," from the relief ranks. They considered such families as in need of steady assistance, until children reached the age of sixteen, and were convinced that only a categorical program like ADC could offer the long-term security, sufficient benefits, and dignity—in short, the standards—families deserved.[65] The emphasis that Abbott and

[62] *Reminiscences of Katharine Lenroot*, pp. 107–11; Lenroot, "Preliminary and Confidential Suggestions," p. 4; Gwendolyn Mink, *The Wages of Motherhood: Inequality in the Welfare State, 1917–1942* (Ithaca: Cornell University Press, 1995); Gordon, *Pitied but Not Entitled*, p. 102; Christopher Howard, "Sowing the Seeds of 'Welfare': The Transformation of Mothers' Pensions, 1900–1940," *Journal of Policy History* 4 (1992): 210.

[63] Wendy Sarvasy, "Beyond the Difference versus Equality Policy Debate: Postsuffrage Feminism, Citizenship, and the Quest for a Feminist Welfare State," *Signs* 17 (1992): 329–62, esp. 348–49 and 360.

[64] *Reminiscences of Katherine Lenroot*, pp. 104–5.

[65] Report by Grace Abbott, September 6, 1934, pp. 3–4, Abbott Papers, box 61, folder 3, UC; testimony of Grace Abbott, House Ways and Means Committee, *Hearings on the Economic Security Act*, p. 495; Gordon, *Pitied but Not Entitled*, p. 105.

Lenroot placed on maintaining "standards" was, however, a two-edged sword: eligibility for such a program had to be narrowly defined in order to justify the better treatment that was supposed to accompany coverage. As Grace Abbott would tell members of Congress, even among female-headed households on relief, probably only one-half or one-third would actually qualify for the program, and they would be "nice children" and "nice families."[66]

Because the bureau's recommendations were so modest and emulated the emphasis of CES leaders on fostering state initiatives in policy development, the CES readily included them, without any of the controversy that surrounded UI plans, into its final report for President Roosevelt. Soon attention turned to developments at the other end of Pennsylvania Avenue, as Congress began to consider the bill.

The Economic Security Bill in Congress

In Congress, where the forces demanding more generous and expansive programs for the elderly were dominating the treatment of the Economic Security Bill, neither UI nor ADC received much explicit attention. Like the OAA program, both were weakened by congressional committees that undermined the force of program standards as a means of curtailing the reach of national government into the affairs of state and local governments. But unlike OAA, the public assistance program for children enjoyed no groundswell of public support. Unemployment compensation, moreover, might have been dropped from the bill entirely were it not for the countervailing pressure of an alternative plan far more radical: the workers' bill, otherwise known as the Lundeen Bill.

The Lundeen Bill

An insurgent sector of the AFL supported the Lundeen Bill, named for its sponsor Representative Ernest Lundeen, a member of the Minnesota Farmer-Labor Party. The plan, which originated in the unemployed councils in 1931, was based on the idea that mass unemployment is caused by social and economic forces that operate on a scale much wider than individual states and thus warrants a national response. Unlike the administration's proposal, the Lundeen Bill called for a fully national system of unemployment benefits that would be financed by a progressive income tax and administered by elected committees of workers and farmers.[67]

---

[66] Testimony of Grace Abbott, House Ways and Means Committee, *Hearings on the Economic Security Act*, January 21, 1935, pp. 495–96.

[67] Richard M. Valelly, *Radicalism in the States* (Chicago: University of Chicago Press, 1989), pp. 168–69; Gordon, *Pitied but Not Entitled*, pp. 236–41; Kenneth Casebeer, "The

The Lundeen Bill promised benefits to all unemployed persons on an explicitly inclusive basis, stating: "The benefits of this Act shall be extended to workers, whether they be industrial, agricultural, domestic, office, or professional workers, and to farmers, without discrimination because of age, sex, race, color, religious or political opinion or affiliation."[68] The plan would also cover workers who were unemployed because of maternity, sickness, accident, or old age. When the House Labor Committee, on which Lundeen served, held hearings on the bill in 1934 and 1935, proponents lauded the plan for deliberately including African American workers and women. In the words of the labor leader "Mother Bloor" (Ella Reeve Bloor), moreover, the Lundeen Bill "would be of great service to . . . working women everywhere."[69]

Roosevelt administration officials cast the Lundeen Bill as a communist plot and urged Congress to act quickly on its own measure to diffuse pressure for the more radical alternative. Though communists and socialists did indeed support the bill, so did several thousand union locals under the auspices of the AFL and many municipal governments. The bill had been drafted, moreover, by Mary Van Kleeck of the Interprofessional Association for Social Insurance and the Russell Sage Foundation.[70] But throughout the debate over social insurance, members of Congress who supported the administrations' bill portrayed the Lundeen legislation as extreme and dangerous. In particular, they argued that the national features of the Lundeen bill would undermine the autonomy of the states.[71]

The leadership of the AFL had hoped for a truly national unemployment insurance policy that would set specific standards for the content of all state laws. AFL spokesman William Green, testifying before Congress, criticized the Economic Security Bill for leaving excessive authority to individual

Workers' Unemployment Insurance Bill: American Social Wage, Labor Organization, and Legal Ideology," in *Labor Law in America*, ed. Christopher L. Tomlins and Andrew J. King (Baltimore: Johns Hopkins University Press, 1992), p. 49.

[68] House Committee on Labor, *Hearings on Unemployment, Old Age, and Social Insurance*, 74th Cong., 1st sess., February 4, 1935, pp. 1–2.

[69] Ibid., pp. 129–35. Also of particular interest are the testimonies of Frieda Pearl, United Council of Working-Class Women, pp. 386–88; Dr. Reuben S. Young, Interprofessional Association, pp. 388–92; Thomas Jefferson Crawford, Agricultural and Cannery Workers Industrial Union of New Jersey, p. 363; T. Arnold Hill, National Urban League, p. 326; Herbert Benjamin, National Joint Action Committee for Genuine Social Insurance, pp. 166–95; Rosa Rayside, Domestic Workers Union, p. 635; L. H. Wittner, National Equal Wealth Society, pp. 424–25; Theresa E. Gold, Brotherhood of Shoe and Allied Craftsmen, p. 440; and Mildred Fairchild, economist, Bryn Mawr College, pp. 397–409.

[70] Altmeyer, *Formative Years*, p. 30; Witte, *Development of the Social Security Act*, p. 85; Gordon, *Pitied but Not Entitled*, p. 237; Casebeer, "Unemployment Insurance Bill."

[71] *Congressional Record*, 74th Cong., 1st sess., April 11, 1935, pp. 5467–68; see also, e.g., pp. 5550, 5536, 5703–4.

states.[72] Still, the organization threw its official support to the administration and denounced the Lundeen alternative supported by rebels from its own ranks.[73] This division in organized labor helped the administration discredit the Lundeen plan.

Although the Labor Committee voted in favor of the Lundeen Bill and reported it out in March 1935, the Rules Committee, which supported the administration's bill instead, did not allow it to advance to the House floor for debate. Congressman Lundeen offered his bill as an amendment to the Economic Security Bill in April. No debate was allowed, however, and the amendment received only fifty-five favorable votes. Meanwhile, however, the administration's fears that conservatives might kill its UI plan dissolved as the specter of the far more comprehensive and nationally uniform alternative prompted Congress to coalesce in support of the moderate CES version.[74]

Unemployment Insurance

Those who had advocated a national or subsidy-type unemployment compensation scheme continued to press their case as Congress began to consider the administration's bill. In hearings before the House Ways and Means Committee, Eveline Burns and Abraham Epstein, and representatives of organizations such as the National Consumers' League and Women's Trade Union League criticized the administration's bill for its lack of national standards.[75] Testifying before the Senate Finance Committee, Paul Kellogg pleaded for the inclusion of national standards as a fundamental right of citizenship: "Such minimum standards should let every wage earner in the United States know, no matter where he lives or works, the least he can count on with respect to the share of his wages that will go to him as benefit, the length of benefit, the waiting period, the work record that will qualify him for benefit, his standing as a part-time worker . . . and the other terms which are the measure of security, or lack of it, to him and his family."[76] A group of businessmen headed by Gerard Swope appealed

[72] Edwin E. Witte, "Organized Labor and Social Security," in *Labor and the New Deal*, ed. Milton Derber and Edwin Young (Madison: University of Wisconsin Press, 1961), pp. 253–54.

[73] Casebeer relates in detail the story of the grass-roots support by union locals and municipal governments for the Lundeen Bill and the conflicts that ensued in the AFL over the disputed visions of unemployment compensation; see Casebeer, "Unemployment Insurance Bill"; see also Witte, "Organized Labor and Social Security."

[74] Gordon, *Pitied but Not Entitled*, p. 240; Valelly, *Radicalism in the States*, p. 169.

[75] House Ways and Means Committee, *Hearings on the Economic Security Act*, 1935, pp. 562–65, 790–95, 1092.

[76] Letter and attachments, Paul Kellogg to Josephine Roche, February 15, 1935, CES, General Records of the Executive Director and Staff, 1934–35, box 1, RG 47, NA.

to the Senate Finance Committee to adopt the subsidy plan instead of the tax-offset plan. They argued that because "American economic society is national in nature" rather than organized within individual state boundaries, so too unemployment insurance should be national in scope and application.[77]

Demands for national standards fell on deaf ears in the Ways and Means Committee and the Finance Committee; in fact the committees took actions that further undermined the few standards the CES had included in the bill. The Ways and Means Committee limited the coverage of UI just as it had for OAI, in this case formally permitting states to bar from UI coverage particular categories of workers who happened to be predominantly female and nonwhite. The exclusion of employees of nonprofit hospitals and religious and educational organizations made UI, like OAI, inaccessible to many workers in the female-dominated fields of teaching, social work, and health care. To reduce the burden on part-time employers, the CES had already recommended that employees working fewer than 13 weeks per year be exempt from coverage; the Ways and Means Committee changed the regulation to apply only to workers who were employed more than 20 weeks annually in order to exempt from coverage the heavily female canning industry.[78] Once again, agricultural and domestic workers were eliminated from coverage. The omission of the mostly female ranks of domestic workers would exclude large segments of the nonwhite population who were in desperate need of UI: in May 1934, a survey by the FERA had found that of persons on relief in forty cities, more than two-thirds of those who described their occupations as servants and allied workers were black.[79]

The CES had proposed that UI be administered by a board within the Department of Labor. Congress chose instead to have UI and other titles of the bill administered by a quasi-independent board, operating outside the auspices of any agency in the executive branch. Altmeyer attributed this alteration to Congress' general distaste for the Department of Labor and particular disdain for Secretary Perkins, largely because "she was a woman and an articulate, intelligent woman at that" and she was "not sufficiently amenable to patronage needs."[80]

[77] Business Advisory Council for the Department on Commerce, "Report of Committee on Social Legislation," April 10, 1935, CES, General Records of the Executive Director and Staff, 1934–35, box 11, RG 47, NA.

[78] Public Law 271, title IX, Sec. 907, parts (a) and (c); Department of Labor, Women's Bureau, "Women Workers and the Social Security Program," address by Mary Anderson before the Indianapolis Council of Women, January 7, 1936, pp. 19–20, LMDC; Witte, *Development of the Social Security Act*, pp. 132–43.

[79] Department of Labor, Women's Bureau, "The Negro Woman Worker," by Jean Collier Brown, bulletin 165 (Washington, D.C.: GPO, 1938), p. 3.

[80] Altmeyer, *Formative Years*, p. 37; see also Perkins, *Roosevelt I Knew*, pp. 300–301.

In other regards, the unemployment insurance section of the bill emerged from Congress in much the same form as the CES had proposed it. By granting a considerable degree of authority to the individual states, particularly for enacting and implementing eligibility restrictions, the CES had already made a law that might seem unconventional in the United States appear to be harmonious with American political traditions. By omitting from coverage several categories of workers, Congress had signaled to state legislatures that the law was not meant to upset state and local autonomy in defining the political economy. In the case of ADC, Congress took even greater measures to make clear the authority and responsibility of the states, in this case for the well-being of female-headed families.

Aid to Dependent Children

Before the ADC proposal was sent to Congress, the program was changed in a fundamental manner that horrified Lenroot and Abbott. Although Harry Hopkins had given his tepid approval to the entire legislative package, his assistants at the FERA started anew the battle for broad, universal relief programs for all needy people. They charged that the Economic Security Bill was elitist because it segregated older people and fatherless children from others on relief. They argued that a national department of public welfare, a permanent version of the FERA, should have been incorporated into the bill. As a concession to their demands, officials rewrote the ADC section of the bill and placed the administration of the program under the FERA rather than within the Children's Bureau as Lenroot and Abbott had planned.[81]

As soon as Lenroot heard the news, she wrote a fervent memo to Perkins, listing several compelling reasons why the Children's Bureau was the most appropriate agency to administer the program. She reminded Perkins of the bureau's experience in the field of mothers' pensions, its experience in administering regular grant-in-aid programs, and the preferability of treating children separately rather than incorporating them into the regular relief case load.[82] Although Perkins agreed, ultimately Congress placed the administration of ADC, like UI, under the independent SSB instead.[83] Thus,

[81] Witte, *Development of the Social Security Act*, pp. 71, 162.

[82] Memorandum, Katharine Lenroot to The Secretary, January 3, 1935, CES, box 1, RG 47, NA. Within a week, Perkins informed Lenroot that Roosevelt intended to place mothers' pensions under the Children's Bureau after all; letter, Katharine Lenroot to Grace Abbott, January 10, 1935, Abbott Papers, box 61, folder 4, UC. Yet, once the final draft was sent to Congress, the FERA was cited as the agency to be charged with administering ADC; see letter, Grace Abbott to Katharine Lenroot, February 21, 1935, Abbott Papers, box 61, folder 4, UC; letter, Katharine Lenroot to Grace Abbott, February 26, 1935, Abbott Papers, box 54, folder 2, UC; and letter, Grace Abbott to Edwin Witte, February 25, 1935, CES, Staff Correspondence, 1934–35, box 16, RG 47, NA.

[83] Witte, *Development of the Social Security Act*, pp. 162–63.

both FERA and Children's Bureau officials lost on the administrative authority issue.

But while the attention of agency representatives was consumed by their efforts to gain future administrative control over ADC, Congress proceeded to, in Witte's words, "all but wreck" other crucial provisions for the program.[84] Just as it had for OAA, the Ways and Means Committee omitted the requirement that state-level agencies charged with administering ADC adopt the merit system. Also parallel to its treatment of the program for the elderly, the committee dropped the clause that would have mandated that states provide for "assistance at least great enough to provide . . . a reasonable subsistence compatible with decency and health." As told by Grace Abbott, "There was much objection to federal determination of adequacy on the part of southern members who feared that northern standards might be forced on the South in providing for Negro and white tenant families."[85] In lieu of the "reasonable subsistence" clause, states were asked simply to provide assistance "as far as practicable under the conditions in such State, to needy dependent children."[86] Both changes undermined Lenroot's and Abbott's hopes for elevating standards, leaving the quality and character of the program to the state and local officials who already administered mothers' pensions in a manner that was highly variable and particular to local norms. Worst of all, however, from Witte's perspective, was the financing and benefit structure the Ways and Means Committee assigned to ADC.

CES officials had overlooked the discrepancy between the matching-grant ratios for ADC and OAA: whereas the OAA title called for a one-to-one grant formula, Lenroot had recommended that national government match the states' expenditures for ADC by only one-third. The Ways and Means Committee, which dealt hastily with ADC, retained the lower funding formula and only worsened the effects by stipulating a strikingly low ceiling for benefits. Representative Fred M. Vinson (D-Ken.) suggested that the law use the same benefit limits as those granted to children through veterans' benefits: $18 per month for the first child and $12 for each additional child. Given the one-third matching formula, the national government would thus pay a maximum of only $6 for the first child and $4 for each additional child.[87] Vinson overlooked the fact that under the veterans' benefits, widows themselves had also received $30 per month. Nonethe-

---

[84] Letter, Edwin E. Witte to Raymond Moley, March 6, 1935, CES, Staff Correspondence, 1934–35, box 15, Witte file 4, RG 47, NA.

[85] Grace Abbott, *From Relief to Social Security* (New York: Russell and Russell, 1966), p. 279.

[86] Public Law 271, title IV, sec. 401.

[87] Grace Abbott, *From Relief to Social Security*, pp. 280–81; Witte, *Development of the Social Security Act*, p. 164.

less, the committee accepted the suggestions, and no caretakers' benefits were included in ADC at all.[88]

Witte, who was respectful of the Children's Bureau officials and concerned that attention to elderly people was distracting Congress from paying sufficient attention to children's needs, was very troubled by the changes. He criticized the inequity between the grant formula and maximum benefits for families with children and for elderly people, and he declared that it would be "simply impossible" for the young families to survive without being on relief as well. He believed that there should be no maximum grant levels written into the bill at all and hoped the administration could restore the bill to its original form in the Senate.[89] Upon reviewing the bill herself, however, Lenroot, perhaps still distracted over the administrative authority issue, left the changes intact.[90] Only later did Grace Abbott observe, "As children eat more and wear out their clothing more rapidly than elderly people, this was obviously an unfair basis for reimbursement."[91] With little pressure to act otherwise, the Finance Committee decided to leave the Ways and Means Committee's alterations to ADC intact. And despite occasional high-flown rhetoric about mothers that punctuated orations in floor debates about the needs of the elderly, such as Representative Sirovich's words about the "queen and angel of the home," both chambers and the conference committee also left the altered ADC provisions in place, and so they remained when the measure was signed into law by President Roosevelt on August 14, 1935.

Congress had made the ADC program, already the most modest plan in the Economic Security Act, even more frugal. The benefit and matching-grant features placed in the bill by Lenroot and Abbott combined with the changes made in Congress to codify inadequate standards for grants to children in law and to place a particularly heavy fiscal burden on state governments. Moreover, though mothers' pensions laws, which sanctified the role of mothers in caring for children, had provided the impetus for ADC, mothers themselves disappeared entirely in the new statute, absent any provision for caretakers. The extremely low benefit structure appeared to dash the maternalist reformers' hopes for a program that would approximate more fully the goal of mothers' pensions: to allow children to stay home with their mothers and to be shielded from the indignities of general relief.

Most important, states' rights advocates on the Ways and Means Committee had outdone the Children's Bureau officials in restricting ADC to the traditional boundaries of federalism. In their reports, Lenroot and Abbott

[88] See Public Law 271, title IV, sec. 403(a), 406(b).
[89] Letter, Witte to Moley, March 6, 1935.
[90] Memorandum, Thomas Eliot to Arthur Altmeyer and Edwin Witte, April 24, 1935, CES, box 56, RG 47, NA.
[91] Grace Abbott, *From Relief to Social Security*, p. 281.

had consistently suggested that federal grants, at least temporarily, be allo-cated according to an "equalization" principle, "with special assistance to States temporarily incapacitated." [92] In this manner, previous governmen-tal matching-grant programs, such as those for highways, agricultural ex-tension work, and vocational education, had been apportioned according to factors such as population and road mileage, rather than left to facile political and economic considerations. [93] In statutory form, however, the "equalization" language was dropped. The matching-grant formula for ADC bore no relationship to the extent of need in particular states but rested instead on the willingness and ability of each state's government to offer assistance.

The efforts of Children's Bureau officials and Congress combined to per-mit tremendous variation in standards and administrative styles in imple-menting the program. Lenroot and Abbott, by no means advocating uni-versal coverage, had nonetheless hoped that permissive federal standards would mean that more children, under more circumstances, would be cov-ered under ADC than had been under mothers' pensions. They had ap-proved the FERA officials' broad language in the bill that defined a "de-pendent child" as "a child under the age of sixteen who has been deprived of parental support or care by reason of the death, continued absence from the home, or physical or mental incapacity of a parent." [94] In keeping with their inclinations to leave substantial authority to the states, however, the bill's definition was not restrictive but only suggested the most inclusive boundaries within which states could determine eligibility to the program. Grace Abbott argued optimistically that although states would not be re-quired to accept the relatively liberal federal definition of a dependent child, the law would prompt states to adopt similar guidelines because they would then be eligible to receive federal grants for more children. [95] In strip-ping merit-system provisions from the bill, however, the Ways and Means Committee made it more likely that ADC would be implemented accord-ing to local and provincial norms rather than those Abbott and Lenroot ad-vocated but were unwilling to mandate.

Thus Children's Bureau officials and members of Congress, with their very different motives, had inadvertently worked in tandem to make ADC the title in the Social Security Act which promised to be most fragmented by federalism. Firm believers in state-level governance, Abbott and Lenroot had sought to build on the decentralized foundation of mothers' pensions

---

[92] CES, "Report of the Committee on Economic Security," p. 36; see also Lenroot, "Spe-cial Measures for Children's Security," p. 3, and Lenroot, "Preliminary and Confidential Sug-gestions," p. 10.

[93] James T. Patterson, *The New Deal and the States: Federalism in Transition* (Princeton: Princeton University Press, 1969), p. 87.

[94] Public Law 271, title IV, sec. 406(a).

[95] Grace Abbott, *From Relief to Social Security*, pp. 279–80.

for the sake of keeping social provision "closer to the people"; the notion of centralized national administration was foreign to their understanding of the proper realm of social policy implementation. States-rights conservatives in Congress, acting on different incentives but for the same result, added more state-level autonomy to ADC. Although Children's Bureau officials were dismayed by some of Congress's manipulations of ADC, they remained optimistic that the program promised a brighter future.

Policies Compared

At the hearings on the Economic Security Act before the House Ways and Means Committee, the proposed ADC program was addressed by Mrs. B. F. Langworthy, president of the National Congress of Parents and Teachers, the organization that had evolved from the National Congress of Mothers, which had steered the passage of mothers' pensions during the 1910s. Describing her organization's efforts over more than two decades to expand mothers' pensions, Langworthy commented:

> In none of our resolutions do we find that mothers' pensions as a Federal project have been considered. We are aware, however, that during the economic depression some States have become so impoverished that Federal assistance of this type seems desirable. We are thoroughly committed to local control and responsibility for child welfare. However, if a method of administration whereby such local control and responsibility may be retained and needs be more adequately met through the use of Federal funds, States desiring this aid, we believe, should be permitted to avail themselves of the opportunity through this or similar legislation.[96]

Langworthy's opposition to national administrative authority for mothers' pensions and her lukewarm support for the use of the federal moneys for the program contrasted sharply with the testimony of most proponents of unemployment compensation. Numerous experts and representatives of organizations insisted that national administrative authority and national standards for UI would be far preferable to the CES plan, which left so much authority to individual states.

Indeed the different discourses on the two programs during the hearings mirrored the extremely dissimilar character of their creations by Roosevelt administration officials. Yet UI and ADC emerged from the policymaking process in 1935 on fairly comparable ground. As seen in Table 4, both had been granted a model of administration in which authority would be shared between the national and state governments. Each offered substantial dis-

---

[96] House Ways and Means Committee, *Hearings on the Economic Security Act*, p. 525.

Table 4. Features and Provisions of UI and ADC, compared

	UI	ADC
Level of governmental administration	Joint national-state	Joint national-state
Contributory v. noncontributory	Contributions by employers; employee contributions optional by state	Noncontributory
Financing arrangement	Tax on employers held by national government	Grant-in-aid, 1:2 ratio
Eligibility determined by	States	States
Merit system	No	No
Annual appropriation for national administration of program, in millions of dollars	49	25

cretion to the individual states for the determination of eligibility standards and benefit rates.

Consequently, compared with the programs for elderly Americans, the two programs for the non-elderly were less distinct from each other in their implications for citizenship. Unlike OAI, the tax-offset plan for UI was infused neither with the language of rights for individuals nor of national standards of citizenship. States were left to define the ideology of their own programs. Similarly, the creation of ADC had nothing to do with individual rights but was grounded instead in ascriptive notions about the appropriate roles of mothers in raising children to be good citizens.

The different politics surrounding the enactment of the two programs had made, however, for distinct financing and administrative arrangements. Though the more centralized versions of UI had been defeated, the final plan still incorporated a federal tax and national control over distribution of funds to states. By contrast, ADC policymakers had allowed state and local officials substantial administrative autonomy. The political forces that had lost the battle for more national versions of UI were still ready to fight, whereas the loss of administrative authority for ADC had dealt a devastating blow to what Robyn Muncy terms "the child welfare dominion." [97] The significance of these differences would only become evident in the course of their implementation.

[97] Robyn Muncy, *Creating a Female Dominion in American Reform, 1890–1935* (New York: Oxford University Press, 1991), pp. 153–54.

CHAPTER SIX

The Development and Implementation of Unemployment Insurance and Aid to Dependent Children

Women as a class, because of marriage and motherhood, can expect to have even more breaks than men have in their employment record and consequent reduction in benefits. Married women must lose time because of the birth and care of children. Moreover, they are apt to lose jobs in depression periods because of unfair discrimination against them on the part of many forces.

> —Mary Anderson, Director, Women's Bureau,
> U.S. Department of Labor, December 1935

Although UI and ADC emerged from the policymaking process in 1935 on fairly equal ground, the status of the two programs diverged sharply during their subsequent development and early implementation. ADC declined in stature from the fairly respectable position held by mothers' pensions, and the originally precarious UI program was fortified and elevated. The coverage of each policy became more rigidly specified, and the experience of the recipients became increasingly distinct. Administrators lifted UI, which had begun with barely a foothold, to the secure status of "insurance," where it became regarded as an earned "right" for white men in particular. ADC became stigmatized as it grew to resemble the sort of "relief" programs its framers had tried to avoid, wherein "standards" had no meaning other than the restrictive criteria through which applicants for assistance were denied. In time, the two programs evolved to have distinct consequences for the citizenship of men and women.

The Early Implementation of UI

During the early years of UI's implementation, national administrators, reform-minded intellectuals, and labor representatives sought to fortify the "first line of defense" for eligible beneficiaries of the program, mostly men.

They worked toward quick and uniform program implementation and national program standards. State-level administrators, meanwhile, developed restrictive measures to limit beneficiaries to a narrow group of long-
term, full-time employees. Women applicants thus became more likely to
be considered ineligible for reasons directly or indirectly related to gender
roles.

Speedy Implementation and National Uniformity

The design of UI gave states strong incentives to implement the program
quickly. The law required all employers, beginning in 1936, to pay a 3 percent tax on salaries and wages to the federal government, but only those
states with their own UI laws approved before January 1, 1937 would be
allowed to recoup those moneys. States that neglected to develop acceptable laws would forfeit entirely the opportunity to gain access to the funds,
and the unemployed in those states would receive no benefits.[1] This feature
alone prompted swift adoption.

Just as the Committee on Economic Security had paid the greatest attention to UI in the planning stages, so too did the SSB and its staff, many
of whom had been involved in the policy's formation, devote greater attention to its implementation, urging widespread application and liberalization.[2] During 1936, the board announced that states which failed to adopt
acceptable programs by the end of the year would lose the 90 percent re-
fund on the payroll tax for the year. Then, in November, two significant
events spurred the states to action: first, Roosevelt was reelected by a landslide, and second, the New York Court of Appeals upheld the state's UI
law.[3] Immediately, eighteen more state legislatures took the SSB's threat seriously and passed UI laws, bringing the total number to thirty-six by the
end of the year.[4] After the Supreme Court held the Social Security Act to

---

[1] Eveline M. Burns, *Toward Social Security* (New York: Whittlesey House, 1936), pp. 55–
56; John G. Turnbull, C. Arthur Williams, Jr., and Earl F. Cheit, eds., *Economic and Social
Security*, 3d ed. (New York: Ronald, 1967), p. 248. States had to send all funds collected for
UI to the federal government, where they were centralized and safeguarded in a trust fund by
the secretary of the treasury. The individual states, however, maintained the "title" to their
own moneys within the larger fund. States with approved laws would recoup 90 percent of
the contributions from employers within their boundaries; the federal government would retain 10 percent to cover administrative costs.

[2] For example, Arthur Altmeyer, Wilbur Cohen, and Thomas Eliot were involved in both
the formation and implementation of UI; see Edward D. Berkowitz, *Mr. Social Security: The
Life of Wilbur Cohen* (Lawrence: University Press of Kansas, 1995).

[3] Charles McKinley and Robert W. Frase, *Launching Social Security: A Capture-and-
Record Account, 1935–1937* (Madison: University of Wisconsin Press, 1970), p. 250; Edwin
E. Witte, "Development of Unemployment Compensation," *Yale Law Journal* 1 (December
1945): 33.

[4] McKinley and Frase, *Launching Social Security*, p. 250; Paul H. Douglas, *Social Security
in the United States*, 2d ed. (New York: Whittlesey House, 1939), pp. 335–36, Bryce M.
Stewart, *Planning and Administration of Unemployment Compensation in the United States*
(New York: Industrial Relations Counselors, 1938), p. 28. Edwin Amenta and his coauthors

be constitutional in May 1937, the two laggard states, Illinois and Missouri, finally enacted acceptable laws.[5]

The SSB also goaded states to establish its preferred type of UI laws. The Bureau of Unemployment Compensation of the SSB distributed drafts of model legislation and actively assisted states in steering such bills toward passage.[6] In some states, serious battles ensued over the choice between the two basic types of unemployment compensation, with employers promoting individual plant reserves and such groups as organized labor, the League of Women Voters, and the Association for Social Security advocating pooled funds that socialized the risk of unemployment.[7] Although the SSB distributed model bills for both types of system, the staff conveyed to governors their preference for "pooled funds." Anxious to pass a bill that would meet with the SSB's approval, forty-four states overwhelmingly enacted pooled-funds systems, and only six adopted the plant-reserve model—a clear victory for proponents of more liberal unemployment compensation.[8] UI began to acquire a fairly uniform character from state to state.

The board's energetic promotion of speedy and uniform development contrasted with its hands-off approach to public assistance programs initiated by the states. As noted in an internal SSB memo:

> In dealing with unemployment compensation, it was assumed that the Board looked forward toward exercising a large measure of control. In the case of Public Assistance, *per contra*, it is assumed that the desire is to establish a real federal-aid activity, in which the states, carrying on activities in which there is less need for uniformity than in the case of unemployment compensation, and with which they have already had considerable experience, are to be made primarily responsible.[9]

The SSB justified these different postures on the grounds that all states except Wisconsin were inexperienced in the implementation of unemployment compensation, whereas a majority had some experience with ADC's predecessor, mothers' pensions.

---

offer insightful and nuanced analysis of the determinants of the timing of the adoption of UI at the state level, but they underestimate the role of what they themselves term "the gun of the federal government"; see Edwin Amenta et al., "The Political Origins of Unemployment Insurance in Five American States," *Studies in American Political Development* 2 (1987): 179.

[5] Witte, "Development of Unemployment Compensation," p. 34.

[6] McKinley and Frase, *Launching Social Security*, pp. 243–51; Witte, "Development of Unemployment Compensation," p. 34.

[7] Douglas, *Social Security in the United States*, pp. 308–10, 400; Burns, *Toward Social Security*, pp. 69–70.

[8] Witte, "Development of Unemployment Compensation," pp. 33–34; Douglas, *Social Security in the United States*, pp. 399–400. Once bills were enacted, the SSB issued specific guidelines on administrative apparatus and budgeting; see McKinley and Frase, *Launching Social Security*, pp. 263–71, 284–94.

[9] McKinley and Frase, *Launching Social Security*, p. 263.

Other distinct features of the two policies also fostered superior development for UI compared to ADC. First, the newness of UI functioned to its advantage in the adoption of the merit system for personnel practices because state legislators were more likely to approve such developments for agencies just being created than for preexisting agencies with established personnel practices and ties to vested interests. Thus, state-level agencies administering UI embraced merit principles for personnel much more quickly than the public assistance agencies: by January 1939, thirty-nine UI agencies had established merit systems compared with only nineteen public assistance agencies. Second, the Social Security Act contained greater specificity regarding the definition of benefit amounts for UI than for ADC, allowing less discretion to the states for determining the former. Third, and most important, UI rested on the foundation of a mandatory, uniform, national tax of employers; ADC depended on state legislators for funding. These financial arrangements gave states an unambiguous incentive to establish UI programs, compared with the matching-grant formula for ADC, which required challenging fiscal decisions about how to raise two dollars in revenue for every dollar from the federal government.[10]

In short, both UI's design and fervent advocacy led to the program's being implemented quickly, quite uniformly, and according to the more liberal of the proposed models. These early efforts were, however, only the first phase of what evolved into a long battle to elevate the program.

Elevating Unemployment Insurance

Once UI programs were in place, administrators continued to seek improvements, urging policymakers to replace the national-state arrangements with fully national administrative authority or, at least, to enact national program standards.[11] In 1939, when the SSB focused predominantly on fortifying OAI, it recommended few major changes for UI other than a mandatory requirement for states to adopt merit systems, which Congress approved, and the inclusion of agricultural and domestic workers, which it did not.[12] But by 1941, the SSB had become, as stated by Altmeyer, "disillusioned regarding the operation of the federal-state system."[13] Just as the

---

[10] Arthur J. Altmeyer, *The Formative Years of Social Security* (Madison: University of Wisconsin Press, 1968), pp. 84–85.

[11] On advocacy by national administrators, see McKinley and Frase, *Launching Social Security*, pp. 263, 271, 284–85, and 267 n. 25. Gerhard Ritter observed a comparable phenomenon in Germany, where federalism initially slowed the development of unemployment insurance, but nationally organized trade unions succeeded in winning higher and more uniform national standards; see Gerhard A. Ritter, *Social Welfare in Germany and Britain: Origins and Development* (New York: Berg, 1986), p. 130.

[12] Altmeyer, *Formative Years*, pp. 103–4; Public Law 379, *Social Security Act Amendments of 1939*, title III.

[13] Altmeyer, *Formative Years*, p. 124.

SSB acted to assert bureaucratic control over the development of OAI during its early years, it also attempted to gain dominance over UI, the program in the Social Security Act that was next most permeable to national influence.[14] Meanwhile, the same intellectual reformers and forces in organized labor that had been disappointed by the federal-state arrangements in the 1935 legislation continued to agitate for a more nationalized program.[15]

At the very least, the SSB and associated groups and individuals hoped to establish a minimum national rate for benefits. Against the wishes of the Women's Trade Union League and other labor representatives, Congress had set no such rate in the original legislation.[16] Officials in the Women's Bureau of the Department of Labor complained that the wage-related benefits structure for UI would especially disadvantage women because of their low status on the wage scale.[17] In fact, the statute provided states with an incentive to keep benefit rates low. Employers could obtain a credit against the UI tax based on their "compensation experience," meaning the relationship between benefits paid out and contributions paid in.[18] Within a decade, forty-five states had adopted these "experience-rating provisions," which effectively reintroduced interstate competition into the system by provoking states to try to keep up with each other in lowering employers' UI taxes to provide a favorable business climate.[19] In resistance to such developments, both the AFL and the CIO began to promote the enactment of national benefit standards and restrictions on experience ratings, and members of Congress introduced bills to that end.[20]

Shortly after the United States entered World War II, the Labor Division of the Office of Production Management recommended to Roosevelt that he order two wartime changes in the handling of unemployment-related programs. The president complied with the first suggestion, notifying all governors by telegram that the state-run public employment offices established in the 1933 Wagner-Peyser Act would be controlled instead by the federal government to facilitate national defense. The other recommendation, that UI be administered by the national government for the duration,

---

[14] Brian Balogh, "Securing Support: The Emergence of the Social Security Board as a Political Actor, 1935–1939," in *Federal Social Policy*, ed. Donald T. Critchlow and Ellis W. Hawley (University Park: Pennsylvania State University, 1988), pp. 55–78.

[15] Katherine Pollak Ellickson, "Labor's Demand for Real Employment Security," *Yale Law Journal* 55 (December 1945): 253–63.

[16] House Committee on Ways and Means, *Economic Security Act: Hearings before the Committee on Ways and Means*, 74th Cong., 1st sess., February 7, 1935, p. 793.

[17] Department of Labor, Women's Bureau, "Women Workers and the Social Security Program," address by Mary Anderson before the Indianapolis Council of Women, January 7, 1936, microfilm 16:0155, p. 18, LMDC.

[18] "Twenty Years of Unemployment Insurance in the U.S.A., 1935–1955," *Employment Security Review* 22 (August 1955): 32–33; Altmeyer, *Formative Years*, p. 85.

[19] Ellickson, "Labor's Demand," pp. 255–56.

[20] Witte, "Development of Unemployment Compensation," pp. 46–47.

Roosevelt rejected. Instead, he assured the states that UI would remain under state auspices.[21]

Meanwhile, however, Chairman Altmeyer and others working for the SSB had become increasingly convinced that as a predominantly state-level system, UI was insufficient to handle the widespread unemployment they expected after the war. Numerous SSB staff reports elaborated the reasons why a fully national system, or at least one with national standards, would be preferable.[22] The SSB began to communicate such ideas to Roosevelt. Also, William Green, president of the AFL, notified the president that his organization supported nationalization of UI.[23] In his 1942 budget message to Congress, Roosevelt recommended the "liberalization and expansion of unemployment compensation in a uniform national system."[24]

Demands for federalization intensified in 1943, when the National Resources Planning Board (NRPB), in its proposal for policies to accommodate the postwar era, called for "replacement of present Federal-State system by a wholly Federal administrative organization and a single national fund."[25] The NRPB report also called for "liberalization" of the current program, meaning the expansion of benefits both in amounts and duration.[26] Later in the year, the Wagner-Murray-Dingell Bill, which would have instituted a national unemployment insurance system, was introduced in Congress with the support of organized labor. Roosevelt had become more preoccupied with the war than with domestic policies at this stage, however, and he never offered his support for the bill. Two years passed without any hearings.[27]

In 1945, the Wagner-Murray-Dingell Bill was introduced again and sup-

---

[21] Ibid., p. 48. On the United States Employment Services, see Desmond King, *Actively Seeking Work? The Politics of Unemployment and Welfare Policy in the United States and Britain* (Chicago: University of Chicago Press, 1995).

[22] See all contents of SSB, Records of the Executive Director, 1941–48, Subject Files, 1935–40, box 283, file 500, "Federalization of UI"; also box 285, file 520, "January 1941–43," and "December 1941 . . . Federalization"; all in RG 47, NA; and "SSB, 1941" and "SSB, 1943–45" files, OF 1710, box 2, FDR.

[23] Letter, William Green to Franklin D. Roosevelt, October 26, 1942, "SSB, 1942" file, ibid.

[24] Altmeyer, *Formative Years*, pp. 132–37; Witte, "Development of Unemployment Compensation," pp. 48–49; memorandum, A. J. Altmeyer to the President, "Material on Social Security for Inclusion in Annual Message to Congress," December 29, 1942, "Social Security" file, PSF, box 165, FDR.

[25] National Resources Planning Board, "National Resources Development, Report for 1943," p. 17, ibid.

[26] William Haber and Merrill G. Murray, *Unemployment Insurance in the American Economy* (Homewood, Ill.: Irwin, 1966), p. 439; Linda R. Wolf Jones, *Eveline M. Burns and the American Social Security System, 1935–1960* (New York: Garland, 1991), pp. 97–109.

[27] Meanwhile, some of the proposals in the NRPB report were narrowed in application to returning veterans and were incorporated in the Servicemen's Readjustment Act of 1944, otherwise known as the G.I. Bill of Rights. The law left the structure of UI intact but permitted veterans twenty dollars per week for up to fifty-two weeks of unemployment, in place of a benefit level that varied from state to state and lasted for twenty-six weeks or less; see Ellickson, "Labor's Demand," p. 255; and Altmeyer, *Formative Years*, pp. 148–49.

ported by the SSB and organized labor, but it faced opposition from the Interstate Conference of Employment Security Agencies and the Council of State Governments.[28] President Truman never offered support for the bill or for any other proposal for a straight national system of unemployment insurance.[29] From the 1950s through the 1970s, critics continued to assail the federal-state system for its inadequacies in promoting employment stability, its tendency to spur rather than to ameliorate interstate competition, and its inability to provide what they considered to be adequate benefits. All amendments to the system, however, left the decentralized structure in place.[30]

Yet, even as proponents of nationalization and national standards failed to meet their stated goals over the course of their long struggle, they still succeeded in elevating the program in most states and in changing the character of the policy until it approximated, for its male beneficiaries, a national right of citizenship. From the 1940s onward, states responded to pressure by changing benefit levels. Rather than raising minimum levels to fortify UI for those who were least well off, however, most states were willing to bend only on the main goal articulated by labor unions: improving the maximum benefit levels.[31] The proponents of such changes argued that "primary beneficiaries" or "breadwinners" needed proportionately higher benefits.[32]

Because UI benefit rates were structured to correspond to previous income, this "liberalization" meant that states began to award higher and more extensive and nationally uniform benefits to workers on the upper end of the wage scale, mostly white men. Meanwhile, states took little action to raise the lowest benefits, those for workers at the bottom of the wage scale, disproportionately women and nonwhite men. The maximum weekly benefit, which had been $15 per week in most states in 1941, was raised by 1945 to $20 in 17 states and even more in another 27 states. The number of states raising the maximum weekly benefit surpassed the number increasing the minimum weekly benefit, which still averaged around

---

[28] Haber and Murray, *Unemployment Insurance in the American Economy*, p. 440; Altmeyer, *Formative Years*, p. 146; Report of the Conference Workshop of Organized Labor on Employment Security, *Labor Looks at Unemployment Insurance* (Chicago: University of Chicago Press, 1946), pp. 25–26.

[29] Altmeyer, *Formative Years*, p. 161.

[30] Edward Harpham, "Federalism, Keynesianism, and the Transformation of the Unemployment Insurance System in the United States," in *Nationalizing Social Security in Europe and America*, ed. Douglas E. Ashford and E. W. Kelley (Greenwich, Conn.: JAI, 1986), pp. 162–78.

[31] Witte, "Development of Unemployment Compensation," pp. 39–40; Joseph M. Becker, "Twenty-Five Years of Unemployment Insurance," *Political Science Quarterly* 25 (December 1960): 489, 498.

[32] Joseph M. Becker, "The Adequacy of Benefits in Unemployment Insurance," in *In Aid of the Unemployed*, ed. Joseph M. Becker (Baltimore: Johns Hopkins Press, 1965), pp. 94–96.

$5 in the median state and $7 for the median worker in any state.[33] In 1949 alone, 24 states acted to increase the maximum benefit levels, but only 9 elevated the minimum benefit levels.[34] At the same time, state governments developed restrictive qualifications that made access all the more difficult for women to attain.

Women Need Not Apply: States Tighten Access

Ever cautious lest they invent an unemployment insurance program that mirrored "relief," CES staff had articulated the goal and limits of their program with care: "Unemployment compensation cannot protect the insured population against the entire risk of unemployment. It must be considered only as the first line of defense. . . . Unemployment compensation must then be limited by strict definition to those persons who are ordinarily employed with a fair degree of regularity. Efforts to extend an unemployment insurance scheme beyond these proper limits have invariably converted it into a relief measure and brought it into disrepute." [35] Soon after the Social Security Act had became law, Mary Anderson, from the Women's Bureau, expressed concern about the use of such principles to guide state-level policy development. She argued that women in particular would be adversely affected because "marriage and motherhood" necessitated that they work for pay on a more intermittent basis than men.[36] As states developed eligibility criteria for UI, the concerns articulated by Anderson in 1935 became realized through an enduring set of measures that acted to exclude women from benefits.

Various factors compelled state officials to put limits on access to benefits. During the early 1940s, judges and administrators took wartime labor shortages into account in defining new limitations on eligibility.[37] During recessions such as those in 1948–49 and 1953–54, many states' UI funds proved insufficient to meet demands for benefits, so officials limited access.[38] The dynamics of interstate economic competition also prompted policymakers to restrict access to ensure a ready and flexible work force.

[33] SSA, *Social Security Yearbook, 1945* (Washington, D.C.: Social Security Administration, 1945), pp. 116–19.
[34] SSB, "Trends in Unemployment Insurance Coverage and Benefit Legislation," by Ruth Reticker, *Social Security Bulletin* 12 (December 1949): 11.
[35] SSB, *Social Security in America: The Factual Background of the Social Security Act as Summarized from Staff Reports to the Committee on Economic Security* (Washington, D.C.: GPO, 1937), pp. 11–12.
[36] Department of Labor, Women's Bureau, "Old Age Security Legislation from the Viewpoint of Women," speech by Mary Anderson before District of Columbia League of Women Voters, December 1935, microfilm 16:0133, LMDC.
[37] SSB, "Trends in Disqualification from Benefits under State Unemployment Compensation Laws," by Ewan Clague and Ruth Reticker, *Social Security Bulletin* 7 (January 1944): 12.
[38] Ibid., pp. 12–23; Harpham, "Unemployment Insurance in the United States," p. 161; Haber and Murray, *Unemployment Insurance in the American Economy*, p. 330.

State officials devised various means of testing for one of the recommended prerequisites for UI eligibility: "attachment to the labor force." Rather than granting UI benefits to any person who was not able to find a job, they typically excluded from coverage those who had never been employed, those who had not been employed recently, and those who had been employed in covered employment only part time and for wages totaling less than a qualifying amount. In 1939, fifteen states measured earnings qualifications by using a flat minimum rate, with levels that ranged from $100 to $300 dollars per year.[39] Other states combined earnings criteria with requirements of participation in the work force for a certain number of weeks in a given period.[40] States also gradually raised the minimum wage levels required of the unemployed to qualify for benefits. The median qualifying amount for UI in all states increased from below $150 in annual earnings in 1940 to $250 in 1955.[41]

These wage eligibility levels excluded women workers from UI disproportionately: the 1940 Census showed that 18 percent of experienced female employees (not including unpaid workers) made less than $199 during 1939, in contrast to 8.8 percent of experienced male workers. Another 17.6 percent of female workers brought in wages between $200 to $399, whereas only 12.5 percent of male employees made such low wages.[42]

States also made UI off limits to women by restricting access to persons deemed "available for work." To demonstrate this quality, one had to be deemed physically and mentally capable of work, registered at the appropriate public employment office, considered to be actively seeking work, and willing to accept any "suitable job" offered so long as it would not present a risk to health, safety, or morals.[43] State administrators exercised discretion as to which cases satisfied those criteria. As observed by Lewis Meriam, "The wide measure of discretion vested in the administrative agency and the extent to which results depend on the integrity, objectivity, judgment, and initiative of the employees of that agency are striking features of this system of insurance."[44] But protections built into the law restrained administrators' discretionary powers over most male workers.

---

[39] SSB, *Social Security Yearbook, 1939* (Washington, D.C.: Social Security Board, 1939), pp. 104–5.

[40] Turnbull, Williams, and Cheit, *Economic and Social Security*, pp. 250–52; Haber and Murray, *Unemployment Insurance in the American Economy*, pp. 113–14. For a description and tabular summary of provisions in state laws determining eligibility for UI in 1941 and 1945, see *Social Security Yearbook, 1945*, pp. 122, 128–29.

[41] "Twenty Years of Unemployment Insurance," pp. 35–36.

[42] Bureau of the Census, *U.S. Census, 1940: The Labor Force* (Washington, D.C.: GPO, 1940), p. 3, table I and p. 12, table VII.

[43] Turnbull, Williams, and Cheit, *Economic and Social Security*, pp. 252–54; Mimi Abramovitz, *Regulating the Lives of Women: Social Welfare Policy from Colonial Times to the Present* (Boston: South End Press, 1989), pp. 293–94.

[44] Lewis Meriam, *Relief and Social Security* (Washington, D.C.: Brookings, 1946), pp. 213–14.

The federal UI statute set apart some exceptional circumstances under which a person could refuse a job and still be considered by any state to be "available for work" and thus eligible for UI. Those special protections, called the "labor standards" provisions, read as follows:

> Compensation shall not be denied in such State to any otherwise eligible individual for refusing to accept new work under any of the following conditions:
>   (A) If the position offered is vacant due directly to a strike, lockout, or other labor dispute;
>   (B) if the wages, hours, or other conditions of the work offered are substantially less favorable to the individual than those prevailing for similar work in the locality;
>   (C) if as a condition of being employed the individual would be required to join a company union or to resign from or refrain from joining any bona fide labor organization.[45]

Clauses A and C reflected the priority given by New Deal policymakers to labor unions, which remained primarily the domain of white, male workers. States interpreted clause B to mean that one would be permitted to refuse a job and still receive benefits if the position was not commensurate with one's skills, experience, and previous pay; if the work place was located too far away; or if the working conditions were unreasonable.[46] This provision protected the status of skilled workers, also predominantly white and male. The large portions of the female labor force, as well as most nonwhite men, already worked in unskilled, nonunionized low-wage occupations and thus gained little from the labor standards provisions.

The national law was designed to uphold the autonomy of labor organizations and to protect the status of skilled workers but it was silent about familial responsibilities outside of the work place. Most states ignored the needs of women to balance domestic and child care responsibilities with paid work. In many states, the availability rule was interpreted to mean that a person was available for full-time work at normal working hours. But women often sought part-time work or shifts during particular times of the day in order to accommodate other responsibilities at home and to arrange child care for their children.[47]

When women in those circumstances sought unemployment benefits, they were often greeted with skepticism. As revealed by a 1940 review of cases involving persons who refused full-time job offers for "domestic" reasons, "If claimant is prevented from accepting full-time work because

[45] Public Law 271, 74th Cong., 1st sess. (August 14, 1935), *Social Security Act of 1935,* title IX, sec. 903 (a)(5).
[46] These provisions are discussed at length in SSB, *Social Security Yearbook, 1940* (Washington, D.C.: Social Security Board, 1940), pp. 41–44.
[47] SSB, "Trends in Disqualification," pp. 18–21.

of domestic circumstances, the question whether claimant is available for work . . . depends upon the views of particular jurisdictions."[48] In other words, women in such instances became subject to parochial norms. In a Delaware case involving a woman who left her job working on a night shift because she could no longer find anyone to take care of her small child, an administrator determined that she had indeed left her job "with good cause" and was truly "available for work." When the employer appealed the case to a commission, it affirmed the earlier decision, declaring, "Faced with the alternative of working at night while her child lay home unattended and completely at the mercy of such dangers as sudden sickness, fire, and the like, or of giving up her job and properly caring for the child, we think the normal parent would choose the latter course."[49]

More typically, however, officials placed priority on the needs of employers to have work done at night during times of peak production and considered the unemployment of women for domestic reasons to be "voluntary," meaning that they had shown themselves to be "unavailable for work." This was the decision of a commissioner in Connecticut in ruling on the case of a mother of two children, aged four and nine, who refused work on the evening and nighttime shifts in an arms plant, despite the fact that she persisted in seeking work during daytime hours. Similarly, a judge in South Carolina determined that a woman who quit work on the night shift, after she lost the help of a relative who had cared for her four young children, was not eligible for UI. He reasoned that the law was not intended to remedy changes in workers' personal circumstances.[50] In short, the willingness of states to acknowledge how women's domestic responsibilities influenced their availability for work varied from place to place, subject to the labor market demands, social norms, and political prerogatives—legislative, judicial, and administrative—of particular states.

States gradually adopted formal measures to deny benefits to women in cases when they left jobs because of domestic responsibilities. These emerged as part of a growing tendency to insist that the cause for unemployment must lie exclusively with the employer and be unrelated to personal "voluntary" reasons on the part of the employee. States increasingly defined "domestic quits," instances in which women left work to assume familial obligations such as pregnancy and childbirth or marital obligations, as grounds to disqualify them from UI benefits.[51] As shown by Table 5,

[48] SSB, *Social Security Yearbook, 1940*, p. 38, also 46.

[49] Benefit Series 7778, Delaware R., vol. 6, no. 2, as quoted in SSB, "Trends in Disqualification," p. 19.

[50] Ibid., pp. 18–19; Gladys Harrison et al., "Eligibility and Disqualification for Benefits," *Yale Law Journal* 55 (December 1945): 120.

[51] See sections titled "Employment Security" or "Unemployment Insurance" in annual editions of Social Security Board/Administration, *Social Security Yearbook* (Washington, D.C.: Social Security Board/Administration).

Table 5. Availability and disqualification provisions: special provisions in State UI laws affecting women, December 31, 1941 and 1945

State	Provision as of Dec. 31, 1941			Provision as of Dec. 31, 1945		
	If unemployment is due to pregnancy	If claimant quit because of marital obligations*	Period of disqualification**	If unemployment is due to pregnancy	If claimant quit because of marital obligations*	Period of disqualification**
Alabama				Unavailable		Not less than 3 months before and after
Alaska				Unavailable		2 months before and 1 after
Connecticut	Disqualified		Not less than 2 months before and after	Disqualified		Not less than 2 months before and after
Hawaii				Unavailable	Unavailable	2 months before and after
Indiana		Disqualified	Duration	Unavailable	Disqualified	Duration
Iowa		Disqualified	Duration		Disqualified	Duration
Maryland				Unavailable		Not less than 2 months before and after
Massachusetts	Unavailable		Not less than 2 weeks before and after	Unavailable		Not less than 4 weeks before and after
Michigan		Disqualified	3–5 weeks	Disqualified	Disqualified	Duration
Minnesota		Disqualified	Duration in benefit year	Disqualified	Disqualified	Duration
Montana		Disqualified	Duration		Disqualified	Duration

Nebraska		Disqualified	Duration	Unavailable	Disqualified	Not less than 12 weeks before and 4 after
New Hampshire				Unavailable		Not more than 8 weeks before and after
Nevada		Disqualified	Duration		Disqualified	Duration
North Carolina				Unavailable		3 months before and after
Ohio		Disqualified	Duration		Disqualified	Duration
Oklahoma		Unavailable	Duration		Unavailable	Duration
Oregon	Unavailable	Unavailable	Duration	Unavailable	Unavailable	Duration
South Dakota		Disqualified		Disqualified	Disqualified	
Utah	Disqualified	Disqualified	Not less than 6 weeks before and 6 after	Disqualified	Disqualified	Not less than 6 weeks before and 6 after
Washington	Disqualified	Disqualified	Duration	Unavailable	Disqualified	Duration
West Virginia		Disqualified		Disqualified		Duration
Wisconsin		Disqualified	Duration		Disqualified	Duration
Wyoming		Disqualified	Duration		Disqualified	Duration

Source: Social Security Board, *Social Security Yearbook, 1945* (Washington, D.C.: Social Security Board, 1945), p. 126.

* Ordinarily the disqualification or unavailability applies if the claimant left work *voluntarily* to marry; in Ohio (1945) if she quit because of marital obligations; in Nebraska, Nevada, and North Dakota (1941) if employment was discontinued because of marriage; in Minnesota (1941) and Wisconsin, if separated pursuant to an employer's rule not to employ married women, unless she proves she is available for work, able to work, and willing to accept work; in Michigan (1941) only if she left work to move with her husband and family to another locality.

** The period of disqualification (or unavailability) for leaving for marital reasons is for the duration of the unemployment. "Before and after" periods are in relation to the date of childbirth; in New Hampshire unavailability may be terminated if worker earns wages of $2 or more than the weekly benefit amount in a week.

special disqualification rules pertaining to women took two forms: mater-
nity-related disqualifications and marital-obligation disqualifications.

First, in implementing UI, states developed a patchwork of restrictions
denying benefits to women who left work to bear a child. In 1941, five
states denied UI benefits to women who left work because of pregnancy;
the number grew to eighteen by 1945. In 1949, the Women's Bureau and
the WTUL urged Congress to amend the Social Security Act to include maternity benefits for working women.[52] The measure failed, and the number
of states excluding pregnant women from UI benefits continued to grow,
reaching thirty-seven by 1966.[53] States generally denied benefits during a
specified period of weeks before and after childbirth during which women
were to be considered "disqualified" or "unavailable for work."[54]

Second, states established restrictions on UI eligibility for cases of "marital quits." Initially, in 1940, women who quit their jobs because their husbands found employment in another locality were regarded to have a
"good cause for leaving" and were considered eligible for UI. For instance,
in 1944 a Pennsylvania court ruled that a woman had "good cause" for
leaving her job to join her husband, who was a soldier, in another community. The judge reasoned, "It is difficult to conceive of a cause more im-
pelling, more humanly justifiable, than the impulse which induces a devoted wife to spend with a husband, who is a member of the Armed Forces
in time of war, what may prove to be the last days they shall ever have together on earth."[55] Yet benefits were generally denied to husbands who left
their jobs when their wives' jobs necessitated the relocation of the household. In such cases, the different treatment of men and women was based
on the "theory that it is for the husband and not for the wife to determine
the marital domicile."[56] Moreover, by 1945, seventeen states had adopted
special restrictions denying benefits to women who left for "marital obligations." Several states, in fact, ruled that women who had been disqualified
for such reasons would remain ineligible until they had been reemployed
for a specific period.

Hence, as national administrators and labor organizations focused on
liberalizing the level and duration of benefits paid to the most well-off

---

[52] See testimony in favor of the amendment submitted to House Ways and Means Committee by Frieda S. Miller, Department of Labor, Women's Bureau, April 15, 1949, in WTUL
papers, LMDC; original at Schlesinger Library, Radcliffe College.

[53] Haber and Murray, *Unemployment Insurance in the American Economy*, pp. 118–19.

[54] The period of disqualification ranged from four weeks before and after childbirth (Massachusetts) to three months before and after childbirth (Alabama and North Carolina); see
SSB, *Social Security Yearbook, 1945*, pp. 125–27.

[55] Teicher Unemployment Comp. Case, 154 Pa. Super. 250, 35 A. (2d) 739 (1944), quoted
in Harrison et al., "Eligibility and Disqualification," p. 159.

[56] SSB, *Social Security Yearbook, 1940*, pp. 54–55.

workers, states were making access particularly difficult for women workers. Women had equal access to UI if they worked in the same types of full-time jobs as men and if they lost their jobs for reasons that could equally pertain to men. They were denied when their need for compensation stemmed from duties particular to their gender role in the domestic sphere. If women tried, unsuccessfully, to enter the labor market after years of work as homemakers or after the birth of a child, or to find part-time work in order to balance wage earning with care of children, they were routinely denied in most states. If a woman left her job to bear a child or to assume domestic responsibilities, most states would define her reasons for quitting as "personal" and therefore as lacking justification for wage compensation. These restrictions carried the assumptions that wage earning was not a necessity for women and that financial burdens related to maintaining the domestic sphere and caring for children lay beyond the responsibility of society at large or of individual employers. Rather, UI as implemented by the majority of states depended on family units headed by male breadwinners to channel financial support to women, children, and others outside the labor market.

More than thirty years after Mary Anderson expressed her concerns about how women would fare under state-defined eligibility rules for UI, William Haber and Merrill G. Murray observed that women workers were still viewed as a "suspect class" when they applied for benefits: "Women who are 'secondary workers,' in the sense that they do not bring the principal income into the home, are especially suspect. It is generally felt that most married women work only to supplement the family income in order to have a higher standard of living. Women move in and out of the labor market more than men, and a high proportion work on part-time jobs. These two facts are pointed to as evidence that women are less firmly attached to the labor market and their 'right' to collect is therefore doubtful."[57] The restrictions that disadvantaged women had been established early in the implementation of UI, and they endured for decades.

The Exalted but Restricted Ranks of the Insured Unemployed

Thus in the course of its early administration, UI acquired a janus-faced character, attributable in part to the manner in which the policy had been designed and in part to the nature of political demands. For men, by virtue of their occupational status and related wage levels, the policy appeared to be national in scope, uniformity, and administration; for women, it seemed to be administered entirely at the state-level, where they encountered the

[57] Haber and Murray, *Unemployment Insurance in the American Economy*, p. 271.

labyrinth of eligibility rules which made their access to benefits so difficult to achieve.

In creating UI, the members of the CES and its staff had been determined to invent a policy distinct from the European need-based models that specified benefits according to tradition-bound conceptions of sex and marital status. These New Deal liberals had fashioned a policy that related purely to work-force participation, avoiding the benefits to wives that other nations had established on the rationale that married women were "doing unpaid work in the home." [58] If UI had retained solely this liberal individualistic and gender-blind identity, women would have been largely excluded because three-quarters did not participate in the paid work force in the 1930s, but at least employed women would have had access to benefits equal to men's, even if the benefits were lower in accord with their wages. And as women increased their numbers in the work force over the decades, they would have gained increased access to benefits.

But besides being molded by the New Deal liberals with their ostensibly gender-neutral vision, UI was also shaped by the gender-particular ideas of traditional and parochial interests at the state level. State legislatures, bureaucrats, and judges across the land—albeit with a nod from national government administrators, wringing their hands over "casual workers"— created particular obstacles to women seeking UI. State officials viewed women as men's dependents, so they turned women workers away from UI benefits, assuming that male breadwinners would provide. Meanwhile, being less well situated than national government to expand the coverage of social benefits, only three American states—Alaska, Arizona, and Nevada—and the District of Columbia acted to establish dependents' benefits for wives of unemployed men.[59] The two forms of governance thus combined to make UI a fairly secure new social right for men as citizens of the nation but a highly inaccessible program for women.

The Early Implementation of ADC

Although reformers hoped that ADC would expand upon the best aspects of mothers' pensions while refining other features, in the first few years of its development, it evolved slowly and unevenly and began to be stigmatized. Having a particularly decentralized design and lacking a popular base of support, ADC steadily fell into a permanent state of disrepute.

---

[58] SSB, "Dependents in Social Security Systems of Great Britain, New Zealand, Australia, and Canada," by Elva Marquard, *Social Security Bulletin* 11 (September 1948): 9.

[59] SSB, "Dependents' Allowances under State Unemployment Insurance Laws," by Olga S. Halsey, *Social Security Bulletin* 14 (February 1951): 4.

Slow and Uneven Implementation

By some indicators, ADC seemed to be off to a fairly promising start in its first two years. Although the program lagged behind UI, which had been adopted in all states by the end of 1937, and OAA, which had been established in all states but Virginia, nonetheless, forty states had enacted ADC laws and received SSB approval.[60] As the Children's Bureau officials had hoped, the old-style poor-relief system was abruptly replaced in some states by a coordinated, professionally administered system of public welfare.[61] Nationally, the number of beneficiaries expanded from some three hundred thousand under mothers' pensions in 1934 to more than seven hundred thousand covered by ADC in 1939.[62] As shown by Table 6, some states began to assist more than twice as many families through ADC than had been covered previously.[63] Mothers' pensions had never been enacted in most of the southern states, and program implementation in states in other regions had been spotty. Only the incentive of aid from the national government prompted these states to develop programs across all localities.

A closer examination, however, shows the beginnings of ADC to have been much less than auspicious. Unlike the policy design for UI, the framework for ADC gave poor states little incentive and limited financial assistance for offering sufficient aid to needy families. Because Congress had stricken from the federal statute the language that would have required that assistance provide "reasonable subsistence compatible with decency and health" and substituted "as far as practicable under the conditions in such State," national administrators were severely constrained from the start in their ability to force states to appropriate adequate funds. Moreover, with ADC grants-in-aid providing one federal dollar for every two state dollars, participation in the program was far more onerous for states than either UI, with its tax arrangement, or OAA, with its one-to-one matching formula. Altmeyer lamented, "It must be confessed that many of the plans were sketchy and the state and local matching funds inadequate to finance a reasonable minimum level of assistance."[64] National, state,

---

[60] Grace Abbott, *From Relief to Social Security* (New York: Russell and Russell, 1966), pp. 282–83.

[61] See John Braeman, Robert H. Bremner, and David Brody, eds., *The New Deal: The State and Local Levels* (Columbus: Ohio State University Press, 1975), 2:332.

[62] Christopher Howard, "Sowing the Seeds of 'Welfare': The Transformation of Mothers' Pensions, 1900–1940," *Journal of Policy History* 4 (1992): 215.

[63] Douglas, *Social Security in the United States*, p. 426; Russell L. Hanson, "Federal State-building during the New Deal: The Transition from Mothers' Aid to Aid to Dependent Children," in *Changes in the State*, ed. Edward S. Greenberg and Thomas F. Mayer (Newbury Park, Calif.: Sage, 1990), p. 98.

[64] Altmeyer, *Formative Years*, p. 59.

Table 6. Number of families receiving aid and average grant per family in dollars by state: Mothers' Pensions, June 1931 versus plans approved by the SSB, June 1936

	Number of families		Avg. grant per family	
States	1931	1936	1931	1936
Alabama	*	4911	*	8.86
Arizona	*	465	*	27.98
Arkansas	131	2301	4.33	6.98
Colorado	650	997	26.50	26.87
Dist. of Columbia	161	1533	65.83	37.50
Idaho	230	1390	13.16	25.94
Maine	608	1185	30.16	35.69
Maryland	121	5494	30.52	29.50
Nebraska	1453	1422	17.81	23.26
New Hampshire	175	346	19.77	34.92
New Mexico	*	32	*	29.28
Oklahoma	1806	15,311	7.29	8.84
Utah	628	1901	11.77	29.07
Vermont	90	291	21.11	17.31
Washington	2517	4370	19.66	26.62
Wisconsin	7052	8047	21.68	28.21
Wyoming	95	502	22.55	28.99

Source: Social Work Yearbook, 1937 (New York: Russell Sage, 1937), p. 287.
* Law not passed or not in operation in 1931.

and local governments spent a total of $30,789,323 for OAA in 1937 compared with only $6,799,001 for ADC.[65]

Given differences in state fiscal capacities and habits in social provision, 1936 ADC benefits could be as low as Arkansas's $6.98 per family per month and Oklahoma's $8.84 (Table 6). In December 1937, ADC grants ranged from a low of $10.40 per family each month in Arkansas to $61.16 in Massachusetts. Six states paid ADC grants between $10 and $20, ten states between $20 and $30, seventeen between $30 and $40, and three states more than $40 per month.[66] These figures fail to show how greatly benefits could vary *within* states. Such distinctions corresponded less to differences in cost of living than to variations in local administrative practices. In Michigan in 1938, for example, grants varied from an average of $22.49 per family a month in Huron County to $45.43 in Wayne County.[67] Over-

[65] Douglas, *Social Security in the United States*, p. 358.
[66] Ibid., p. 428.
[67] Altmeyer, *Formative Years*, pp. 80–82; Marcia Dancey, "Mothers' Pensions and the Aid to Dependent Children Program in Michigan," *Social Service Review* 3 (1939): 643–44; Martha Derthick, *The Influence of Federal Grants* (Cambridge: Harvard University Press, 1970), p. 80.

Table 7. Proportion of children aided by ADC in January 1938 by states

State	Number per 1,000 under 16	State	Number per 1,000 under 16
Maryland	40	Arkansas	19
Oklahoma	40	New York	18
Idaho	35	Hawaii	18
Utah	34	Delaware	16
Washington	34	Minnesota	16
Louisiana	33	Ohio	16
Arizona	32	Alabama	15
Colorado	29	Pennsylvania	15
District of Columbia	29	Maine	14
Indiana	27	Kansas	13
Wisconsin	27	Rhode Island	13
New Mexico	26	North Carolina	10
Montana	25	Oregon	10
Nebraska	24	Georgia	8
West Virginia	24	New Hampshire	8
New Jersey	22	South Carolina	7
Wyoming	22	Vermont	7
Tennessee	21	North Dakota	4
California	20	Average of all states	19
Michigan	20		

Source: Paul H. Douglas, *Social Security in the United States*, 2d ed. (New York: Whittlesey House, 1939), p. 428.

all, the number of beneficiaries grew dramatically under ADC, but the level of public assistance benefits increased little from average levels under mothers' pensions in most localities, even decreased in some (including the District of Columbia, Maryland, and Vermont, as shown in Table 6), and remained extremely low in all but a few states.

Despite the growth in the overall number of beneficiaries, furthermore, the proportion of needy persons assisted by ADC still varied tremendously from state to state, as shown by Table 7. In 1938, the number of children aged 16 or younger receiving ADC benefits ranged from 40 per 1,000 in Maryland and Oklahoma to 10 or fewer in North Carolina, Oregon, Georgia, New Hampshire, South Carolina, Vermont, and North Dakota. In

1939, eight states still had not established ADC, though some continued to grant assistance through mothers' pensions laws.[68]

Besides the obstacles to development embedded in the statutory design, the program was crippled by its treatment in the hands of the Bureau of Public Assistance, the SSB agency charged with reviewing state-level implementation. Whereas national administrators had provided states with model bills and assistance for the development of UI, the BPA offered little support to states developing ADC. Starting out with a team of only three people, the agency lacked a field organization to assist states in designing their own plans. Instead, in December 1935, the BPA convened a meeting in Washington, D.C., of delegates from forty-two states and territories. Wary of the FERA's reputation for exerting federal control, the BPA refrained from providing too much direction. According to BPA staff member Helen Bary, the December meeting was regarded as successful because it "had seemed to dispel the fear of federal dictation and the idea entertained by many state people that the board expected to set up many meticulous or unreasonable requirements."[69]

The BPA's hands-off approach reflected the early position of the SSB's top officials. In 1937, an SSB staff member wrote in a draft of the annual report to Congress that perhaps the board should deny federal grants to states where benefit levels were exceedingly "meager." His superior, Wilbur Cohen, who was then a special assistant to Altmeyer, insisted that the language be dropped. He explained, "From my own personal information, I am under the impression that the current attitude . . . of the Board itself is that we must go slow in making any suggestions for the revision of the public assistance program and leave the responsibility pretty much to the States from both the fiscal and administrative aspects in working out their own problems."[70] At the same time the SSB was beginning to assert new federal control over both OAI and UI, it was being cautious lest it seem too ready to encroach on the states in other areas of policy implementation.[71] Accordingly, the SSB approved several state laws for ADC even though they

[68] Blanche D. Coll, "Public Assistance: Reviving the Original Comprehensive Concept of Social Security," in *Social Security: The First Half-Century*, ed. Gerald D. Nash, Noel H. Pugach, and Richard F. Tomasson (Albuquerque: University of New Mexico Press, 1988), p. 231.

[69] McKinley and Frase, *Launching Social Security*, pp. 144, 140–45.

[70] Quoted in Jerry Cates, *Insuring Inequality: Administrative Leadership in Social Security, 1935–1954* (Ann Arbor: University of Michigan Press, 1983), p. 133.

[71] Whereas Jerry Cates sees a long-term effort by the SSB/SSA to limit and restrict public assistance, neither my own research in agency records nor Blanche Coll's work bear out his interpretation. As early as 1939, after all, the SSB advocated variable grants for states. I view the SSB's greater attention to OAI and UI than to OAA and ADC as reflecting the politics of national versus state control rather than antipathy toward public assistance per se. See Cates, *Insuring Inequality*, and Blanche D. Coll, *Safety Net* (New Brunswick: Rutgers University Press, 1995).

retained old features of mothers' pensions and failed to meet conditions that Children's Bureau officials had written into Title IV of the Social Security Act to raise standards.

The ADC title required that to qualify for federal funds, a state's program must be established across all localities and administered either by a single state agency or through state-level supervision of local units. State officials contended, however, that the wording of the law did not mandate the application of uniform statewide standards. They faced vested interests and entrenched patterns of policy implementation far more extensive than those associated with OAA and UI, so instead of overhauling mothers' pensions, they mostly built on the old administrative framework. Thus arose a wide variety of county-state administrative and cost-sharing arrangements.[72]

Administrative models ranged from highly centralized administrative authorities, such as those in New England states with long-established patterns of state-run welfare programs, to decentralized authorities amid powerful county agencies, found particularly in western and midwestern states. The midwestern states had typically vested local authority for mothers' pensions in the judicial system, particularly in juvenile judges. Against the better judgment of Edith Abbott and Sophonisba Breckinridge, who viewed judges as ill disposed to administer public welfare, such arrangements persisted under ADC.[73] The model characterized by substantial local control and responsibility became much more common than the centralized version: by the end of 1936, seventeen states used local administration complemented by state supervision, compared with ten states that relied exclusively on state-level administration. Similarly, eighteen states relied on a combination of state and local funds for the program, and only nine used the more reliable form, purely state-level financing.[74]

Contrary to the hopes of Children's Bureau officials for a categorical assistance plan that would elevate needy children from the indignities of relief, ADC became entangled with general public assistance and other social services. Such fusion occurred because of economic necessity, administrative convenience and tradition, and the clash in perspectives between professional social workers at the national level and frequently untrained and

---

[72] On administrative development and organizational forms in state public welfare agencies during the 1930s, see Marietta Stevenson, "Public Welfare, State and Local Agencies," *Social Work Yearbook, 1937* (New York: Russell Sage, 1937), pp. 392–403.

[73] Letter, Sophonisba Breckinridge to Mr. Altmeyer, December 13, 1935, SSB, box 19, file 631, RG 47, NA; memorandum, Office of the General Counsel and the BPA to Mr. A. J. Altmeyer, October 12, 1936, "Re: Court Participation in Public Assistance Administration," SSB, Chairman's Files, Subject Files, 1935–40, box 93, file 631, RG 47, NA.

[74] Memorandum, Joseph Meyers to Wilbur Cohen, December 3, 1936, SSB, Chairman's Files, Subject Files, 1935–40, box 92, file 620, RG 47, NA.

inexperienced local and state administrators. ADC benefits failed to provide enough money for families to survive, so local poor-relief officials sometimes tried to supplement the funds with moneys from general relief.[75] State and local agencies that assumed responsibilities for the various grants-in-aid programs were frequently charged with carrying out other public assistance programs as well.[76] The shortage of professional social workers, coupled with the tradition of political appointments for civil service jobs in many areas meant that ADC was frequently implemented by staff lacking in training and knowledge.[77]

Meanwhile, unlike the staff that oversaw state development of UI programs, the BPA staff failed to insist on the standards of compliance intended by framers of the national statute.[78] Thus, local agencies persisted in utilizing the same restrictive eligibility rules as they had in implementing mothers' pensions. Suitable-home or fit-mother criteria continued to be used to evaluate mothers' behavior, character, reputation, housekeeping standards, and ability to manage cash.[79] Although the new federal statute promised matching funds for children who were "deprived of parental support" owing to the broad criterion called "continued absence from the home," actual coverage remained fairly exclusive, favoring the children of widows who measured up to particular cultural norms. Only 2 percent of the children accepted for aid in 1938 lived with unmarried mothers, though seventy-five thousand children were born out of wedlock annually. Five states offered no ADC funds to such children, and in eleven other states, fewer than fifty children of unmarried mothers were assisted. No states had formal laws excluding such children from coverage, but local officials adhered to preexisting practices and personal discretion in making such determinations.[80] For example, a Juvenile Court Official in Cook County, Illinois, explained, "There is never a pension granted for an ille-

---

[75] Dancey, "Mothers' Pensions," pp. 640–41; Illinois Department of Public Welfare, *An Appraisal of ADC in Illinois* (Springfield, Ill.: State Department of Public Welfare, 1943), p. 2.

[76] In many states, the implementation of the popular OAA program occupied the same administrators who were charged with responsibility for ADC. Though in some ways OAA served as a vehicle for lifting standards for public assistance in general and thus promoting the lower-status ADC program, the program for the elderly jeopardized the program for children in that the matching-grant formula of the former made it more attractive to states. See Hanson, "Federal Statebuilding during the New Deal," pp. 105–8; and Derthick, *Influence of Federal Grants*, pp. 54–57, 80–81.

[77] Winifred Bell, *Aid to Dependent Children* (New York: Cambridge University Press, 1965), pp. 37–38; Jane Hoey, "Some Administrative Problems in State Assistance Programs," *Public Welfare News* 10 (1937): 4; Derthick, *Influence of Federal Grants*, pp. 79–80; McKinley and Frase, *Launching Social Security*, p. 156.

[78] McKinley and Frase, *Launching Social Security*, pp. 194–97.

[79] Derthick, *Influence of Federal Grants*, pp. 84–87; Dancey, "Mothers' Pensions," pp. 647–49.

[80] Louise McGuire, "Compilation of Material on Aid to Dependent Children," December 7, 1938, p. 19, SSB, Records of the Executive Director, Subject Files, 1935–40, box 273, file 600, RG 47, NA.

gitimate child but a pension may be granted to other children in the family where the mother married after the birth of the illegitimate child or where the illegitimate child is more than a year old at the time the pension is granted."[81] In several states, a woman who was found to be "immoral," meaning that she was having an affair, would be prohibited from receiving ADC for her children for one year. In Fall River, Massachusetts, an SSB inquiry into administrative practices found that "apparently the case worker is puritanical in her viewpoint to the apparent detriment of the needy children. She stated, 'Parents must be fit to care for children. Mothers with illegitimate children should not be eligible. The home must be clean. Children must attend church to be eligible for relief.'"[82] In New York, a woman who kept a "slovenly home" risked losing eligibility.[83]

The decentralized style of ADC implementation was characterized by a racial bias as well. Usually the denial of assistance was carried out through the application of suitable-home rules, exercised with discretion.[84] Georgia, however, utilized a racial quota system, which stayed in place until federal administrators withheld funds. Similarly, Arizona, New Mexico, and Nevada excluded Indians and Latinos from public assistance through techniques including a formal resolution banning assistance, citizenship requirements, and the purposeful negligence of agency staff toward applications from those groups.[85]

Like all programs that left authority to the states, ADC depended on the decisions of state legislators, but unlike UI and to a greater extent than OAA, ADC was subject to especially contentious political battles on the state level, in part owing to policy design. For public assistance, states had to agree to appropriate money from their own general revenues.[86] Most state treasuries had been depleted by the depression; states therefore financed the new grants-in-aid programs largely through regressive and volatile sales taxes.[87] They had a greater incentive to appropriate funds for OAA than ADC, given the stronger public pressure for the former program and its' more favorable grant formula. Thus, for example, in 1939 the state of Colorado spent $12.91 per capita for OAA compared with $1.61 for ADC.[88]

[81] Ibid., p. 21.

[82] Memorandum, A. G. Thomas to Francis A. Staten, "County Reports of Administration of Public Assistance Programs," February 2, 1939, SSB, Records of the Executive Director, Subject Files, 1935–40, box 274, file 620.6/1940, RG 47, NA.

[83] McGuire, "Compilation of Material on Aid to Dependent Children," pp. 26–27.

[84] Bell, *Aid to Dependent Children*, pp. 41–42.

[85] *Reminiscences of Jane Hoey*, pp. 42–47, OHC.

[86] Altmeyer, *Formative Years*, p. 85.

[87] George Brown Tindall, *The Emergence of the New South* (Baton Rouge: Louisiana State University Press, 1967), pp. 490–91; Braeman, Bremner, and Brody, *New Deal*, pp. 184, 286, 365.

[88] Geoffrey May, "Aid to Dependent Children," in *Social Work Yearbook, 1941* (New York: Russell Sage, 1941), pp. 52–53.

Finally, ADC lacked the support of either a strong, organized popular constituency or devoted bureaucrats who could have pressured state legislators to improve the program. Whereas mothers' pensions had begun with momentum and legitimacy through the efforts of widespread federated women's organizations, ADC had no visible supporters.[89] Serving on the SSB in 1937, Mary Dewson wrote to an old friend who shared her maternalist approach to social reform, expressing her expectation that women and women's groups would press for the development of the programs left to the states:

> Of course, two-thirds of our work comes under the federal-state provision and the manner in which the states cooperate will depend tremendously on the public opinion in those states and the demand for first-class administration. That is the place where the women can help all over the country and I shall look to them to do so. . . . It is a beautiful job for the women and one that can be handed on to their grand-daughters and great grand-daughters for so long as we have a democratic form of government, we must be eternally at it.[90]

But no such rallying forces materialized. Realizing the disadvantaged position of ADC, SSB officials attempted to mobilize the citizenry through public relations efforts in the late 1930s.[91] They remained convinced, however, that it was not their place to advocate the program directly, as they did for OAI and UI, where the statutory mandate for national control was more clear.

The 1939 Amendments

Meanwhile, beginning in 1937, plans were already underway in the SSB and the newly appointed Advisory Council for changes to the Social Security Act that would dramatically alter ADC. In seeking to fortify and broaden the base of the contributory program for the elderly, bureaucrats and council members considered not only how those in the ranks of OAA might be incorporated but also how widows and children currently on ADC might be covered by OAI as well. The SSB's research staff found that the death of one or both parents in a family was a contributing factor to

---

[89] Theda Skocpol, *Protecting Soldiers and Mothers: The Political Origins of Social Policy in the United States* (Cambridge: Harvard University Press, 1992), chap. 8.

[90] Letter, Mary W. Dewson to Mrs. P. S. Nagle, September 23, 1937, Dewson Papers, Subject Files, "Social Security Board, 1937–38," box 8, FDR.

[91] Memorandum, Robert Huse to Mr. W. L. Mitchell, May 15, 1939, "Background Information for a Conference on Public Relations Problems of State Public Assistance Agencies"; and memorandum, Lavinia Engle to Mr. Huse, March 5, 1937, "Re: State Conferences"; both in SSB, Records of the Executive Director, Subject Files, 1935–40, box 274, file 620, RG 47, NA.

dependency in nearly 50 percent of the ADC cases.[92] Advancing the notion that "good citizenship" is inherently tied to personal or familial independence as achieved through the breadwinner's employment status, the Advisory Council reasoned that widows and surviving children of workers who had been covered by OAI might better be included in an extension of the contributory program:

> A democratic society has an immeasurable stake in avoiding the growth of a habit of dependency among its youth. The method of survivors' insurance not only sustains the concept that a child is supported through the efforts of the parent, but affords a vital sense of security to the family unit. . . . While the expansion of aid to dependent children under the Social Security Act has been gratifying, there is great need for further protection of dependent children. In many instances, the aid is insufficient to maintain normal family life or to permit the children to develop into healthy citizens. . . . Survivors' insurance must be looked upon as current protection, closely related to the current earning status of the insured worker.[93]

Congress readily enacted these recommendations as it transformed OAI into Old Age and Survivors' Insurance through the 1939 amendments.

In effect, the amendments rescued mostly white, middle-class women and their children from the miserly benefits and intensive scrutiny of ADC and granted them coverage in a program with national, uniform standards, and rights-based benefits. These changes meant, however, that ADC was robbed of its middle-class constituencies and primary basis for public support. Left behind would be the children of mothers who were unmarried, divorced, or separated and those whose parents either were among the long-term unemployed or were workers in those low-wage occupations not covered by OASI.

The SSB had hoped that ADC might, simultaneously, be strengthened through amendments. Agency staff members were exasperated with the states over their eligibility criteria, but in reviewing the congressional hearings from 1935, they reconfirmed their understanding that Congress had not intended to make ADC broad enough to cover all children on relief and thus refrained from proposing such changes in 1939.[94] Officials also knew

---

[92] Memorandum, Wilbur J. Cohen to Arthur J. Altmeyer, November 28, 1938, "Reasons for Dependency: Aid to Dependent Children," SSB, Chairman's Files, Subject Files, 1935–40, box 92, file 600.03, RG 47, NA.

[93] "1937–1938 Advisory Council on Social Security: Final Report," in *The Report of the Committee on Economic Security and Other Documents relating to the Development of the Social Security Act,* 50th anniversary ed., National Conference on Social Work (Washington, D.C.: National Conference on Social Welfare, 1985), pp. 173–204, esp. 191–93.

[94] Memorandum, Helen Jeter to Ewan Clague, October 27, 1937, "Memorandum on Suggested Amendment to Definition of Dependent Child in Title IV," SSB, Chairman's Files, Subject Files, 1935–40, box 92, file 600.03, RG 47, NA.

that the Abbott sisters and others who still championed categorical assistance would oppose changes to ADC that would significantly broaden coverage.[95] The agency decided to recommend instead that Congress raise the age limit for children on ADC from 16 to 18 and increase funds for the program both by changing the grant formula to the 50 percent matching basis used for OAA and by increasing maximum allowable payments.

As in 1935, however, Congress paid little attention to ADC in the course of the amendment process. The Ways and Means Committee did raise the age and change the grant formula, but it refrained from raising benefit levels. In other matters, the committee dealt with ADC similarly to OAA. A provision requiring that states adopt a merit system was included, and SSB's wish for variable grants was denied.[96] Most important, the Ways and Means Committee amplified the need-based character of ADC. As recommended by the BPA, policymakers inserted the word *needy* in front of the statutory definition of dependent children and mandated that henceforth states subtract all income and assets from each applicant's resources to evaluate eligibility. Thus ADC became inscribed with means testing.[97] In sum, through the 1939 amendments the "gilt-edged widows," whose coverage had won respectability for mothers' pensions, were safely transferred to the ranks of contributory OASI. ADC emerged severely weakened—and altered in ways that would further distance recipients from the rights of social citizenship.

No More "Queens and Angels of the Home"

In 1947, in an article entitled "Second-Class Children," Gilbert Laue wrote:

> In the United States, in the bread-basket of the world, there are children who can never have a second helping of food; children who never had a whole apple or a whole orange; babies who can't have the cod liver oil the clinics prescribe; little girls who never wore a dress that wasn't second hand. These are the children whose fathers have died or deserted them, or whose parents were not married, or whose homes were broken up by divorce or the father's physical or mental incapacitation. These are the recipients of "aid to dependent children," as provided by the Social Security Act.[98]

Laue concluded the essay with a plea to the public to consider the costs of ADC in terms of citizenship, observing, "The cost of raising a fatherless

---

[95] Coll, *Safety Net*, p. 107.

[96] On the merit system, see *Reminiscences of Bernice Bernstein*, pp. 87–88, and *Reminiscences of Frank Bane*, p. 207, both in the OHC; and Altmeyer, *Formative Years*, pp. 104–5.

[97] Public Law 379, title IV, sec. 401(b) and 403(a); Meriam, *Relief and Social Security*, p. 53; Derthick, *Influence of Federal Grants*, p. 47.

[98] Gilbert Laue, "Second-Class Children," *The Nation*, October 11, 1947, p. 381.

child is too often illogically balanced against taxes. It can really be balanced only against the cost of having failed our future citizens, the greatest resource of our democracy." [99]

The 1939 amendments had by then hastened and intensified the stigmatizing of ADC beneficiaries. Mothers of children in the program were declining in the public eye from the status of "queens and angels of the home" to that of the undeserving poor. These developments occurred as the program came to accentuate its predecessors' worst features: localism, restrictive standards, and notoriously low benefits. [100]

During the 1940s, the proportion of children covered under ADC increased by 36 percent, and the composition of the program changed. [101] As widows and children of the mostly white men covered by OAI came under OASI, and as whites benefited from the postwar economic boom more than African Americans, the proportion of white families aided by ADC declined, and that of African Americans increased, from the 14 to 17 percent of the caseload in the late 1930s to 31 percent in 1948. The proportion of families who were on ADC because the father was deceased declined from 37.2 percent in 1942 to 22.8 percent in 1948, and the numbers of children with incapacitated or estranged parents grew. As the postwar escalations in marriage and birth rates coupled with increases in rates of divorce and births outside of marriage among people of all races, the rates of children of unmarried mothers on ADC rose from 2 percent of all individual children in 1938 to 14.1 percent of all ADC families in 1948. [102] Even so, in many states African Americans and children whose parents were unmarried, divorced, or separated remained underrepresented on the ADC rolls.

In 1947 the President's Committee on Civil Rights requested information from the Social Security Administration on the extent to which its services were able to "impartially reach all qualified recipients, despite local and regional differences." The agency reported that eligibility procedures for OASI were "determined by factors that are entirely or largely objective," without "considerations of race, religion, sex, country of birth, or national origin." In the case of public assistance programs, however, it only urged states to avoid "subjective judgement" in decisions on eligibility. [103] The federal agency still lacked the ability to impose national standards or even to conduct sufficient oversight to guarantee fair treatment for program applicants and beneficiaries. Neither could state and local agencies be

[99] Ibid., p. 382.

[100] *Reminiscences of Katherine Lenroot*, OHC, pp. 108–11.

[101] SSA, "Old Age Assistance and Aid to Dependent Children, 1940–1950," by Ellen J. Perkins, in *Social Security Bulletin* 14 (November 1951): 13.

[102] SSA, "Aid to Dependent Children in a Postwar Year," by Elizabeth Alling and Agnes Leisy, in *Social Security Bulletin* 13 (August 1950): 3–12.

[103] SSA, "Equality of Rights to Social Security," in *Social Security Bulletin* 10 (November 1947): 20–22.

relied on to regulate themselves effectively because, although the 1939 amendments to the Social Security Act had called for states to develop their own personnel merit systems, such programs were still in their infancy.[104]

State and local officials persisted in applying discretionary eligibility criteria to discriminate against nonwhites, despite the fact that need was typically higher among such groups. A 1942 SSB study of families receiving ADC in sixteen states showed that though the rolls included a higher proportion of nonwhite than white children, in several states needy nonwhite applicants were more underrepresented on ADC rolls in all states except Massachusetts.[105] State agencies in all sixteen states except Massachusetts denied assistance to many more individual children in nonwhite families already on the ADC rolls than those in white families. On average, 12.3 percent of nonwhite applicants in such circumstances were denied assistance compared with 7.7 percent of white applicants. The exclusion of needy African American children from ADC appeared to be most pronounced in southern states, and the exclusion of needy "Indian" (Latino and Native American) children was most dramatic in Arizona.[106] Though the SSB cracked down on explicit means of discrimination, the agency lacked the power to intervene in more typical instances, where state and local officials excluded nonwhites through the enduring suitable-home or fit-mother practices. By 1941, thirty-one of the forty-five states incorporated some variant of such criteria in their ADC programs.[107] Although the SSB granted them its reluctant approval, it attempted to discourage states from using such rules, pointing to their typically vague and imprecise character and the problems posed by such subjective measures of administrative discretion. The BPA in particular decried the manner in which the rules made children's eligibility for aid conditional on their parents' behavior and tried instead to advance the idea that many homes would become more "suitable" if offered the necessary income assistance of ADC.[108] In 1945, after a difficult two-year drafting process, the bureau sent a letter to state agencies recommending that they work to repeal the suitable-home provisions, but the results were less than impressive: fifteen states responded positively, but five new programs included versions of the rules.[109]

---

[104] SSA, "Merit System Objectives and Realities," by Albert H. Aronson, in *Social Security Bulletin* 13 (April 1950): 3–19.

[105] SSB, Bureau of Public Assistance, *Families Receiving Aid to Dependent Children, October 1942*, by Agnes Leisy, pt. 1, Public Assistance Report No. 7 (Washington, D.C.: Social Security Board, Bureau of Public Assistance, 1943), pp. 3–5.

[106] Ibid., pp. 15–18.

[107] Bell, *Aid to Dependent Children*, pp. 30–31.

[108] SSA, "'Suitable Home' Provisions of State Plans for Aid to Dependent Children," in *Social Security Bulletin* 8 (April 1945): 19–21; *Reminiscences of Dean Jack B. Tate*, OHC, pp. 10–11, 72–73; *Reminiscences of Jane Hoey*, p. 42.

[109] Bell, *Aid to Dependent Children*, pp. 50–51, 44–45.

Table 8. Reason for lack of support or care by father, ADC families, for 16 States, October 1942

		Percent ADC families lacking support or care by the father for specified reason					
			Estranged from family				
State	Deceased	Total	Parents divorced or legally separated	Deserting or parents separated without court decree	Not married to mother and deserting	Incapaci- tated	Other*
Total	37.2	35.8	11.1	15.0	9.7	22.1	4.9
Arizona	42.9	26.4	8.0	12.3	6.1	25.5	5.2
Arkansas	37.4	33.2	9.7	15.9	7.6	26.8	2.6
Dist. of Columbia	30.6	46.9	2.2	28.4	16.3	14.4	8.1
Illinois	37.4	47.8	9.6	23.2	15.0	11.4	3.4
Kansas	34.3	37.6	16.3	15.6	5.7	21.6	6.5
Louisiana	32.7	30.1	4.3	14.7	11.1	33.1	4.1
Massachusetts	47.4	30.1	15.0	10.8	4.3	16.9	5.6
Missouri	35.1	37.9	13.0	15.5	9.4	24.5	2.5
Montana	33.4	35.4	16.4	14.3	4.7	23.7	7.5
Nebraska	29.4	40.2	16.4	16.3	7.5	24.8	5.6
North Carolina	55.6	18.5	2.6	10.2	5.7	20.2	5.7
Oklahoma	27.6	46.2	18.2	14.7	13.3	18.1	8.1
South Dakota	47.0	31.6	16.6	9.1	5.9	18.0	3.4
Utah	32.1	28.6	17.4	8.6	2.6	33.9	5.4
West Virginia	32.9	25.3	2.3	13.0	10.0	36.1	5.7
Wisconsin	46.2	30.3	14.7	8.5	7.1	19.8	3.7

Source: Social Security Board, Bureau of Public Assistance, *Families Receiving Aid to Dependent Children, October 1942,* by Agnes Leisy, pt. 1, Public Assistance Report No. 7 (Washington, D.C.: Social Security Board, Bureau of Public Assistance, 1943), p. 55.

* Includes imprisonment, serving in armed forces, absent for other reasons, unemployed or with insufficient earnings, not legally responsible, and needed in home.

Many states also established rules that excluded children whose parents were unmarried, divorced, or separated, as shown in Table 8. The 1942 study by the BPA noted that differences in "illegitimacy rates" from state to state, for example, were not sufficient to account for the disparity in eligibility rules pertaining to children of unmarried mothers.[110] Using highly interventionist methods of surveillance applied most rigorously to southern blacks, some states and localities prohibited women receiving ADC from

[110] SSB, *Families Receiving Aid to Dependent Children,* p. 30.

having any "male callers" and withdrew aid if such man-in-the-house rules were violated.[111]

Some southern states denied assistance to "employable mothers" whose children were no longer infants, forcing such women to work, usually in the fields.[112] As one field supervisor explained, cultural norms and labor market demands accounted for the small proportion of African Americans awarded public assistance in the districts she serviced:

> The number of Negro cases are few due to the unanimous feeling on the part of staff and board that there are more work opportunities for Negro women and to their intense desire not to interfere with local labor conditions. The attitude that "they have always gotten along" and that "all they'll do is have more children" is definite. . . . There is hesitancy on the part of the lay boards to advance too rapidly over the thinking of their own communities which see no reason why the employable Negro mother should not continue her usually sketchy seasonal labor or indefinite domestic service rather than receive a public-assistance grant.[113]

Such practices laid the groundwork for "work rules" for mothers on ADC, which became more widespread in subsequent years.

Benefit levels for ADC continued to vary greatly between states and localities. Although the matching-grant formula had been changed to the more favorable 50–50 ratio in 1939, only three states, Louisiana, Michigan, and Tennessee, responded by increasing their own contributions. Other states simply scaled back their contributions accordingly.[114] As the cost of living rose, states gradually increased their ADC spending. In 1946 and again in 1948, Congress agreed to mildly variable grant arrangements, approved by President Truman, enabling the federal government to boost the benefit levels in poorer states by making more generous grants.[115] As shown by Map 2, however, 1950 ADC benefits still varied more from state to state than benefits for any other major social program, ranging from $9.80 per child in Mississippi to $49.46 per child in

[111] Bell, *Aid to Dependent Children*, pp. 42–48.

[112] Frances Fox Piven and Richard A. Cloward, *Regulating the Poor* (New York: Random House, Vintage Books, 1971), pp. 134–41.

[113] Quoted in Mary S. Larabee, "Unmarried Parenthood under the Social Security Act," in *Proceedings of the National Conference on Social Work, Selected Papers, Sixty-Sixth Annual Conference, Buffalo, N.Y., 18–24 June 1939* (New York: Columbia University Press, 1939), p. 454.

[114] Memorandum, Division of Plans and Grants to Jane M. Hoey, January 16, 1940, "Savings in State and Local Funds Available for ADC," SSB, Chairman's Files, Subject Files, 1935–40, box 93, file 622.03, RG 47, NA.

[115] Gilbert Y. Steiner, *Social Insecurity: The Politics of Welfare* (Chicago: Rand-McNally, 1966), pp. 50–51.

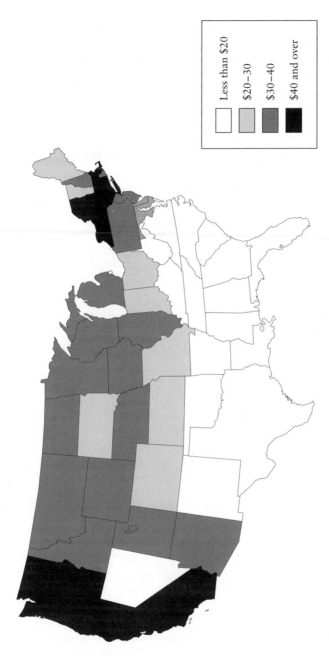

Map 2. Average ADC benefits by state, 1950. From Social Security Administration, *Social Security Bulletin* 13 (August 1950): 32.

Less than $20

$20–30

$30–40

$40 and over

Connecticut. Average payments had risen over the decade by slightly less than one-third in real terms.[116]

Though the framers of the program had intended for caretakers of children to be freed from participation in the work force, allowing them to devote their full attention to their children, the benefits were too low to make that hope a reality. In 1942, about three-fifths of the families supplemented the payments with earnings, especially in the states offering the lowest benefits.[117] In 1945, one state noted that its benefits provided "about one-third of each family's minimum needs for food, clothing, shelter, and medical care."[118]

Without fervent promoters in either government or among the public, characteristics given to ADC in its formation became its weaknesses and, unaddressed, its fatal flaws. Witte reports that the absence of a caretaker grant was simply an oversight attributable to the haste of the committee's treatment of the program; yet fifteen years passed before the law was amended to include such a grant. Suitable-home rules persisted until the 1960s.[119] States retained residence requirements until the Supreme Court declared them unconstitutional in 1969.[120] Only the mildest form of variable-grant provisions were enacted successfully, so that from the 1940s to the 1990s, the variation in ADC and AFDC benefits between states has been much greater than differences in wages or the cost of living.[121]

Perhaps the dream of the Children's Bureau officials could have been realized if they themselves had won administrative authority over ADC and if their efforts could have been joined by a revival of the federated women's clubs across the country to bolster and support the program. Without advocates, the program easily became a pawn in legislative decisions over funding at the state level, and local officials encountered little resistance as they scrutinized the behavior of ADC applicants and recipients. ADC thus left many of the poorest women at the mercy of the states, subject to the

---

[116] SSA, *Social Security Bulletin* 13 (August 1950); 32; SSA, "Old Age Assistance and Aid to Dependent Children, 1940–1950," p. 13; For Map 2, the average benefit levels per child in each state were figured by dividing the number of children on ADC in each state by the number of families in the program in that state, and then by dividing the average benefits per family by that amount. Eveline M. Burns, *The American Social Security System* (Cambridge, Mass.: Houghton-Mifflin, 1949), pp. 360–63.

[117] SSB, *Families Receiving Aid to Dependent Children*, pt. 2, p. 22.

[118] Quoted in Emma Octavia Lundberg, *Unto the Least of These: Social Services for Children* (New York: Appleton-Century, 1947), p. 179.

[119] SSA, " 'Suitable Home' Provisions," pp. 19–21; Derthick, *Influence of Federal Grants*, pp. 80–93.

[120] SSA, "People on the Move: Effect of Residence Requirement for Public Assistance," by Arthur J. Altmeyer, *Social Security Bulletin* 9 (January 1946): 3–7; *Shapiro v. Thompson*, 394 U.S. 618 (1969).

[121] Turnbull, Williams, and Chiet, *Economic and Social Security*, chap. 3; Altmeyer, *Formative Years*, pp. 80–82; Paul E. Peterson and Mark C. Rom, *Welfare Magnets: A New Case for a National Standard* (Washington, D.C.: Brookings Institution, 1990).

variable benefits, morals restrictions, means tests, and administrative supervision of each locality. More than any other program in the Social Security Act, ADC rendered its beneficiaries into vassals whose duties were defined by the political geography of federalism.

Retrospectively, observers of the American welfare state have surmised that UI earned respectability by virtue of its "earned," wage-related character, whereas ADC faltered because public assistance rests on principles out of sync with American values. Such conclusions were by no means obvious, though, when the Social Security Act was enacted in 1935. Unemployment compensation, virtually untried but long contested in the United States, would have seemed likelier to fail than the successor to the reputable mothers' pensions programs.

But although UI and ADC were both to be administered jointly by the national and state governments, it was their designs that propelled them toward their separate fates. The model of administration chosen for UI short-circuited the multiple layers of federalism and produced national uniformity. ADC's design, by contrast, allowed the program to be easily compromised by the weakest link in intergovernmental relations.[122] In time, the two policies had evolved so as to separate non-elderly men from women as if they were citizens of distinct sovereignties.

[122] See Hanson, "Federal Statebuilding during the New Deal," pp. 93–114. For more on the implications of federalism for ADC's development in the mid-twentieth century, see Steiner, *Social Insecurity*.

CHAPTER SEVEN

The Formation of the Fair Labor Standards Act of 1938

I had one experience in the campaign. . . . We got into New Bedford and in that park there . . . must have been 20,000 people. . . . There was a girl six or seven feet away who was trying to pass an envelope to me . . . I said to [an aide], "Get the note from that girl." He got it and handed it to me and the note said this: "Dear Mr. President: I wish you could do something to help us girls. . . . We have been working in a sewing factory, a garment factory, and up to a few months ago we were getting our minimum pay of $11 a week. . . . Today the 200 of us girls have been cut down to $4 and $5 or $6 a week." . . . Something has to be done about the elimination of child labor and long hours and starvation wages.

—President Franklin D. Roosevelt, Press Conference, December 29, 1936

Women workers remained in need of labor standards. Occupational segregation persisted, keeping them disproportionately employed in low-wage jobs. Their underrepresentation in labor unions meant they gained little from the NLRA. Reformers in the women's organizations that had been struggling for labor standards for decades still hoped their goals would be realized nationally in the New Deal.[1] Many maternalists who still favored a high degree of state and local authority in social policymaking had come to regard national regulations as indispensable in matters of labor policy. In their New Deal–era campaign for national wage-and-hour laws, child labor prohibitions, and the regulation of industrial homework, they were joined by male advocates of women workers in the garment and textile industries. Departing from the protective labor law tradition of covering women only, these reformers sought gender-neutral legislation that would, at least in theory, apply to workers regardless of sex. But ironically, al-

---

[1] Landon R. Y. Storrs, "Civilizing Capitalism: The National Consumers' League and the Politics of 'Fair' Labor Standards in the New Deal Era" (Ph.D. diss., University of Wisconsin-Madison, 1994); Vivien Hart, *Bound by Our Constitution: Women, Workers, and the Minimum Wage* (Princeton: Princeton University Press, 1994).

though they won their case in principle, the labor standards legislation that came out of the tumultuous politics of the late New Deal actually circumvented the women workers who most needed it.

The Fair Labor Standards Act of 1938, America's first and enduring national labor standards law, which mandated a floor under wages and a ceiling on hours for employees in covered occupations, epitomized the revised boundaries of national and state authority that separated men and women into different jurisdictions of governance. The law rested on the principle of interstate commerce, recently reinterpreted by the Supreme Court from its older, restrictive meaning that applied to the literal "flow" of goods across state lines, to a broader definition that included all those industries "affecting commerce." Yet though gender-neutral on the surface, in fact the contours of "interstate commerce" excluded the vast majority of the female work force who most needed such measures. The reinterpreted commerce clause still evaded the terrain wherein most women's occupations were located, leaving them under the provincial, uneven, and generally paternalistic rule of state legislatures.[2]

Momentum for National Labor Standards: The Early New Deal

When the newly elected Roosevelt had asked Frances Perkins to be secretary of labor, she had tested him by outlining a plan of labor legislation that included a goal to which she had long been committed, the establishment of federal minimum wages and maximum hours. Although Roosevelt was typically conservative in fiscal matters, as seen in his views on spending for social policy, he was usually willing to apply the force of federal government authority in the realm of regulatory policy, where little government spending was involved.[3] Without hesitation, he pledged his hearty support for her entire plan. She quickly reminded him that such goals had not been sanctioned by the courts: "But," I said, "have you considered that to launch such a program we must think out, frame, and develop labor and social legislation, which then might be considered unconstitutional?" "Well, that's a problem," Mr. Roosevelt admitted, "but we can work out something when the time comes."[4]

[2] See also Vivien Hart, "Minimum Wage Policy and Constitutional Inequality: The Paradox of the Fair Labor Standards Act of 1938," *Journal of Policy History* 1 (1989): 319–43; Eileen Boris, "(En)gendering the New Deal Order: Labor Standards' Alternative Stream" (paper presented at the Thirteenth Annual North American Labor History Conference, Wayne State University, October 17–19, 1991). On industrial homework regulations in the FLSA, see Eileen Boris, "The Quest for Labor Standards in the Era of Eleanor Roosevelt: The Case of Industrial Homework," *Wisconsin Women's Law Journal* 2 (spring 1986): 53–74.
[3] Author's conversation with James MacGregor Burns, May 6, 1993, Richmond, Va.
[4] Frances Perkins, *The Roosevelt I Knew* (New York: Harper and Row, 1964), p. 152.

Besides Perkins, the labor standards agenda was also promoted by leaders of the textile and garment workers unions, both the Amalgamated Clothing Workers of America and the International Ladies Garment Workers Union. Despite internal ambivalence on gender issues, these unions stood out in the early 1930s for representing industries composed largely of unskilled women who worked for extremely low wages.[5] Their leaders necessarily had different views from other labor chieftains regarding government intervention in labor markets and the needs of unskilled workers and unorganized workers.

Sidney Hillman, general president of the ACWA, had long-established ties with the women's reform associations that championed the minimum wage, including the National Consumers' League and the Women's Trade Union League. During the 1930s, he was the labor leader most welcome at the White House, having been drawn into cooperation with the political leadership of Roosevelt's campaign and his future administration in 1932. Hillman, like various Keynesians, interpreted the depression in underconsumptionist terms and sought public policy measures designed to spur mass consumption.[6] At the June 1933 meeting of the general executive board of the Amalgamated, he told his colleagues:

> Some months ago the discussion of hours and wages was taken as a joke. . . . But it developed to be a serious matter. Since the moment Roosevelt was elected I was in constant touch with Felix Frankfurter. I knew he was close to the President. I had prepared an outline on stabilization of industry and had Frankfurter show it to Roosevelt. I have also spent a great deal of time with Frances Perkins. At first Frankfurter seemed to discourage me saying that the scheme will be considered unconstitutional. When Frances Perkins was appointed Commissioner of Labor she called a conference [of labor leaders]. . . . at which I presented . . . a plan for hours and wages, which in turn was presented to the President.[7]

---

[5] For the ACWA's stance on gender issues, see Records of the Amalgamated Clothing Workers of America, LMDC, collection 5619: (1) Dorothy Bellanca Records, box 8, file 26, various; box 35, file 6, "The Convention-Woman Problem" by Dorothy Bellanca, May 1918, also 1937 speech; box 28, file 17, correspondence with Mary Anderson, Department of Labor, Women's Bureau; box 29, file 8, letters to E. Christman of WTUL; and (2) Sidney Hillman Records, box 1, file 19, letter from Dorothy Bellanca to Sidney Hillman, March 30, 1915; box 7, file 23, telegram to Hillman from Women's Civic and Educational Club of the ACWA, August 1918. See also Steve Fraser, *Labor Will Rule: Sidney Hillman and the Rise of American Labor* (New York: Free Press, 1991), pp. 46, 57–58, 64, 116, 224; Nina Lynn Asher, "Dorothy Jacobs Bellanca: Feminist Trade Unionist, 1894–1946" (Ph.D. diss., State University of New York, Binghamton, 1982).

[6] Fraser, *Labor Will Rule*, pp. 284–85.

[7] General Executive Board Meeting, ACWA, Hotel Wardman Park, Washington D.C., June 5, 1933, Records of the Amalgamated Clothing Workers of America, collection 5619, box 165, file 18, LMDC.

Hillman's initial letter to Roosevelt, which was well received, called for industrial regulation and a federal labor board to enforce wage-and-hour legislation. Only later would AFL opposition come to bear on political leaders.[8]

Labor Standards in the National Industrial Recovery Act

The earliest version of minimum wage-and-hour standards in New Deal legislation appeared in the National Industrial Recovery Act of June 1933. The purpose of the NRA was to increase consumer purchasing power by mandating wage increases and to promote the creation of more jobs for adults by limiting the hours in the work week and outlawing child labor. Frances Perkins proudly noted that the NRA codes were the first labor standards in the United States which recognized equality between the sexes, as most of the codes in principle applied to both men and women.[9]

The NRA was short lived, however: on May 27, 1935, the Supreme Court declared the law unconstitutional. In *Schecter Poultry Co. v. United States*,[10] the Court found the NRA to be unconstitutional primarily because Congress delegated too much discretionary power to the executive branch for the implementation of the law. Immediately, wages fell in many industries, and sweatshop conditions returned in workplaces that had reformed under the NRA.

Perkins had anticipated the court's decision and had already begun to seek a means to restore wage-and-hour provisions. She had called on the solicitor's office in the Department of Labor (DOL) to draft two wage-and-hour bills, and she assured Roosevelt that she had something "up [her] sleeve":

> "I've got two bills which will do everything you and I think important under NRA," I said. "I have them locked up in the lower left-hand drawer of my desk against an emergency."
>
> He threw his head back and laughed. "There's New England caution for you, I declare."

---

[8] Fraser, *Labor Will Rule*, pp. 284–85.

[9] Perkins, *Roosevelt I Knew*, p. 208. Enforcement of the NRA, however, proved to be an administrative disaster, especially notorious for the failure to establish any uniformity in the minimum wage. Many women missed the opportunity to obtain minimum wages because their industries were slow to adapt codes; others were paid lower wages than men through sex-based differentials. Though most NRA industry codes mandated a forty-cent-per-hour minimum wage, about one-quarter of the codes, covering nearly 17 percent of workers in code industries, provided for lower rates for women. See Irving Bernstein, *A Caring Society* (Boston: Houghton Mifflin, 1985), pp. 119–20; Alice Kessler-Harris, *Out to Work* (New York: Oxford University Press, 1982), p. 262.

[10] 295 U.S. 495 (1935).

"But you and I agreed in February 1933," I reminded him, "that putting a
floor under wages and a ceiling over hours was essential and that it would be
a wise and necessary program to be carried out on the federal level, if possible.
We've explored the NRA. It is fine, but if it doesn't work or breaks down, we
have to be prepared for something else."

"You're pretty unconstitutional, aren't you?" he said.[11]

The first of Perkins' two bills, which required federal contractors to meet
minimum labor standards in the production of goods that were to be sold
to the government, passed through Congress with relative ease and, in
1936, became law as the Walsh-Healey Public Contracts Act.[12] The second
bill was intended to regulate wages and hours broadly, in all industries engaged in interstate commerce. Early in 1936, however, the Supreme Court
erected a stone wall in the way of any efforts to enact social and labor
legislation, and the prospects for the wage-and-hour bill grew very dim
indeed.

The Supreme Court Obstructs the Path

In two decisions handed down over a two-week period, *Carter v. Carter
Coal Company* and *Morehead v. N.Y. ex rel Tipaldo*,[13] the Supreme Court
insisted that the Constitution prohibited both Congress and state legislatures from regulating the conditions of labor. First, in the *Carter* decision,
the Court vehemently reiterated its traditionally narrow interpretation of
the commerce clause, once again forbidding workplace regulations. The
justices declared unconstitutional the Bituminous Coal Conservation Act
of 1935, a law pushed through Congress by the United Mine Workers in
the wake of the *Schecter* decision in an effort to salvage some labor standards in the coal industry. Justice George Sutherland, writing the opinion
for the majority in the 6–3 decision, contended that interstate commerce
refers strictly to "intercourse for the purpose of trade" and does not include economic activities that precede or follow trade, such as agriculture,
manufacturing, and mining.[14] Sutherland reasoned further that regulation
of wages, hours, and collective bargaining pertained to production, not
commerce, and therefore did not fall within the domain of congressional
powers. This decision, wrote Perkins, "revived beyond any doubt the doctrine of *Hammer v. Dagenhart*," straitjacketing the commerce clause.[15]

Second, with the *Tipaldo* decision, the Court once again set aside state-

---

[11] Perkins, *Roosevelt I Knew*, p. 249.
[12] Bernstein, *Caring Society*, pp. 126–27.
[13] 298 U.S. 238 (1936) and 298 U.S. 587 (1936), respectively.
[14] 298 U.S. 238 (1936).
[15] Perkins, *Roosevelt I Knew*, p. 255.

level minimum wage laws for women and children, deciding, as in *Adkins*, that such laws violated freedom of contract. When the depression had brought on a resurgence of sweatshop labor, particularly affecting working women and children, NCL leaders had asked Felix Frankfurter and another lawyer to draft new minimum wage legislation for the states. The two thought they had found a loophole in *Adkins* through which such laws could be upheld: the derivation of a "fair wage" based on the value of the service performed and the industry's ability to pay.[16] Seven states had enacted such laws; the Court struck down the New York version in *Tipaldo* on the basis that "the state is without power by any form of legislation to prohibit, change, or nullify contracts between employers and adult women workers as to the amount of wages to be paid."[17] Echoing the *Adkins* decision, the majority opinion once again drew on liberal principles of abstract equality between the sexes to show the arbitrary nature of laws pertaining solely to women, insisting that they were equally capable actors in the labor market. In his dissent, Justice Harlan F. Stone retorted, "There is a grim irony in speaking of the freedom of contract of those who, because of their economic necessities, give their services for less than is needful to keep body and soul together." He charged the majority of the Court with falsely interpreting the Constitution to protect a particular set of economic beliefs.

Public Outrage and Roosevelt's Reelection

The Supreme Court had once again slammed the door on constitutional validation of both national and state minimum wage laws, but this time the response was public outrage. Prominent members of both parties protested vociferously. Though most newspapers had been far from sympathetic to the New Deal, 80 percent of those commenting on *Tipaldo* opposed the Court's decision.[18] Critics decried the spurious identification of freedom of contract with the bargaining position of workers earning miserly wages. Elinore Herrick, who served as a regional director of the National Labor Relations Board and was active in the NCL, called the decision a verification of "women's constitutional right to starve."[19] The NCL won the support of the Amalgamated and other groups in launching a campaign for a constitutional amendment to overhaul the structures of restraint, "giving

---

[16] Bernstein, *Caring Society*, p. 130.

[17] 298 U.S. 587 (1936).

[18] John Chambers, "The Big Switch: Justice Roberts and the Minimum Wage Cases," *Labor History* 10 (winter 1969): 54–55, text and nn. 47–49.

[19] Elinore Herrick, address over Station WEAF, National Broadcasting Company, March 13, 1936, Records of the National Consumers' League, collection 5235, box 1, LMDC.

both the federal and state governments power to enact labor and social legislation, with the federal standard controlling unless the states create higher standards." [20]

The women's reform groups and labor unions interested in labor standards did their utmost to mobilize support for Roosevelt's reelection in 1936. The president, capitalizing on popular sentiments, made national labor standards legislation a central issue in his campaign. Roosevelt won a landslide victory, with the widest electoral margin of any candidate since James Monroe. [21]

A Switch in Time Clears the Way for Economic Regulations

Soon after his reelection, Roosevelt summoned Perkins and asked her, "What happened to that nice unconstitutional bill you had tucked away?" [22] The president, according to Perkins, was confident that the country was behind such measures as a national minimum wage and maximum-hours law. But the administration and the coalition working toward social and labor legislation had no reason to believe that the Supreme Court had altered its stance. Roosevelt proposed to pack the Court. That idea provoked an angry debate in Congress, divided the Democratic Party, and was ill received by the country at large. Roosevelt notified Perkins that the wage-and-hour bill would once again have to be delayed. [23]

Some months later, however, the Supreme Court surprised almost everyone when it handed down a series of decisions harkening what has been called "the first constitutional revolution" and the end, in judicial terms, of dual federalism. First, in the *West Coast Hotel v. Parrish* of late March in 1937, [24] the Court upheld a Washington state minimum wage law for women and children, overturning the *Adkins* decision of 1923 and denying the existence of a constitutional principle of "freedom of contract." In the majority opinion, Chief Justice Oliver Otis Hughes wrote:

> What is this freedom? The Constitution does not speak of freedom of contract. It speaks of liberty and prohibits the deprivation of liberty without due process of law. . . . Liberty under the Constitution is thus necessarily subject to the restraints of due process, and regulation which is reasonable in relation

[20] Minutes, Sixty-Second Meeting of the Board of Directors, National Consumers' League, June 11, 1936, p. 3, collection 5235, LMDC; John A. Salmond, *Miss Lucy of the CIO* (Athens: University of Georgia Press, 1988), pp. 61–62, 72; Storrs, "Civilizing Capitalism," p. 344.

[21] William E. Leuchtenburg, *Franklin D. Roosevelt and the New Deal* (New York: Harper and Row, 1963), p. 195.

[22] Perkins, *Roosevelt I Knew*, p. 255.

[23] Ibid., p. 256; Bernstein, *Caring Society*, p. 132.

[24] 300 U.S. 379 (1937).

to its subject and is adopted in the interests of the community is due process. But the liberty safeguarded is liberty in a social organization which requires the protection of law against the evils which menace the health, safety, morals and welfare of the people.[25]

The Court thus moved away from an abstract notion of freedom in which the state is rarely allowed to intervene in economic relationships and toward a substantive notion of freedom which would justify the action of governments, at least at the state level, to regulate the economy and the conditions of workers.

Just two weeks later, in *National Labor Relations Board v. Jones and Laughlin Steel Corporation*, the Supreme Court upheld the National Labor Relations Act. The decision seemed to affirm the revised interpretation of the commerce clause in which all stages of the production process were understood to be interdependent and thus within Congress's power to regulate.[26] The majority opinion read: "Although activities may be intrastate in character when separately considered, if they have such a close and substantial relation to interstate commerce that their control is essential or appropriate to protect that commerce from burdens and obstructions, Congress cannot be denied the power to exercise that control."[27] By broadening the legitimate realm of "interstate commerce" and hence the government's role in regulating the economy, the decision further prepared the ground for the FLSA.

At last, the Supreme Court had dismantled the structural supports of dual federalism, both the strict interpretation of the commerce clause and the reverence for freedom of contract. In late May of 1937, with the judicial obstacles to a national labor standards law cleared, Roosevelt sent to Congress a comprehensive wage-and-hour bill.

Formation of the Wage-and-Hour Bill in the Roosevelt Administration

The labor standards' bill fashioned by the Roosevelt administration appeared to be an unprecedented example of gender-neutral regulation of American labor conditions. In contrast to both the Progressive Era laws for women only and the NRA, with its sex differentials for wages, the interstate commerce criteria in the FLSA displaced the sex-based rationale for labor standards. This new basis of legitimacy meant that the bill could, in

[25] Ibid.
[26] 301 U.S. 1 (1937); See also Alexander Feller and Jacob E. Hurwitz, *How to Operate under the Wage-Hour Law* (New York: Alexander, 1938), pp. 91–99.
[27] 301 U.S. 1 (1937).

theory, be applicable to both men and women. When questioned about sex differentials in the bill during congressional hearings, Perkins would be able to answer unequivocally that the bill did not provide for any and that she disapproved of such a concept. She praised the concept of equal pay for equal work: "I think the wage is an economic factor, and it should be the same no matter who does the work."[28] At those same hearings, Lucy Mason, representing the NCL, also lauded the bill for its coverage of men as well as women.[29] Yet whereas protective labor laws had overtly applied to women only, the seemingly gender-neutral labor standards created in 1937 implicitly left most low-wage women beyond their reach.

Accounts of the formation of the FLSA typically focus on the law's turbulent journey through Congress; the policymaking role of the executive branch has received little attention.[30] But it was in the quiet drafting of the bill by administration officials that the majority of low-paid women workers and nonwhite men, those who could have benefited most from national labor standards, were exempted from coverage. In this process, policymakers were reined in not simply by the Constitution itself, as scholars have tended to assume, but also by political and strategic considerations.

The basis of coverage in protective labor laws had been derived politically, through the triumph of particular ideas about the role of the state and through social constructions of the meaning of female citizenship. Similarly, the new criteria for coverage by national labor standards were also formulated through a political process, only this time in a different institutional context. On this occasion, when the old structures of dual federalism no longer applied, policymakers had to decide which categories of work would qualify as interstate commerce and which would not. The Constitution as interpreted in recent Court decisions provided the basic framework but by no means a definitive blueprint. As administration officials determined the delineation between covered and excluded occupations, political imperatives necessarily came into play.

Earlier, when Secretary Perkins directed the drafting of a bill to restore the wage-and-hour provisions, she had drawn on the model of the Black-Connery Thirty-Hour Bill which had proposed to fine industrialists who ship, in interstate commerce, goods that had been produced under substandard labor conditions. The terms of that bill's coverage ("any mine, quarry, mill, cannery, workshop, factory, or manufacturing establishment") had pertained to mostly male-dominated occupations (with the notable excep-

[28] Senate, Committee on Education and Labor, *Joint Hearings on FLSA*, 75th Cong., 1st sess., June 2, 1937, pp. 187–88, 190–91, 205.

[29] Ibid., p. 404.

[30] Bernstein, *Caring Society*, pp. 116–45; Jonathan Grossman, "Fair Labor Standards Act of 1938: Maximum Struggle for a Minimum Wage," *Monthly Labor Review* 101 (June 1978): 22–30.

tions of canneries and mills).[31] Through the convulsions of the Supreme Court over the next two years, Perkins consulted with numerous constitutional lawyers and administration officials about the viability of the interstate commerce approach.[32]

The bill produced by the administration, though clearly going beyond the extremely restrictive approach of the 1936 *Carter* case, set the terms of coverage cautiously, with limits suggested by the definitions of interstate commerce used in the earlier *Schecter* decision from 1935, on the one hand, and in the 1937 *NLRB* case, on the other. In *Schecter*, Justice Hughes had written that Congress's commerce power pertained only to the direct effects of interstate transactions, whereas indirect effects "remain within the domain of State power." Seeming to define interstate commerce far more broadly, the *NLRB* case had upheld the extension of congressional power over even those industries that merely "affect" commerce. But rather than assume the *NLRB* decision canceled *Schecter*, administration officials steered a prudent middle course. They drafted a labor standards bill that applied to employees "engaged in commerce or in the production of goods for commerce," stating clearly an intent to include the manufacturing sector that preceded trade.[33] But in deference to the earlier exemption in *Schecter* of enterprises in which the "flow" of interstate commerce had come to a final rest, they assumed that distributional activities following trade should be excluded from coverage under the law.[34]

Thus officials marked off the terrain they considered beyond the scope of the FLSA, established the territory clearly within the bill's coverage, and suggested a middle ground that would remain subject to qualifications by Congress and subsequent administrative judgments. Conceding to *Schecter*, policymakers omitted the heavily female retail occupation from coverage.[35] They considered other jobs, especially female occupations in the service sector, to be so firmly embedded in "intrastate" commerce that clarification of their exemption was barely required. Conversely, coverage was widely understood to include the mostly male occupations associated most directly with industry: manufacturing, mining, transportation, and public utilities. The ambiguity in the law lay in the definition of "production of goods for commerce."

The fact that the administration's drafting process was shaped by politics as well as by the new interpretation of the Constitution is illustrated

[31] *Congressional Record*, 72nd Cong., 2d sess., December 21, 1932, vol. 76, pt. 1, 820.
[32] Perkins, *Roosevelt I Knew*, pp. 249–55.
[33] Public Law 718, *Fair Labor Standards Act of 1938*, 75th Cong., 3d sess., June 25, 1938, sec. 6(a).
[34] Bernstein, *Caring Society*, pp. 125–26, 133; Perkins, *Roosevelt I Knew*, pp. 151–52; Paul Douglas and Joseph Hackman, "The Fair Labor Standards Act of 1938, I: The Background and Legislative History of the Act," *Political Science Quarterly* 53 (1938): 499.
[35] Douglas and Hackman, "Fair Labor Standards Act," pp. 499, 514.

by the situation of agricultural workers in the law. Though, in previous cases, agriculture had been considered as falling within the realm of interstate commerce and could certainly be considered within the realm of "production for commerce," the administration made agricultural workers exempt from the wage-and-hour provisions of the bill.[36] Already in the battles over the Social Security Act, the administration had discovered the extreme resistance to regulation of agriculture among southern and rural Democrats in Congress, whose support for New Deal legislation was so critical for passage. The exclusion of agricultural workers meant the omission of more than 50 percent of southern African American employees, men and women, from coverage.[37] Because poll taxes, literacy tests, and other voting restrictions were used to severely limit electoral participation by African Americans during the period, their needs could easily be ignored by the Democratic Party. The combined exclusion of agricultural and domestic workers also omitted near majorities of "Mexican American and American Indian women and men, as well as substantial numbers of Filipino-Americans and other Asian Americans" from coverage as Phyllis Palmer indicates.[38] The child labor prohibition of the FLSA was extended to agriculture (except in instances where children were "not legally required to attend school"), underscoring the groundswell of political support for that provision in contrast to the lack of interest in the plight of nonwhite workers.[39]

The status of most low-paying women's occupations in the FLSA similarly reflected political considerations regarding the reach of the Constitution. Among the greatest beneficiaries of the new law were women workers in the garment and textile trades. As New Deal policies granted government sanction to union activities, the representatives of organized labor gained political influence in the realigned Democratic Party. Sidney Hillman worked closely with Perkins to assure coverage of "sweatshops."[40] The masses of low-paid women in nonunionized service occupations were, by contrast, excluded: the bill failed to extend to workers in laundries, hotels, hairdressing, restaurants, and domestic service. Although it could have been argued that those jobs "affected" commerce, administration officials

[36] Richard A. Epstein, "The Proper Scope of the Commerce Power," *Virginia Law Review* 73 (November 1987): 1440, 1449–50.

[37] This figure is based on Robert Lieberman's detailed analysis of the exclusion of agricultural workers in parts of the Social Security Act; the reference groups are fairly equivalent. See Robert Charles Lieberman, "Race and the Development of the American Welfare State from the New Deal to the Great Society" (Ph.D. diss., Harvard University, 1994), p. 130.

[38] Phyllis Palmer, "Outside the Law: Agricultural and Domestic Workers under the Fair Labor Standards Act," *Journal of Policy History* 7 (1995): 420.

[39] Public Law 718, sec. 13 (a) (6); sec. 12 (a); sec. 13 (c).

[40] Fraser, *Labor Will Rule*, p. 391.

went on the assumption that such work lay well within the confines of intrastate commerce.

Given the new flexibility in legal interpretations in 1937, what can explain the seemingly unquestioning assumption by Perkins and others that so many women's occupations lay beyond the realm of interstate commerce? First, though women reformers and some northern Democrats had hoped for more expansive labor standards legislation, they lacked the ability to alter the debate.[41] As well, the NCL and its affiliates were not about to propose that national laws displace state initiatives; for they were anxious to protect the hard-earned state-level protective labor laws they had achieved over the previous decades.[42]

Second, although Perkins herself advocated national regulatory powers for labor standards, she was influenced once again, as with the Social Security Act, by advice from that staunch defender of state-level governance, Felix Frankfurter. Frankfurter had represented the NCL in protective labor legislation cases during the Progressive Era. He did consider the commerce clause to be a flexible instrument and thought that national labor standards could be held constitutional. He believed, however, that state-level laws were generally preferable for such purposes, and he wanted to preserve the possibilities for further experimentation in public policy in the states. National labor standards with narrow coverage, he was convinced, could serve the positive function of promoting additional state-level initiatives that would cover workers in those large categories he regarded as intrastate commerce.[43]

Third, some women's occupations were considered to belong to an entirely different realm than those industries of "production" that had become a target of state action. When concerns arose among southerners that the FLSA would mandate that housewives "pay your negro girl eleven dollars a week," Roosevelt was clear: "No law ever suggested intended a minimum wages and hours bill to apply to domestic help." As noted by Vivien Hart, "the fact that the President thought of these women as help, not as labor, sums up their problem."[44]

[41] This situation held constant in the decades ahead; see Jerry Voorhis, *Confessions of a Congressman* (Garden City, N.Y.: Doubleday, 1947), p. 94.

[42] Minutes of the Board of Directors, National Consumers' League, March 17, 1937, p. 3, LMDC, collection 5235.

[43] Liva Baker, *Felix Frankfurter* (New York: Coward-McCann, 1969), pp. 114–15; Helen Shirley Thomas, *Felix Frankfurter: Scholar on the Bench* (Baltimore: Johns Hopkins Press, 1960), pp. 315–19, 324–25; Michael E. Parrish, "Felix Frankfurter and American Federalism," in *Federalism: Studies in History, Law, and Policy: Papers from the Second Berkeley Seminar on Federalism*, ed. Harry N. Scheiber (Berkeley: University of California, 1988), pp. 27–35; Felix Frankfurter, *The Commerce Clause* (Chapel Hill: University of North Carolina, 1937), pp. 21–22.

[44] Hart, "Minimum Wage Policy," pp. 336–37.

The original FLSA bill was lengthy and cumbersome. It vested broad powers to fix minimum wages and maximum hours in a labor standards board to be made up of five members. Though the bill contained no figures, Administration officials suggested that Congress adopt a minimum wage level of forty cents per hour and an hours limit of forty hours per week as national standards. Beyond that, the board would be empowered to fix higher wages up to eighty cents per hour in particular industries if it evaluated collective bargaining to be ineffective therein, or if the cost of living, value of services, and other factors necessitated higher pay for a minimum "fair" wage. Labor by children under age sixteen was outlawed. No regional differentials were to be included in the bill, but administrative flexibility was assumed for making allowances for economic differences between geographic regions.[45]

Roosevelt's administration had failed to seize the opportunity to promote broad coverage of national labor regulations. On first seeing the bill, Merle Vincent, counsel to the ILGWU, wrote to union president David Dubinsky, "It has a very narrow definition of interstate commerce which will exclude several million workers from the benefits of the Act."[46] Women and nonwhite men fell disproportionately into those categories, in agriculture, as domestics, and in retail and service work. In short, the Roosevelt administration had delineated the new expanse of interstate commerce in a manner that would make for a gender divide in the coverage of labor standards.

The FLSA's Tumultuous Journey through Congress

Roosevelt submitted the wage-and-hour bill to Congress in May 1937. Given widespread popular support and the cautious drafting process, administration officials were optimistic that the bill would pass quickly. Such hopes dissipated, however, early in the congressional hearings, as conflicts arose in the ranks of organized labor. Though advocates for female workers offered enthusiastic support for the bill, advocates for male workers began to voice strong reservations.[47]

Hearings on the FLSA: Conflicts in the Ranks of Labor

In congressional hearings on the wage-and-hour bill, most parties testified in a predictable manner. Administration officials advocated for the bill;

---

[45] Bernstein, *Caring Society*, p. 137.

[46] Letter, Merle Vincent to David Dubinsky, May 22, 1937, Records of the International Ladies Garment Workers Union, collection 3/10/2, box 81, file 7B, LMDC.

[47] Perkins, *Roosevelt I Knew*, p. 257; James MacGregor Burns, *Congress on Trial: The Legislative Process and the Administrative State* (New York: Harper, 1949), p. 70.

the National Association of Manufacturers and Chamber of Commerce opposed it; and representatives of employers in the textile industry divided on a north/south regional basis. Key elements of organized labor caught policymakers by surprise, however, when they began to criticize the bill.[48] Although the recent dismantling of dual federalism had allowed labor organizations to acquire a place in national politics, in the FLSA battles they quickly joined the forces that opposed further alterations of federalism. Specifically, labor leaders feared a policy that would expand the domain of national government to nonunionized workers.

The national leadership of the AFL had long opposed minimum wage laws, though some state-level federations had supported protective labor laws for women only. The organization feared that the "minimum would become the maximum" and would undermine efforts for better wages through collective bargaining. During the hearings, AFL official William Green did, at least, "faintly endorse"[49] the labor standards bill. He did so on the condition that the wage standard be adopted at a rock-bottom level, too low to have adverse effects on the efforts of organized workers who sought to improve their wages through collective bargaining. Yet he argued for amendments to clarify that the bill would act to encourage rather than to supplant collective bargaining.[50]

John L. Lewis of the CIO offered more support than Green for the wage-and-hour bill, but he articulated various reservations as well, and he made his concerns about gender-related issues quite explicit. He voiced strong support for the principle of equal pay: "I believe the committee should add to the bill, namely, that women doing the same work as men should receive the same pay as men."[51] But he went on to argue that the ultimate interest of the CIO was not in fighting for a miserly minimum wage of forty cents an hour, which would necessitate that both husbands and wives and sometimes their adolescent children work to support a family:

This practice is destructive to all that we cherish most in our American institutions. Normally, a husband and father should be able to earn enough to support his family. This does not mean, of course, that I am opposed to the employment of women, or even of wives, when this is the result of their own free choice. But I am violently opposed to a system which by *degrading the earning of adult males*, makes it economically necessary for wives and children to

[48] Senate, *Joint Hearings on the Fair Labor Standards Act*; also, Fraser, *Labor Will Rule*, p. 399; Bernstein, *Caring Society*, p. 138; James MacGregor Burns, *Congress on Trial* (New York: Gordian, 1966), p. 70; Douglas and Hackman, "Fair Labor Standards Act," pp. 508–13; Voorhis, *Confessions of a Congressman*, p. 88.
[49] Frances Perkins as quoted in George Martin, *Madam Secretary: Frances Perkins* (Boston: Houghton Mifflin, 1976), p. 390.
[50] Senate, *Joint Hearings on the Fair Labor Standards Act*, p. 221.
[51] Ibid., p. 273.

become supplementary wage earners, and then says, "See the nice income of this family." [52]

Lewis insisted that the struggle to ensure a "living wage" to all adult males, enabling them to support their families single-handedly, must go forward. But though he voiced clearly his belief that women should be allowed to work if they wished and to earn fair wages, his overriding concern was that men must be able to exercise economic independence, ensuring the well-being of a middle-class family model with distinct gender roles. If the "minimum became the maximum," Lewis worried, labor standards might undermine that traditional family model. At the same time, to protect the autonomy of working men, he urged elimination of the section of the bill which proposed a secondary "minimum fair wage" set by a labor standards board, complaining that the principle sounded like "wage fixing" and threatened to interfere in the relationship between employer and employee. [53]

Representatives of organizations in the low-paid, female-dominated garment and textile industries, namely the ACWA and ILGWU, and NCL voiced enthusiastic support for the FLSA including the minimum wage standard and the minimum fair wage. [54] When Sidney Hillman, speaking for the ACWA, was questioned as to why his view conflicted dramatically with Lewis's, he answered that he spoke from his years of experience with workers in the textile and garment industries, who would surely benefit from such legislation, whereas Lewis spoke from his experience in the coal industry, which already provided wages well above "sixty cents or eighty cents an hour." [55] He could have added that in the various garment and textile industries, women were between 50 and 80 percent of operatives, whereas the mining industry employed nearly all men. [56] From the perspective of the Amalgamated, the proposed minimum wage was sufficiently low that it would not endanger unions' efforts in collective bargaining, and it would establish a necessary wage floor to protect unorganized women and to keep factories from relocating. Merle Vincent, counsel for the ILGWU, argued similarly. [57]

Both Perkins and the NCL representatives articulated the values of labor standards in terms similar to those used by themselves and their forebears in the Progressive Era women reformers' tradition, but with an updated,

---

[52] Ibid., p. 275. Emphasis mine.

[53] Ibid., pp. 273–74.

[54] Senate, *Joint Hearings on the Fair Labor Standards Act*, p. 946.

[55] Ibid., p. 948.

[56] Bureau of the Census, *Census of the Population, 1940: The Labor Force*, vol. 3, (Washington, D.C.: GPO, 1940), table 58.

[57] Senate, *Joint Hearings on the Fair Labor Standards Act*, pp. 262–69.

Keynesian twist. Perkins appealed in part to humanitarian reasons to pass the bill, citing the "evils of child labor, sweatshops and low wages,"[58] but she also argued that the bill would do away with the problem of "wage cutters," of businesses that could sell their products at a lower cost than the competition because they paid the most miserly wages.[59] Female employees most often became the underpaid or unemployed victims of these "gypsy industries," which typically moved from state to state to escape both labor laws and labor unions. Speaking for the NCL, Mason derided such industries as "parasites" that not only exploited workers but also drained profits from businesses elsewhere which paid workers more and failed to improve the quality of life in the communities where they became established.[60] The FLSA would not only protect employees and grant more security to businesses but through the minimum wage, grant more purchasing power to many citizens and thus spark economic growth.[61]

Later, at its October 1937 convention, the AFL came out firmly against the FLSA, arguing that the proposed labor standards board would become too powerful and undermine the power of organized labor to engage in collective bargaining. After two years of experience with the NLRB, the federation had begun to consider such administrative arrangements as constraints on labor autonomy.[62]

In sum, advocates for women workers understood labor standards as empowering for those who needed them and as insignificant for workers who already earned better wages. Working men's advocates perceived them as fundamentally disempowering. They conceded that such measures might be a legitimate means of protecting women, whom they considered difficult to organize, but they insisted that national labor standards were a dangerous threat to the political and economic agency of organized workers. Perkins, Hillman, and other advocates of labor standards waxed eloquent about how such measures would help create better citizens and a healthier democracy owing to the greater freedom and improved quality of life of those whose social status had rendered them economically vulnerable in the work force.[63] The AFL convention in October 1937 countered with:

> The most essential right of free men is that of voluntary association for lawful purposes. . . . This priceless right and the freedom to bargain collectively with employers would be injuriously affected by any Federal Board or Commission

[58] Ibid., p. 174.
[59] Ibid., p. 175.
[60] Ibid., pp. 405–6.
[61] Several articulated this Keynesian theme, including Hillman, ibid., p. 956.
[62] Christopher L. Tomlins, *The State and the Unions: Labor Relations, Law, and the Organized Labor Movement in America, 1880–1960* (New York: Cambridge University Press, 1985), p. 165.
[63] Senate, *Joint Hearings on the Fair Labor Standards Act*, pp. 173, 180, 943, 957.

. . . who had the power to in any measure replace the function of the members of the AFL to bargain collectively with their employers. . . . It would be definitely injurious . . . if the principle of voluntarism in the activism of free men was interfered with.[64]

For those with the pro–labor standards perspective, action by the state could liberate women from the slavery of the sweatshops; for those with the anti–labor standards perspective, such action constituted an infringement of men's liberty.

The FLSA under Siege: Regional Conflicts in Congress

Though the political climate for the wage-and-hour bill had seemed quite favorable when it was first introduced, opposition mounted as the bill became bogged down amid conflicts in the ranks of organized labor. As 1937 proceeded, the economy sank yet again, causing mills in the South to close, jobs to disappear, and wages to fall. Opposition to the New Deal hardened in the increasingly conservative Congress, and not only among southerners.[65]

In early July the Senate Committee on Education and Labor completed work on the bill by adding several weakening amendments. The primary changes were dramatic curbs on the power of the proposed board and a lowering of child labor standards.[66] When the bill reached the Senate floor, senators committed to acting on behalf of organized labor became confused by the ambivalence of the CIO and a division in the leadership of the AFL. Vincent wrote to Dubinsky, "Five A.F. of L. Board members are dogging Senators to kill the bill."[67] In the South opposition was organized by the Southern Pine Industry Committee, the National Association of Manufacturers, and the Chamber of Commerce, who swayed southern members of Congress to oppose the bill.[68] This time, Vincent informed Dubinsky, "The Labor Bill [FLSA] has been pretty thoroughly mangled by the Southern group. The Southern Manufacturers counsel is laying down a barrage of demands and threats."[69] Senators finally passed a version of the FLSA, but only after adding dozens of exemptions: for local retailing, railroad employees, forestry, farming, dairying, and fishing.

[64] Report of Proceedings, *American Federation of Labor: 57th Annual Convention* (n.p.: American Federation of Labor, 1937), p. 285.

[65] Fraser, *Labor Will Rule*, p. 399; James T. Patterson, *Congressional Conservatism and the New Deal* (Lexington: University of Kentucky Press, 1967), pp. 149–54, 179–80, 196.

[66] Burns, *Congress on Trial*, p. 71.

[67] ILGWU records, collection 3/10/2, box 81, file 7B, LMDC.

[68] See *Effects of Black-Connery Wage and Hour Bill*, pamphlet of the Southern Pine Industry Committee, New Orleans, LMDC.

[69] Letter dated July 8, 1937, in ILGWU records, collection 3/10/2, box 81, file 7B, LMDC.

In early August the House Labor Committee acted on the Senate version of the bill under the new leadership of Representative Mary Norton (D-N.J.). Though generally sympathetic to the position of the predominant labor unions, she had been influenced by the "women's network" to support labor standards.[70] At Roosevelt's request, her committee added some of the concessions requested by Green to protect collective bargaining.[71] The bill failed to come to the House floor for a vote, however, because it was held hostage by the House Rules Committee, which was dominated by southern Democrats.[72]

Finally, by early December, after a variety of vote "trades" and other deals, enough members had signed a discharge petition to force the Rules Committee to surrender the bill. Norton, intending to make a significant concession to the AFL, replaced the bill's proposed independent board with an administrator in the DOL. She failed to realize that AFL leaders held that department in disdain, largely because of its nonlabor, female head. In December, the AFL opposed Norton's bill and supported its own, which placed the law's administration in the Department of Justice instead. The AFL's bill was defeated in the House on December 12 by 162 to 131. Then, on December 17, Norton's bill was defeated by 216 to 198.[73]

The defeat marked the first time that legislation with Roosevelt's support had failed on the House floor since early in 1933, and the president was outraged. He vowed to continue to press for passage of the bill and asked Perkins to simplify and shorten it during Congress's recess. Early in 1938, he urged the new Congress to pass a revised version that proposed to create a division of wages and hours under an administrator who would appoint tripartite boards to investigate, hold hearings, and recommend wage-and-hour standards within the limitations of forty cents per hour and forty hours per week.[74] The AFL continued to thwart the plan, however, still fearing overly broad powers vested in a federal administrator.[75] Norton appointed a subcommittee to devise a version acceptable to labor. After the

[70] Gary Mitchell, "Women Standing for Women: The Early Political Career of Mary T. Norton," *New Jersey History* 96 (1978): 27–42; letters, Clara Beyer to Molly Dewson, February 10, 1937, and Molly Dewson to Clara Beyer, July 12, 1958, both in Dewson Papers, General Correspondence, box 1, FDR. See also Eileen Boris, *Home to Work* (New York: Cambridge University Press, 1994), pp. 287–89.

[71] Bernstein, *Caring Society*, p. 139.

[72] Burns, *Congress on Trial*, pp. 73–74; Patterson, *Congressional Conservatism and the New Deal*, pp. 153–54, 179–80.

[73] Burns, *Congress on Trial*, pp. 72–77; Bernstein, *Caring Society*, pp. 140–41.

[74] Burns, *Congress on Trial*, p. 79.

[75] The treatment of the FLSA in Congress illustrates Terry Moe's observation that groups opposing a piece of legislation tend to press for fragmented procedures of administration and other features aimed at undermining the chances of the law's success; see Terry Moe, "The Politics of Bureaucratic Structure," in *Can the Government Govern?* ed. John E. Chubb and Paul E. Peterson (Washington, D.C.: Brookings, 1989), p. 326.

AFL rejected yet another version, Green, under pressure from both the administration and the rank and file, finally gave reluctant support to a second revision. Once again, the Rules Committee blocked the bill.

The NCL, ACWA, and ILGWU rallied for the bill. On April 27, a group of garment and textile workers from the ACWA and the ILGWU, nearly all women, went to Washington to testify before a conference of New York congressmen on the need for the FLSA. Some reported that their employers had already purchased factories in the South, where they could pay lower wages, and said they feared they would lose their own jobs if the trend continued. Others cited instances in the Northeast of a resurgence of sweatshops, competing with union shops.[76] An ACWA report about the workers' subsequent visits to their own members of Congress related a story that foreshadowed both the scope and the limits of labor standards for women workers:

> Speaking to Congressmen who had voted against the bill [in December 1937], they urged them to reconsider their position and told them that the organized workers regarded a vote against the bill as a vote against the best interests of labor. One $10,000 a year Congressman told a delegate that he would not vote for the bill because that might make him pay his maid $15.00 a week. The delegate replied that *she was not talking about how she could pay a maid. . . . but how she could get $15.00 a week to support a family on.*[77]

Throughout the spring of 1938, articles in ACWA's *Advance* urged the rank and file to press their representatives to support the wage-and-hour bill. The NCL made mobilization of support for the legislation the primary task for the season, urging its own members to contact their representatives to support the bill and attempting to broaden public support through speeches, editorials, and radio talk show appearances.[78]

Meanwhile, the Roosevelt administration formulated a strategy to make popular support for the FLSA evident in the South through primary election returns. A Gallup poll in February had already shown that a large portion of the public, including the South, favored the enactment of a national labor standards law. Political experts knew that Claude Pepper would win the nomination for the Senate in the Florida primary on May 3. Through Tom Corcoran, a donation of ten thousand dollars was turned

---

[76] Document dated April 30, 1938, Records of ACWA, collection 5619c, box 546, file B702, LMDC.

[77] Memo dated April 30, 1938, ibid. Emphasis mine.

[78] Minutes, National Consumers League Board of Directors Annual Meeting, December 1938, Records of the National Consumers League, LMDC, collection 5235. For a thorough treatment, see Storrs, "Civilizing Capitalism," pp. 351–72.

over to Pepper to urge him to speak vigorously for the wage-and-hour bill.[79] When Pepper won a decisive victory, the tide turned at last: large numbers of representatives signed a discharge petition immediately, and finally, on May 24, the House passed the House Labor Committee's version of the FLSA by a vote of 314 to 97.[80]

The divisions within labor plagued the bill to the bitter end, as the AFL continued to denounce the Senate version once the conference committee tried to iron out the vast differences between the bills. At last, on June 11, the committee agreed on a bill providing for a single administrator in the DOL, provisions for industry advisory committees, a number of exemptions, and extremely low minimum wage rates: twenty-five cents an hour in 1938 increasing to a maximum of forty cents an hour by 1945. With such paltry standards, the FLSA posed almost no threat to southern industrialists, who had feared they would have to close shop, and was irrelevant for male union constituencies who earned far more generous wages already. The House and Senate accepted the conference report on June 14, and Roosevelt signed the act into law on June 25, 1938.[81]

Just one month later, Women's Bureau officials summed up the outcome of the policymaking process in their publication, *Woman Worker*. They applauded the advances for women employed in industries to which the law applied, especially in the garment and textile trades. They pointed out, however, that large portions of the female labor force were exempt from the law's coverage, including the low-paid jobs of retail workers, laundry and dying and cleaning operatives, cannery workers, waitresses and other hotel and restaurant employees, beauty operators, agricultural laborers, household employees, and many clerical workers.[82] In short, the judicial vestiges of dual federalism had combined with the politics of the New Deal to exempt from coverage under national labor standards the majority of women workers in the lowest-paid jobs, leaving them to plead their case to the individual states.

---

[79] Claude Denson Pepper with Hays Gorey, *Pepper* (Boston: Hall, 1988), pp. 96–97; Burns, *Congress on Trial*, p. 81.

[80] George Brown Tindall, *The Emergence of the New South, 1913–1945* (Baton Rouge: Louisiana State University Press, 1967), pp. 534–35; Patterson, *Congressional Conservatism*, pp. 242–46.

[81] House, *Conference Report: Fair Labor Standards Act of 1938*, June 11, 1938, 75th Cong., 3d sess., Rep. 2738; Bernstein, *Caring Society*, p. 142.

[82] Department of Labor, Women's Bureau, "The Federal Wage-Hour Law and Women Workers," *Woman Worker*, July 1938, p. 3.

CHAPTER EIGHT

The Implementation of the Fair Labor Standards Act of 1938

Every man has a right to life; and this means that he has also a right to make a comfortable living. He may by sloth or crime decline to exercise that right; but it may not be denied to him. We have no actual famine or dearth; our industrial and agricultural mechanism can provide enough and to spare. Our Government formal and informal, political and economic, owes to everyone an avenue to possess himself of a portion of that plenty sufficient for his needs, through his own work.

— President Franklin D. Roosevelt, campaign address on progressive government, Commonwealth Club of San Francisco, September 23, 1932

The early administrators of the Wage and Hour Division in the Department of Labor interpreted the coverage of the Fair Labor Standards Act as liberally as its definition of inclusion would appear to permit. Nonetheless, the FLSA's delineation between coverage and exemption still resulted in a two-tiered system of governmental regulation with gender-specific consequences. In time, the boundaries of the FLSA came to exemplify how New Deal policymakers had restructured federalism in a manner that reorganized governance along the lines of gender, creating qualitatively different forms of citizenship for men and women in the following decades.

The Early Implementation of the FLSA

The framers of the FLSA did succeed in creating a law that would be found constitutional: the statute was upheld in the 1941 decision *U.S. v. Darby Lumber Co.*[1] The Supreme Court, by then having a majority of justices appointed by Roosevelt, at last overturned *Hammer v. Dagenhart*,[2]

[1] 312 U.S. 100 (1941).
[2] 247 U.S. 251 (1918).

canceling the need for a constitutional amendment. Wrote Justice Harlan F. Stone in the majority opinion: "It is no longer open to question that the fixing of a minimum wage is within the legislative power and that the bare fact of its exercise is not a denial of due process. . . . Nor is it any longer open to question that it is within the legislative power to fix maximum hours." [3] Furthermore, in contrast to earlier decisions that affirmed laws for women only, based on a rationale of gender difference, the court affirmed the application of the law to both sexes.

Long before the judiciary offered an approving nod to the legislation, proponents of labor standards, well aware of the narrow scope of the FLSA, had sought to make the implementation of the provisions as far-reaching as possible. They knew that the manner in which the new Wage and Hour Division administered the law could make a real difference in the number of workers affected. As Merle Vincent had written to David Dubinsky when Congress finally passed the FLSA, "It's a weak beginning, but if we are lucky in getting a good administrator, he can make the law realize the best possible results under it and assemble facts to show the necessity of amendments to expand and strengthen it." [4] The first administrators were selected by Frances Perkins in consultation with Sidney Hillman. By 1941 there were nearly twelve hundred inspectors in the field, and they made 48,449 investigations, which had resulted in approximately 19,000 establishments paying ten million dollars in additional wages to their employees. [5]

Already, in the first years of implementation, administrators could safely interpret the statute in the most liberal fashion its categories would permit because, during the period, the Supreme Court handed down several more decisions that clarified and further expanded the national government's role in regulating interstate commerce. In the 1938 decision *Santa Cruz Fruit Packing Company v. National Labor Relations Board*,[6] the Court upheld a ruling by the NLRB even though it pertained to a company that sold only 37 percent of its goods in interstate commerce. The reach of the commerce clause was broadened still further in *Consolidated Edison Co. v. NLRB*, also in 1938, and even more dramatically in *NLRB v. Fainblatt* in 1939.[7] The first decision confirmed NLRB's jurisdiction over a power company that sold entirely within one state, on the basis that many of the purchasers (such as radio stations, airports, etc.) were themselves engaged in

---

[3] 312 U.S. 100 (1941).

[4] Letter, Merle Vincent to David Dubinsky, June 11, 1938, Records of the International Ladies' Garment Workers Unions, LMDC, box 81, file 7A.

[5] Steve Fraser, *Labor Will Rule: Sidney Hillman and the Rise of American Labor* (New York: Free Press, 1991), p. 411; George Martin, *Madam Secretary: Frances Perkins* (Boston: Houghton Mifflin, 1976), pp. 392–93.

[6] 303 U.S. 453 (1938).

[7] 305 U.S. 197 (1938); 306 U.S. 601 (1939).

interstate commerce. In the second case, the Court upheld NLRB rulings in regard to a small-scale clothing producer who sold all goods within the state.[8] Indeed, in the course of a few short years, the commerce power had been expanded enormously.

Work-Force Coverage under the FLSA

Given that the leadership of the Wage and Hour Division and the judicial climate of the late 1930s permitted a relatively expansive interpretation of the FLSA, how much of the work force would actually come under the coverage of the FLSA in the early years of implementation, and what would the implications be in terms of gender? To answer these questions, it is necessary to examine how administrators interpreted the reach of the law and to analyze the composition of the affected occupations by sex. Past scholarship on the FLSA's coverage has utilized data calculated in 1939 from employers' responses to questionnaires returned voluntarily to the DOL.[9] Not only were DOL officials themselves dubious about the quality of this data, but, moreover, the findings relied on the perspectives of employers, who may have had limited understanding of the terms of the statute and who could only guess as to the manner in which it would be interpreted by administrators. More recently, Ronnie Steinberg has evaluated FLSA coverage in terms of sex.[10] Although she did examine judicial and administrative decisions in making her evaluations about employee coverage, Steinberg omitted a significant portion of the work force from her examination, and thus her findings do not adequately portray the situation of all working persons, by sex, in relation to the FLSA provisions.[11]

---

[8] Alfred H. Kelly, Winfred A. Harbison, and Herman Belz, *The American Constitution: Its Origins and Development*, 7th ed. (New York: Norton, 1991), 2:489–90.

[9] Department of Labor, Bureau of Labor Statistics, *Estimated Number of Workers in April 1939 Subject to Provisions of FLSA, Effective October 24, 1939*, by A. F. Hinrichs and A. Sturges (Washington, D.C.: Department of Labor, 1939). The method of data collection yielded very conservative estimates of the law's coverage, claiming that only about one-fifth of the labor force (eleven million workers) would be covered. The report suggested, moreover, that the minimum wage provisions would have nearly negligible consequences: of workers to whom the law applied, only about 300,000 would actually see an increase in their wages under the 25¢ per hour minimum in the first year under the law and 650,000 when the 30¢ per hour minimum took effect.

[10] Ronnie Steinberg, *Wages and Hours: Labor and Reform in Twentieth-Century America* (New Brunswick: Rutgers University Press, 1982), pp. 99–100. Steinberg shows inverse proportions of male and female workers covered, respectively, by national versus state labor standards from 1938 to 1970.

[11] Because minimum wage laws excluded some entire categories of workers, namely, owners and managers and professional, executive, administrative, and public employees, Steinberg dropped those occupational groupings from her analysis altogether. Because those groups included a disproportionate number of male workers, their omission from the analysis skews Steinberg's evaluation of FLSA coverage in terms of sex. Another shortcoming of Steinberg's data is that she does not clarify how extensively she disaggregated occupational groupings in making judgments about their coverage. Ibid., pp. 37, 30–31.

For this book, then, data has been compiled anew, focusing on the minimum wage component of the FLSA. The actual coverage of the provision was determined by examining the language of the statute and definitions of interstate commerce used by the Wage and Hour Division, both as articulated by the division's counsel in 1940 and as exercised in cases in the early 1940s.[12] The results of this analysis, when applied to categories of occupations used in the 1940 census, yielded a classification of occupations covered and exempt from the FLSA.[13] On this basis, the total number of workers covered by the law appears to have been 15,467,760.[14] Overall, 34% of the work force was covered and 66% were exempt. Next, the data were used to figure the number of covered versus exempt workers by sex.

To put FLSA coverage in the appropriate context, the occupational divisions of the 1940 work force by sex must be examined.[15] As shown in Table 9, the 1940 census reveals that occupational segregation persisted: women and men were quite differently situated in the work force. The five occupational groupings employing the greatest proportion of men included, in diminishing order, factory operatives, farmers and managers, craftsmen and foremen, clerical and sales workers, and proprietors. By contrast, women's jobs were found most often in clerical and sales work, followed by factory work, domestic service, professional and semiprofessional employment, and service work.

Scholars have often assumed that the law covered a far lower percentage of women than men.[16] Despite the disparity in occupations between

---

[12] See House, *Conference Report: Fair Labor Standards Act of 1938, H.R. 2738*, 75th Cong., 3d sess., June 11, 1938; Department of Labor, *Opinion Manual of the General Counsel, Wage and Hour Division* (Washington, D.C.: GPO, 1940), vol. 1; Raymond S. Smethurst and Reuben S. Haslam, *Cases on the Fair Labor Standards Act of 1938* (Washington, DC: Smethurst, 1949); Department of Labor, *First Annual Report of the Administrator of the Wage and Hour Division, 1939* (Washington, D.C.: GPO, 1940); Louis Weiner, *Federal Wage and Hour Law* (Philadelphia: American Law Institute, 1977).

[13] Bureau of the Census, *Census of the Population, 1940: Summary Report* (Washington, D.C.: GPO, 1940), Occupations, table 58, pp. 75–80. Some workers were considered to be entirely exempt from coverage regardless of the relation of their particular job to interstate commerce; for instance, all professionals, agricultural workers, and service and domestic workers were excluded. Much more detailed analysis and discretionary judgments were required to determine the status of some other occupational groups: 49 percent of clerical and sales workers were exempt from the FLSA, as well as 43 percent of craftsmen and foremen, 22 percent of nonfarm labor, and 24 percent of factory operatives. See Suzanne B. Mettler, "Divided Citizens: State-Building, Federalism, and Gender in the New Deal," (Ph.D. diss., Cornell University, 1994), App. A.

[14] Since the data were derived through judgments about the legal and administrative interpretations of coverage rather than payment of the minimum wage in actual practice, they tend to overestimate the number of workers who actually received minimum wages as a result of the law.

[15] Coverage evaluations rely on census data that disaggregate each of these general occupational categories into very detailed job classifications.

[16] For example, see Vivien Hart, "Minimum Wage Policy and Constitutional Inequality: The Paradox of the Fair Labor Standards Act of 1938," *Journal of Policy History* 1 (1989): 337.

Table 9. Occupational groups of employed persons, by sex, 1940 (in percentages)

	Males	Females
Professional and semiprofessional	5.5	13.0
Farmers and managers	14.7	1.4
Proprietors	9.7	3.8
Clerical and sales	12.8	28.3
Craftsmen and foremen	14.5	0.9
Factory operatives	18.2	18.4
Domestic service	0.4	17.7
Protective service	2.0	0.0
Service (excluding domestic and protective)	4.5	11.3
Farm labor	8.1	2.9
Labor (excluding farm)	8.7	0.9
Occupation not reported	0.7	1.2

Source: Bureau of the Census, *Census of the Population: 1940: Summary Report,* (Washington, D.C.: GPO, 1940), table 58, pp. 75–80.

Table 10. Status of workers under FLSA, covered versus exempt, by sex, 1940 (in percentages)

	Males	Females
Covered	34.9	32.1
Exempt	64.9	67.9

Sources: House, *Conference Report: Fair Labor Standards Act of 1938, H.R. 2738,* 75th Cong., 3d sess., June 11, 1938; Department of Labor, *Opinion Manual of the General Counsel Wage and Hour Division* (Washington, D.C.: GPO, 1940), vol. 1; Raymond S. Smethurst and Reuben S. Haslam, *Cases on the Fair Labor Standards Act of 1938* (Washington, D.C.: Smethurst, 1949); Department of Labor, *First Annual Report of the Administrator of the Wage and Hour Division, 1939* (Washington, D.C.: GPO, 1940), p. 20; Louis Weiner, *Federal Wage and Hour Law,* (Philadelphia: American Law Institute, 1977), p. 113; Bureau of the Census, *Census of Business, 1940: Summary on Retail Trade* (Washington, D.C.: GPO, 1940); and Department of Labor, Women's Bureau, *Office Work in Houston,* Bulletin No. 188-1, *Office Work in Los Angeles,* No. 188-2, *Office Work in Kansas City,* No. 188-3, *Office Work in Richmond,* No. 188-4, and *Office Work in Philadelphia,* No. 188-5 (Washington, D.C.: GPO, 1942).

Table 11. Status of workers under the minimum wage provisions of the FLSA, by sex and occupational group, 1940 (in percentages)

Occupational group	Males		Females	
	Covered	Exempt	Covered	Exempt
Professional and Semiprofessional	0.0	5.5	0.0	13.0
Farmers and managers	0.0	14.7	0.0	1.4
Proprietors	0.0	9.7	0.0	3.8
Clerical and sales	6.0	6.8	16.3	12.0
Craftsmen and foremen	8.3	6.2	0.4	0.5
Factory Operatives	13.7	4.5	14.7	3.7
Domestics	0.0	0.4	0.0	17.7
Protective service	0.0	2.0	0.0	0.0
Service (excluding domestic and protective)	0.0	4.5	0.0	11.3
Farm labor	0.0	8.1	0.0	2.9
Labor (excluding farm)	6.9	1.8	0.7	0.2
Occupation not reported	0.0	0.7	0.0	1.2

Sources: see sources for Tables 9 and 10.

the sexes, however, the data analysis for this study reveal that the FLSA minimum wage provisions actually covered nearly equal proportions of the male and female work force. As seen in Table 10, there existed only about a 3 percent difference in coverage, with approximately 35 percent of all men in the work force covered compared with 32 percent of all women.

The occupational breakdown by sex of workers covered versus exempt is shown in Table 11. Among male workers, the minimum wage provisions of the FLSA were interpreted to apply to 13.7 percent who worked as factory operatives, 8.3 percent who were craftsmen and foremen, 6.9 percent who worked as nonfarm laborers, and 6.0 percent in clerical and sales work. In the female work force, 16.3 percent of employees were covered because of the status of their jobs in clerical and sales work, and 14.7 percent were covered who were factory operatives. The task remains, however, to analyze what difference the FLSA actually made for those who were covered by its provisions, and what difference it could have made if those who were excluded had come under its provisions.

Effectiveness of the FLSA in Increasing Wages

A DOL report noted that women had higher average hourly earnings in March 1940 than one year previous in nearly all of the industries employing large numbers of women. The report credited the FLSA with influencing these wage raises, citing an increase of 10 percent in women's wages in the cotton-dress industry and 6 percent in the cotton-goods,

Table 12. Subminimum wage workers and percentage of women employed in twelve industries most affected by FLSA minimum wage provisions

	Number of wage earners earning less than 30¢ an hour (1939)	Percentage of women employed in industry (1940)
Sawmills	96,200	2.3
Furniture	9,300	14.4
Millwork	10,000–11,000	*
Boots and shoes	20,400	46.1
Clothing, men's	*	77.4
Clothing, women's	28,000	77.4
Shirts and Collars	10,500	77.4
Cotton	51,300	47.0
Knit goods	28,100	66.9
Silk and rayon	10,500	55.4
Cottonseed oil	15,100	*
Fertilizers	12,500	*

Sources: Department of Labor, Bureau of Labor Statistics, *Estimated Number of Workers in April 1939 Subject to Provisions of the Fair Labor Standards Act, Effective October 24, 1939*, by A. F. Hinrichs and A. Sturges (Washington, D.C.: Department of Labor, 1939), pp. 25–26; Bureau of the Census, *Census of the Population, 1940: The Labor Force* (Washington, D.C.: GPO, 1940), table 58, p. 78.
* Data unavailable.

candy, women's undergarments, rubber boots and shoes, and hosiery industries.[17]

Data limitations preclude reaching a conclusive answer to the question of how many workers, male and female, saw an increase in their wages because of the minimum wage provisions of the FLSA.[18] Nonetheless, the demographics of work-force participation in those low-wage industries for which the labor standards law forced changes can be examined. According to the 1939 DOL report, twelve industries employed more than three-quarters of the wage earners in the manufacturing sector who earned less than thirty cents per hour. These data have been paired in Table 12 with the percentages of men versus women in each industry.

Although these data are somewhat incomplete and fail to specify the sex of workers whose wages actually increased under the FLSA, comparison with occupational data in the 1940 census suggests that women figured prominently in several of the industries most affected by the FLSA mini-

[17] Bureau of Labor Statistics, "Women in Industry" (Bulletin 694), *Handbook of Labor Statistics* 1 (1941): 969.

[18] The 1940 census data are not very useful for determining which workers benefited from the new minimum wage because several industries had already improved conditions while the NRA was in effect earlier in the 1930s, and others raised wages as soon as the FLSA took effect, either voluntarily or in response to specific industry codes.

mum wage provisions. Considering that women represented 24.7 percent of the total work force in 1940, the various textile and clothing-production industries shown in the table clearly employed disproportionate percentages of women workers. Given that most women's jobs in industry in 1940 were found at the bottom of the pay scale, it is fair to assume that the majority of workers in the textile and clothing industries who benefited from the minimum wage provision were women.[19]

By most accounts, the number of workers receiving immediate gains were few. Nonetheless, for women workers in the sweatshops as well as men in the low-wage sawmill and furniture industries who did benefit, national labor standards surely were a most welcome reform.

Significance of Exemption for Men and Women

With only about a third of the work force covered by the FLSA, the more important question becomes: Of workers whose occupations were exempt from the minimum wage, for how many would coverage have meant an increase in wages? Here, wage data from the 1940 census were used to calculate average salaries for each employment classification.[20] In the early 1940s, a standard annual minimum wage salary for full-time work would have been $800: 40¢ an hour, 40 hours a week, 50 weeks a year. The calculations revealed that whereas 35.6 percent of male workers exempt from the FLSA earned wages below this minimum annual salary, 62.1 percent of exempt female workers did. In other words, as summarized in Table 13, women suffered in far greater proportions than men as a consequence of exemption from coverage.[21] For most men, exemption from FLSA coverage was irrelevant except for those 22.8 percent of the total male work force who were engaged in agriculture, who did earn extremely low wages and among whom nonwhite men figured disproportionately.[22] The other 42.1 percent of male workers who worked in exempt occupations tended to earn the highest salaries offered in 1940, as professionals, businessmen, government workers, skilled craftsmen, and in managerial positions. By contrast, 42.2 percent of all female employees, nearly twice the proportion

[19] See Bureau of Labor Statistics, "Women in Industry," noting that in every industry reported, women had lower earnings than men and in half of the industries reported, women's average hourly earnings were less than the lowest average for men.

[20] This was done by figuring weighted averages of the numbers of workers of each type per income group and then adding them together.

[21] For a detailed discussion of covered and exempt groups within each broad occupational category, see Mettler, "Divided Citizens," App. B.

[22] It should be noted, however, that though 8.1 percent of this group were "farm laborers," the other 14.7 percent were "farmers and managers," who presumably derived various non-cash benefits, namely, food, from farming.

Table 13. Average annual wages in dollars for workers exempt from the FLSA, by sex and occupational group, 1940

Occupational Group	Males: average annual		Females: average annual	
	% exempt	Wages ($)	% exempt	Wages ($)
Professional and semiprofessional	5.5	1,661	13.0	1,152
Farmers and managers	14.7	86	1.4	67
Proprietors	9.7	1,362	3.8	628
Clerical and sales	6.8	1,557	12.0	910
Craftsmen and foremen	6.2	1,264	0.5	993
Factory operatives	4.5	1,108	3.7	573
Domestics	0.4	579	17.7	359
Protective service	2.0	1,431	0.0	
Service (excluding domestic and protective)	4.5	836	11.3	518
Farm labor	8.1	269	2.9	78
Labor (excluding farm)	1.8	887	0.2	686
Occupation not reported	0.7	1,164	1.2	648
Total and weighted average salary	64.9	901	67.9	653
Total minus farmers and farm labor and weighted average salary	42.1	1,307	63.6	694

Source: Bureau of the Census, *Census of the Population, 1940: Summary Report* (Washington, D.C.: GPO, 1940), table 72, pp. 120–22.

of men, were both exempt from FLSA coverage and earning wages well below the minimum level in a variety of occupations.

Of exempt workers, men earned an average of $901 annually to women's $653. The omission of farmers and farm laborers shows the average pay of other exempt men to have been $1,307, to women's average of $694, still well below the minimum wage level of $800 annually. Women workers' wages were particularly low in the service sectors, where they figured so prominently: fully 17.7 percent of all women workers, including the vast majority of black women, were employed in domestic service work for average annual wages of $359; other women employed in service occupations, who made up 11.3 percent of the female labor force, made $518 per year on average.

In short, though women workers had the most to gain from FLSA coverage, the vast majority of those who could actually have benefited from the minimum wage had been eliminated from the jurisdiction of labor standards. The gender-neutral language of the law, though a tribute to equality between the sexes in an abstract sense, contrasted sharply with the gender-specific effects of the statute. Given that a majority of low-paid women workers were left out of the FLSA, what was to become of the women's reform organizations after the law's passage? The answer to this question illuminates the distinct burdens of citizenship imposed on women by their place in the New Deal order.

Women's Work Is Never Done: The Post-FLSA Agenda of Women's Organizations

In the American polity as restructured by the New Deal, men's working conditions had become the legitimate object of the new rational and efficient administrative procedures of national government. Authorized by the Wagner Act, unionized men now possessed the agency in organizations sanctioned by the state to improve their wages, pensions, and working conditions through collective bargaining. But because women workers were largely unaffected by the NLRA and circumvented in critical ways by the FLSA, their advocates had to return to much the same agenda they had pursued for the three decades before the New Deal.

Groups like the National Consumers' League, the Women's Trade Union League, and the YWCA had to redouble their efforts on behalf of exploited women workers who had gained nothing from the passage of the FLSA. The activities of the reform groups were almost totally absorbed in state-by-state efforts for minimum wage laws and other labor standards aimed at sectors of female employment considered by New Dealers to be in the realm of "intrastate commerce." The new willingness of the Supreme Court to uphold economic regulation placed reformers, theoretically, in a better position to achieve their goals. Yet despite the new style of government born at the national level in the 1930s, state governments remained extremely resistant to such governmental activism.

The NCL took the lead in calling for states to enact labor standards that would cover groups unaffected by FLSA. In late October 1938, in the same week that the FLSA took effect, the NCL announced plans for a national drive to promote the adoption of a model bill.[23] In promoting the bill, NCL general secretary Mary Dublin lamented the social and economic costs to communities when people tried to survive and raise families on the low wages paid in many industries. She told a *New York Times* reporter, "When the population lives on a desperately low income, results can be clearly traced in unemployment caused by the breakdown of purchasing power, destitution, dependency and low standards of health."[24] Though twenty-five states and the District of Columbia already had minimum wage laws in operation, Dublin noted that most of the laws pertained to women

---

[23] Minutes, Annual Meeting of the National Consumers' League, December 1938, LMDC, collection 5235.

[24] Anne Petersen, "National Drive to Broaden Wages and Hours Law," *New York Times*, October 30, 1938.

workers only and needed to be broadened to include men.[25] Legislation for women workers remained the priority of the league, however, as it also sought to safeguard the already existing sex-specific wage laws.[26]

Reformers had expected that the removal of judicial obstacles and the example set by the FLSA would create some momentum for states to enact labor legislation more readily and to make laws apply to both sexes.[27] Yet most state governments continued to obstruct such efforts, remaining extremely resistant to enacting minimum wage laws well beyond the New Deal.[28] After one year, the NCL's model bill had been introduced in 30 states and passed in none. The organization set out to have a new bill drafted which would clarify problems of the original bill.[29] Even by 1949, however, the NCL lamented that twenty-two states still lacked minimum wage laws.

The difficulties of state-by-state efforts are not surprising, given that despite the enormous change in the character and capabilities of the national government in the New Deal, most states continued to be dominated by conservative forces reluctant or unable to use governmental power to improve workplace and social conditions. As Clara Beyer, chief of the Division of Labor Standards, wrote in 1939: "The State legislatures, in almost every instance, are dominated by farmers and big business. Very little labor legislation will be enacted." James Patterson has observed that by the start of World War II, "the gap between state and federal labor law was widening, and standards in all too many states remained weak and poorly enforced."[30]

Beyer and NCL leaders had hoped that the Wage and Hour Division would work to promote the development of effective labor departments at the state level, but they quickly grew pessimistic about the abilities and willingness of the new administrators to engage in such tasks.[31] In his comprehensive study of state labor departments in 1950, Robert Erwin Berry

---

[25] On existing state minimum wage laws, see Department of Labor, Women's Bureau, "A Year of the Minimum Wage," by Mary Andersen, *American Federationist*, March 18, 1938.

[26] Ibid.

[27] Paul Douglas and Joseph Hackman, "The Fair Labor Standards Act of 1938, II: The Act as Finally Passed," *Political Science Quarterly* 54 (1939): 54–55; Michael E. Parrish, "Felix Frankfurter and American Federalism," in *Federalism: Studies in History, Law, and Policy*, ed. Harry N. Scheiber (Berkeley: University of California, 1988), pp. 28–29.

[28] Steinberg, *Wages and Hours*, pp. 99–100.

[29] Minutes, Annual Meeting of the National Consumers' League, December 1939, collection 5235, LMDC.

[30] Both quotations appear in James T. Patterson, *The New Deal and the States* (Princeton: Princeton University Press, 1969), pp. 125–26.

[31] Landon R. Y. Storrs, "Civilizing Capitalism: The National Consumers' League and the Politics of 'Fair' Labor Standards in the New Deal Era" (Ph.D. diss., University of Wisconsin-Madison, 1994), pp. 378–80.

found that although a few were "meeting their responsibilities admirably," most "must be judged as falling somewhere between fair and poor, according to standards established in most cases by the labor commissioners themselves." He attributed the poor record of most state departments to their lack of "the necessary tools, in terms of organization, statutory authority, personnel and finances."[32]

Most of the laws achieved and preserved by the reformers, moreover, continued to be for women only. The majority opinion in *West Coast Hotel*, though backing away from biological criteria, had still emphasized women's special needs as a justification for sex-specific protection in the workplace. During the decades between 1937 and the enactment of the Equal Pay Act and the Civil Rights Act in the early 1960s, courts continued to uphold female-specific legislation in what Judith Baer has termed "an almost infinite expansion of the *Muller* principle."[33]

The limits of the FLSA thus defined a long-term agenda for women reformers, concentrating their efforts on arduous state-by-state campaigns for labor legislation to the exclusion of other goals they might have pursued had their hopes been realized in the first national labor standards law. The path followed by the reform groups after 1938 kept them quite isolated from the mainstream labor movement, which was mostly preoccupied with collective bargaining efforts and trying to preserve the gains made in the New Deal.[34] The defenders of protective labor legislation also remained at odds with the other wing of the women's movement because the latter group favored the Equal Rights Amendment, which threatened to undermine the female-specific, state-level measures that reformers had worked so hard to achieve. Accordingly, the energies of the reform groups became absorbed as well in maintaining an organized opposition to the ERA.

Since the early 1920s, animosity had characterized the relationship between groups that sought to improve the lives of women workers through protective labor legislation and the small cadre of women's groups who opposed their efforts. The FLSA, with its principle of equal application to both sexes, received the support of both camps, but the two contingents continued to battle each other at the state level. At the NCL's annual meeting in 1939, several state chapter representatives complained that the

---

[32] Robert Erwin Berry, "The State Labor Departments: Organization, Functions, Personnel, Finances, and Relations with the Federal Department of Labor" (Ph.D. diss., University of Wisconsin, 1950), p. 255.

[33] 300 U.S. 79 (1937); Judith Baer, *The Chains of Protection* (Westport, Conn.: Greenwood, 1978), p. 6.

[34] Frances Fox Piven and Richard A. Cloward, *Poor People's Movements: Why They Succeed, How They Fail* (New York: Random House Vintage, 1979), chap. 3. The NCL did, however, participate in efforts to protect the NLRA from weakening amendments in 1939–40; see Storrs, "Civilizing Capitalism," pp. 388–411.

National Woman's Party and the Business and Professional Women's Clubs were the arch opponents of their legislative goals.[35]

The coalition of women's reform groups that favored the protective laws and were closely associated with the New Deal Democratic Party had continued to oppose the ERA when it was once more introduced in Congress in the late 1930s, and they maintained their stalwart opposition in the 1940s.[36] Their representatives argued that the legal equality implied by the ERA would undermine labor laws for women only and would thus cause women's economic and social position to decline. Though the Republican Party endorsed the ERA in 1940, the Democrats held off until 1944, and even then, prominent Democratic women such as Eleanor Roosevelt and Frances Perkins objected.[37] The two branches of the women's movement did manage to coalesce in support of an equal pay bill in 1945. Some of the leaders of the protective labor law camp began to grow weary and skeptical of the approach. In 1946, Clara Beyer wrote to Molly Dewson:

> I can't get excited any more about separate legislation for women and believe we are losing a lot of the push for real improvement of conditions by the emphasis on sex. . . . Men need seats, lunch rooms, toilet rooms, etc. just as much as women do. But if, as a Labor Department, we emphasize the need for such facilities for women only we are doing a great disservice to workers in general. In the same way the movement for wage and hour legislation for women has certainly held back the possibilities of getting such laws for all workers.[38]

Nonetheless, the fundamental divisions remained for several more years and prevented a full-scale women's movement from emerging for another quarter-century.[39]

As women remained politically weak and divided, efforts at the national level to expand the FLSA continued to be stymied as well. Sporadically, the reform coalition pushed for increases in the national minimum wage standard and the inclusion of more categories of work under the FLSA's coverage, but such efforts encountered persistent obstacles. In 1945, the NCL

[35] Minutes, Annual Meeting of the National Consumers League, December 1939, collection 5235, LMDC; letter, Lavinia Engle to Molly Dewson, April 8, [year missing], Dewson Papers, General Correspondence, box 1, FDR.

[36] Resolutions adopted at Annual Meeting of National Consumers League, January 18, 1947, collection 5235, LMDC.

[37] Ethel Klein, *Gender Politics* (Cambridge: Harvard University Press, 1984), chap. 1.

[38] Letter, Clara Beyer to Molly Dewson, August 24, 1946, Dewson Papers, General Correspondence, box 1, FDR.

[39] File on ERA and National Committee on the Status of Women, Records of the National Consumers League, collection 5235, LMDC; letter, Mary Andersen to President Mosher, National Association of Manufacturers, May 11, 1945, Papers of the Women's Trade Union League, collection 3, Mary Andersen Papers, microfilm 3:74, LMDC, original at Schlesinger Library, Cambridge, Mass.

organized the Committee for a Fair Minimum Wage, headquartered in Washington, to campaign for improvements in the FLSA.[40] The ACWA joined in the campaign and again sent several women workers to testify before Congress, but support for expanding the law was thin.[41] In 1949, when Congress belatedly increased the minimum wage to seventy-five cents per hour, new stipulations were added to the FLSA to make coverage more restrictive.[42] Henceforth administrators were to interpret the provisions as excluding "fringe" occupations, meaning the heavily female-employing clerical and service jobs in firms selling goods in interstate commerce, unless those positions passed the tests of being "closely related" and "directly essential" to the production of goods for interstate commerce; no longer would the broader "necessary to production" qualification suffice.[43]

Not until groups excluded from the FLSA gained political power did Congress act to broaden coverage significantly. The exemption of agricultural workers was finally lifted in 1966, in response to the civil rights movement. Retail, service, and domestic service employees were finally granted coverage in 1974, after the "second wave" of the women's movement had emerged.[44] Indeed, the burdens of citizenship imposed on women by their lack of significant inclusion in the FLSA had preoccupied women's groups for several decades beyond the New Deal and had, throughout that long period, preempted many possibilities for the improvement of women's lives.

The FLSA represented an entire restructuring of American federalism and a brand new posture in the political economy for a government that had long eschewed such intervention. Workers covered by the law gained new economic rights, guaranteed by the national government, assuring them of certain minimal labor standards. The law also signified a new means of promoting active citizenship, through enhanced incorporation of citizens through economic rights. In the course of the congressional hearings on the law, proponents Sidney Hillman and Frances Perkins had argued that it would enable the development of better citizens by improving the quality of life of the most low-paid workers and thus granting them greater freedom to participate in public life.[45] Yet the law, in essence, missed

---

[40] See "Some Milestones" and "Minimum Wage and Collective Bargaining," by Solomon Barkin, May 22, 1946, Records of the National Consumers League, collection 5235, LMDC.

[41] Records of the ACWA, collection 5619c, box 546, file B702, LMDC.

[42] Jerry Voorhis, *Confessions of a Congressman* (Garden City, N.J.: Doubleday, 1947), pp. 94–95.

[43] Louis Weiner, *Federal Wage and Hour Law* (Philadelphia: American Law Institute, 1977), pp. 8, 63–64, 72–74.

[44] Ibid., pp. 122–24.

[45] Senate, *Joint Hearings on the Fair Labor Standards Act, Senate Committee on Education and Labor and House Committee on Labor*, 75th Cong., 1st sess., June 1937, pp. 173, 180, 943, 957.

its target, excluding from coverage the vast majority of exploited workers, especially women and minority men.

One critic of the New Deal revision of the commerce clause has charged that decisions such as *U.S. v. Darby* "showed that the 'internal concerns of a state' had become an empty vessel." [46] But although Supreme Court rulings of the late 1930s and early 1940s affirmed the potential of somewhat broader definitions of "interstate commerce," in fact the individual states still retained substantial powers, particularly in regard to the welfare of those excluded from national policies. Even the FLSA left women citizens subject to the uneven but generally unyielding and paternalistic state governments, where their advocates had to continue to work, state by state, year by year, for hard-earned and meager reforms.

[46] Richard A. Epstein, "The Proper Scope of the Commerce Power," *Virginia Law Review* 73 (November 1987): 1447.

CHAPTER NINE

Divided Citizens

That central feature is to end the absolute entitlement to welfare, to end the detailed Federal regulation of the way in which welfare policies are administered by the State . . . and to encourage—for that matter, to require—a wide range of experimentation in welfare policies among our 50 states. . . . In fact, in a relatively short period of time after the passage of this bill, we will have 50 distinct and different systems of welfare in the United States.

> —Senator Slade Gorton (R-Wash.), *Congressional Record*, August 1, 1996

The great achievement of the New Deal was the broadening of American citizenship, through social and labor legislation, to more fully incorporate citizens as full members of the polity. President Franklin D. Roosevelt, in his call to further "the security of the citizen and his family," had advanced the idea that citizens should be endowed with some protection against the insecurities that could emerge in a modern, industrial economy.[1] Policy officials in his administration concurred that a floor of social and labor standards, a minimum assurance of well-being, ought to be guaranteed. They fashioned policy on the premise that for people to be meaningfully included as free, equal, and potentially active members of the citizenry, political and civil rights should be complemented by social dimensions of citizenship.

To New Dealers, the development of expanded rights of citizenship was intrinsically connected to a vibrant, democratic polity. Frances Perkins and Sidney Hillman, in presenting the case for the Fair Labor Standards Act to Congress, argued that the proposed law represented the "hallmark of

---

[1] Franklin D. Roosevelt, "Message to Congress Reviewing the Broad Objectives and Accomplishments of the Administration, June 8, 1934," in *The Report of the Committee on Economic Security of 1935 and Other Basic Documents relating to the Development of the Social Security Act*, 50th anniversary ed., National Conference on Social Welfare (Washington, D.C.: National Conference on Social Welfare, 1985), p. 138.

modern democracy," which would in turn lead to the development of better citizens.[2] John L. Lewis called for labor legislation that would enable "the unfortunate victims of our existing economic system to rise to industrial citizenship."[3] Protection against the vagaries of the marketplace and the servitude of the sweatshops, these policy entrepreneurs believed, would offer citizens greater freedom and well-being, fostering the modicum of social equality that is required for a democratic system of government to persist. As well, the enhanced quality of life that would follow from social citizenship, they suggested, would enable citizens to participate more actively in civic and political life.

Thus, through New Deal social and labor policies, political officials transformed and enriched the meaning of American citizenship. The metamorphosis of citizenship in the 1930s nonetheless had its limits, imposed by prevailing ideologies pertaining both to ascribed gender roles and to the proper realm of governance for public policies, the political imperatives of a Democratic Party that represented diverse industrial and agricultural interests, and the institutional arrangements of federalism. First, New Dealers aimed their most innovative policymaking efforts at the concerns of the "forgotten man," who had, indeed, been long neglected in social and labor policy. Earlier in the twentieth century, efforts to build a "paternalist" welfare state in the United States had failed while modest "maternalist" efforts succeeded; during the 1930s and in subsequent decades of policy implementation, policies directed primarily toward male breadwinners took center stage and policies targeting women and children received only marginal attention from political leaders and administrators.[4] Second, and more deliberately, policymakers refashioned intergovernmental arrangements but stretched the realm of national governance only far enough to incorporate full-time, long-term wage earners under its auspices. Inadvertently, these two developments combined in such a way that mostly white men came to be incorporated into fully national programs, while women and nonwhite men were left in programs administered primarily by the states. As a result, the New Deal established divided citizenship, separating the governance of men and women between two sovereignties, each with its own particular ideological, institutional, and administrative character.

---

[2] Senate, *Joint Hearings on the Fair Labor Standards Act, Senate Committee on Education and Labor and House Committee on Labor*, 75th Cong., 1st sess., June 1937, pp. 173, 180, 943, 957.

[3] Ibid., pp. 272–73.

[4] Theda Skocpol, *Protecting Soldiers and Mothers: The Political Origins of Social Policy in the United States* (Cambridge: Harvard University Press, 1992); Linda Gordon, *Pitied But Not Entitled: Single Mothers and the History of Welfare, 1890–1935* (New York: Free Press, 1994).

Persons incorporated as national citizens came to experience governance that was quintessentially liberal and operated according to modern administrative practices. National regulatory and redistributive policies, including the NLRA, OASI, FLSA, and UI (to the extent that it was developed according to uniform, national standards), all included citizens on the basis of liberal criteria: they bestowed status on persons defined as "independent," meaning that they were long-term, full-time, wage earners. Although these statutes treated persons abstractly, not differentiating on the basis of characteristics such as sex, the social organization of the work force of the era limited their reach to a predominantly male group. Such persons were regarded, in law and administrative policy, as free, equal, rights-bearing citizens. The policies applied to them were administered according to the rule of law, through standardized, routinized procedures, in agencies that operated under the merit system for the civil service.

Policies administered chiefly by the states, by contrast, incorporated citizens on the basis of a variety of nonliberal rationales, and they were implemented according to procedures belonging to an earlier era of governance. The public assistance programs, OAA and ADC, were established on the basis of a combination of republican and ascriptive hierarchical ideals. Rather than treating beneficiaries as abstract individuals, they incorporated persons on the basis of their membership in a community or a relationship, often in roles ascribed to them by virtue of personal characteristics such as sex. Policymakers considered the program beneficiaries as the "deserving poor." Single mothers were accepted as worthy of ADC because they were responsible for raising future citizens and because they could perform that function best if they could assume their "natural" status as housewives and remain out of the work force. Protective labor laws were rooted in ascriptive ideologies about "women's place" and the need to protect all women as potential mothers. Besides having distinct ideological characteristics, state-run programs were administered according to the discretion of state and local officials who scrutinized and supervised beneficiaries' personal lives. Typically, such personnel had been hired through the patronage traditions; in most states, the civil service was barely in its infancy. Citizens left to state-level governance, furthermore, were endowed with rights and obligations that varied from state to state according to political demands, cultural norms, and the economic needs of local employers.

Because the national policies were ostensibly gender neutral, women who met the appropriate eligibility criteria or fell within the regulatory purview of such laws stood to be included in the same manner as similarly situated men. Given the social organization of gender in the 1930s, combined with occupational exclusions in the policies that circumvented women,

relatively few would gain such access except through the spousal and survivors' benefits of OASI. Still, the policies each constituted the historic enactment of a principle, establishing the possibility that coverage could be
broadened through subsequent political struggles.

Once established, however, divided citizenship endured in the United
States for decades, with manifold implications. Most important, though
men and women had unequal forms of social status before the 1930s, New
Deal policies had institutionalized those disparities and inscribed them
with political significance. Governed under separate sovereignties, men and
women, further differentiated by class and race, gained very different and
unequal forms of status in the political community. Those incorporated as
primary beneficiaries in the national realm were viewed as worthy, independent, and free; those relegated to the states were considered dependent
persons subject to evaluation to determine whether they were deserving.
What it meant to be an "American citizen" meant very different things to
the retired male breadwinner, who came to expect his monthly social security check from the national government, and to the poor mother who
hoped that the social worker assigned to evaluate her eligibility for a meager welfare check would find her child-rearing and housekeeping efforts
worthy. The first was treated with dignity and respect, as an entitled person; the latter, with suspicion and scrutiny. The bureaucracy that came to
surround the administration of national programs assured beneficiaries of
routine treatment, whereas citizens whose experience was defined at the
state and local level could be certain only of variation, as politics shifted
within the state or if they moved to a different locality.

The Zenith of Divided Citizenship

Divided citizenship, as established by the New Deal, flourished throughout the mid-twentieth century owing to a combination of factors. First,
though by some indications the United States in the early 1940s seemed to
be moving toward a more universal form of national social citizenship and
greater parity between men and women, in fact most proposed reforms
failed to materialize, those that did emerged slowly, and wartime shifts in
women's status proved to be only temporary. Second, though policymakers
had expected that the dramatic changes in national government during the
1930s would act to promote change at the state level, instead governance
in the states remained distinct from national governance for many years.
Third, the division of citizens in terms of status promoted separate avenues
and forms of political participation, which in turn reinforced the distinctions between men's and women's citizenship.

The National Level

In the early 1940s, the mobilization of women into the war effort and new national policy initiatives and rhetoric suggested that citizenship divided by gender and federalism might be on the wane. As the nation entered World War II and male workers were needed for the armed services, the War Labor Board actively encouraged women to serve on the "home front" by entering the work force. There, they were allowed to work in high-paying, skilled jobs traditionally reserved for men. Government-sponsored child care programs were arranged to accommodate working mothers. Female labor-force participation climbed from 27.9 percent in 1940 to 35.8 percent in 1945.[5] At the same time, officials in the National Resources Planning Board, who had been asked by President Roosevelt to formulate social and economic policy for after World War II, proposed building on the beginnings of social citizenship as established in the New Deal to fashion a more inclusive and comprehensive form of citizenship for all Americans. Drawing in part on plans put forward by the Social Security Board, NRPB officials suggested broadening OASI coverage, nationalizing and expanding the public assistance programs and unemployment insurance, establishing national health insurance, and providing measures for full employment.[6] An NRPB report noted, "Women and men . . . have shared similar responsibilities during the period of the war as workers in the war industries or as members of the armed forces [and] should enjoy similar rights and privileges with respect to demobilization and readjustment."[7] In his state of the union message in 1944, President Roosevelt adopted the NRPB's rhetoric, calling for an "economic bill of rights" for all Americans. Yet, the promise to replace divided citizenship with universal social citizenship—regardless of sex—failed to materialize.

First, when soldiers returned home from the front, government-sponsored wartime propaganda efforts were reversed: women were encouraged to leave paid work and return to domestic responsibilities. Child care

---

[5] Karen Anderson, *Wartime Women: Sex Roles, Family Relations, and the Status of Women during World War II* (Westport, Conn.: Greenwood, 1981); Susan M. Hartmann, *The Home Front and Beyond: American Women in the 1940s* (Boston: Twayne, 1982); Susan E. Riley, "Caring for Rosie's Children: Federal Child Care Policies in the World War II Era," *Polity* 26 (1994): 655–75; Francine D. Blau and Marianne A. Ferber, *The Economics of Women, Men, and Work* (Englewood Cliffs, N.J.: Prentice-Hall, 1986), p. 70.

[6] Edwin Amenta and Theda Skocpol, "Redefining the New Deal: World War II and the Development of Social Provision in the United States," in *The Politics of Social Policy in the United States*, ed. Margaret Weir, Ann Shola Orloff, and Theda Skocpol (Princeton: Princeton University Press, 1988), pp. 87–90.

[7] National Resources Planning Board, *Demobilization and Readjustment*, report of the *Conference on Postwar Readjustment of Civilian and Military Personnel* (Washington, D.C.: GPO, June 1943), p. 49.

programs were dismantled. The Management and unions cooperated in efforts to reinstate traditional divisions of occupational segregation, forcing women to return to clerical and service-sector jobs so that men could regain high-skilled ones. Women lacked the seniority to compete with their male counterparts for jobs, and, regardless, veterans were granted preferential treatment in hiring.[8] By 1947, female labor-force participation had declined to 31.9 percent. Over the next few decades, women gradually increased their numbers in the work force through a moderated but steady growth pattern.[9] The wage gap and divisions between men's and women's jobs in terms of status and security, however, had already been reestablished. Those divisions meant that, once again, men and women were incorporated separately into social and labor policies.

Second, the hopes of the NRPB failed, for the most part, to pan out. The most generous new form of social provision established during the period was the G.I. Bill, which was targeted narrowly to returning veterans of World War II, primarily men. Health insurance efforts floundered, and hopes for a genuine full-employment bill dissipated when the modest Employment Act of 1946 was enacted.[10]

Public assistance programs in the Social Security Act were altered only slightly, eclipsing the plans of the NRPB and the provisions of the Wagner-Murray-Dingell bills of the mid-1940s, which would have gone far to expand eligibility and to remove the aspects of financing that disadvantaged poorer states. In 1946, Congress adopted a modified version of a variable-grant formula for OAA and ADC. But instead of providing for at least a minimum standard of public assistance in the poorest states, the plan only changed the matching-grant ratio to depend more heavily on funds from the national government.[11] In effect, the scheme meant that federal efforts to promote more generous benefit levels in the poorest states were contingent on higher financial obligations toward the wealthiest states, hardly a redistributive solution. As a result, wide disparities in benefits persisted: in 1947, OAA benefits ranged from $17.32 per recipient per month in Mississippi, to $53.02 in Washington state; for ADC, benefits ranged from $26.29 per family per month in Mississippi, to a high of $104.63 in Wash-

[8] Anderson, *Wartime Women*; Hartmann, *Home Front*; Riley, "Caring for Rosie's Children."

[9] Blau and Ferber, *Economics of Women, Men, and Work*, p. 70.

[10] Margaret Weir, "The Federal Government and Unemployment: The Frustration of Policy Innovation from the New Deal to the Great Society," in *Politics of Social Policy*, ed. Weir, Orloff, and Skocpol, p. 156.

[11] Amenta and Skocpol, "Redefining the New Deal," p. 91; Eveline M. Burns, *The American Social Security System* (Boston: Houghton Mifflin, 1949), p. 370; Jill Quadagno, *The Transformation of Old Age Security: Class and Politics in the American Welfare State* (Chicago: University of Chicago Press, 1988), p. 141.

ington state.[12] In 1950, a benefit for caretakers of children on ADC, a provision omitted by policymakers in 1935, was finally included in the program. Even with these changes in fiscal matters, however, the public assistance programs continued to be run according to the same patterns of governance long utilized in the states.[13]

The nationalization of UI never came about, and the consequences were most severe for women and nonwhite men. Both groups suffered from unemployment rates consistently higher than those of white men and they typically fared the worst at the hands of the states as well.[14] UI was altered slightly in 1954 to apply to employers of four or more workers instead of eight or more. As late as 1963, however, state laws still exempted some fifteen million workers from coverage, including workers in state and local government, domestic service, farm and agricultural processing, and nonprofits.[15] In 1971, moreover, twenty-three states still disqualified women from collecting UI if they left work for reasons categorized as "domestic quits," including pregnancy, childbirth, or other family responsibilities.[16]

Most women's jobs were still concentrated in low-wage occupations excluded from coverage under the FLSA. Despite repeated attempts at reform, expansion of the FLSA to include more categories of workers remained beyond the reach of women's reform organizations throughout the 1940s and 1950s. In fact when an increase in the minimum wage was finally achieved in 1949, half a million other workers, particularly in the female-dominated clerical and service sectors, were newly excluded from the law's provisions.[17]

The primary advances in the expansion of national social citizenship in the mid-century involved the improvement of OASI, and even those reforms came slowly. Officials in the SSB, which was reorganized as the Social Security Administration in 1946, pressed for amendments to the program throughout the 1940s. At last, in 1950, Congress expanded OASI to include about ten million more persons, primarily the self-employed and employees in nonprofit agencies, and in 1954 the law was amended once again to include agricultural and domestic workers, thus erasing the racial

---

[12] Burns, *American Social Security System*, pp. 306–7, 324–25.

[13] SSB, "Assistance Expenditures per Inhabitant, 1940–1950," by Frank J. Hanmer and Ellen J. Perkins, *Social Security Bulletin* 14 (March 1951): 12.

[14] Bureau of the Census, *Statistical Abstract of the United States*, 91st ed. (Washington, D.C.: GPO, 1970), p. 213.

[15] William Haber and Merrill G. Murray, *Unemployment Insurance in the American Economy* (Homewood, Ill.: Irwin, 1966), pp. 144–45.

[16] Diana M. Pearce, "Toil and Trouble: Women Workers and Unemployment Compensation," *Signs* 10 (1985): 452–54.

[17] Phyllis Palmer, "Outside the Law: Agricultural and Domestic Workers under the Fair Labor Standards Act," *Journal of Policy History* 7 (1995): 424; Louis Weiner, *Federal Wage and Hour Law* (Philadelphia: American Law Institute, 1977), pp. 8, 63–64, 72–74.

cleavages that had formerly excluded most African Americans and many other nonwhites from OASI.[18]

The status of older women continued to confound reformers throughout the period, however, because many still qualified for neither OASI nor OAA. In the early 1950s, the SSA research staff found that among a group of 2.6 million older Americans who had access to neither benefit type and who lacked earnings, fully 80 percent were women, and three-quarters of them were widows.[19] In 1956, Congress attempted to remedy the situation somewhat by lowering the age for OASI eligibility from sixty-five to sixty-two for women.[20] As a result of the mid-century expansions in OASI, demand for OAA slowly began to shrink: the number of recipients dropped from 2.8 million in 1950 to 2.2 million in 1964.[21] But even then, older people who did not fit the acceptable mold for status in OASI, still mostly women, remained subject to the states and experienced citizenship in a manner that had grown distant from that of OASI beneficiaries.

Why was the reform momentum of the 1930s curbed so quickly, preventing the expansion of national social citizenship during the next two decades? First, the NRPB had to contend with the SSB and the increasingly powerful Veterans' Administration, both of which had different priorities for policy development. Then, in 1943, Congress, seeking to restore congressional dominance over wartime planning, abolished the NRPB as well as several other executive planning agencies.[22] Second, though Democrats continued to dominate Congress, conservative southern and rural Democrats became increasingly inclined to part ways with northern and urban members of their own party, and in the House their numbers made them especially powerful. Without sufficient numbers of urban Democrats to promote the social policy proposals of the NRPB and SSB, measures such as the Wagner-Murray-Dingell bill of 1943 simply died in committee. Wartime strike activity, furthermore, weakened the sympathy for labor that had existed during the 1930s, and southern Democrats began to block the efforts of their northern colleagues on labor legislation, developing what Ira Katznelson and his collaborators have called the "southern veto."[23]

[18] O. C. Pogge, "Old-Age and Survivors Insurance: The 1950 Amendments," *Social Casework* 32 (March 1951): 95–101; Arthur J. Altmeyer, *The Formative Years of Social Security* (Madison: University of Wisconsin Press, 1968), pp. 280–83.

[19] Jerry Cates, *Insuring Inequality: Administrative Leadership in Social Security, 1935–1954* (Ann Arbor: University of Michigan Press, 1983), pp. 71–72.

[20] Edwin E. Witte, "Organized Labor and the Social Security Act of 1935," in *Labor and the New Deal*, ed. Milton Derber and Edwin Young (Madison: University of Wisconsin Press, 1961), p. 264.

[21] Gilbert Y. Steiner, *Social Insecurity: The Politics of Welfare* (Chicago, Ill.: Rand McNally, 1966), p. 250.

[22] Amenta and Skocpol, "Redefining the New Deal," pp. 107–8, 111, 117–18.

[23] Ira Katznelson, Kim Geiger, and Daniel Kryder, "Limiting Liberalism: The Southern Veto in Congress, 1933–1950," *Political Science Quarterly* 108 (1993): 283–306.

At the same time, Roosevelt became preoccupied with the war and ceased to push domestic policy initiatives as he had in the 1930s. In fact, even after his rousing 1943 budget message advocating "freedom from want" and his 1944 address calling for an "economic bill of rights," Roosevelt neglected to send specific proposals to Congress. Then, on April 12, 1945, Roosevelt died in Warm Springs, Georgia. The task of broadening the New Deal was left to Harry S. Truman, who faced an uphill battle with Congress. His administration achieved only modest victories on social policy and suffered important setbacks on labor policy.[24] When Republicans took back the presidency with the election of Dwight D. Eisenhower in 1952, hopes for the expansion of the New Deal became increasingly dim, leaving the framework of divided citizenship undisturbed for yet another decade.

The State Level

For those citizens whose status was still defined primarily by the states after the New Deal, the character of governance in the realm of social citizenship changed little, remaining relatively conservative well into the 1960s. Despite the liberalization of the national government in the 1930s and the willingness of the Supreme Court to allow both the national and state governments to intervene in the economy as never before, states seemed little affected. The particular features of state politics and the structure of federalism still stymied the development of governance that could have enhanced the status of women.

Even in the new era of "cooperative federalism," political factors limited the capacity of individual states to develop social and labor policies. Because of outdated apportionment, many state legislatures were dominated by rural interests. One-party dominance and factionalism, particularly in the South, impeded programmatic policymaking.[25] States had difficulty attracting administrative talent owing to the continuation of the patronage tradition.[26] Besides the political obstacles to social provision, many state constitutions retained features that made innovative policies impossible, particularly if increased spending was involved.

---

[24] Bartholemew H. Sparrow, *From the Outside In: World War II and the American State* (Princeton: Princeton University Press, 1996), p. 41.

[25] V. O. Key, *Southern Politics in State and Nation* (New York: Knopf, 1949), chap. 14.

[26] See Jane Perry Clark, *The Rise of a New Federalism* (New York: Columbia University Press, 1938), chaps. 8 and 10; Leonard D. White, *The States and the Nation* (Baton Rouge: Louisiana State University Press, 1953), pp. 35–64; Grant McConnell, *Private Power and American Democracy* (New York: Knopf, 1967), chaps. 4 and 6; James T. Patterson, *The New Deal and the States: Federalism in Transition* (Princeton: Princeton University Press, 1969); and Theodore J. Lowi, "Party, Policy, and Constitution in America," in *The American Party System: Stages of Political Development*, ed. William Nisbet Chambers and Walter Dean Burnham (New York: Oxford University Press, 1967), pp. 238–76.

The dynamics of federalism also continued to deter change at the state level. Compounding the fact that state budgets had been devastated by the depression, the threat of interstate economic competition hindered state legislators from establishing more generous programs. Southern states, anxious to protect their low-wage economies, provided particularly low public assistance benefits and had the most limited labor protections. Such tendencies, in turn, acted as a drag on the policies of states concerned that higher taxes and regulations might discourage businesses from operating within their borders.[27] Also, states remained the predominant holders of the police power, and its preliberal character still shaped the manner in which states governed. In fact, states distinguished by relatively high social spending and administrative capacity often wielded the police power in a particularly scrupulous and paternalistic fashion. For example, states such as Wisconsin, Massachusetts, and Washington inscribed ADC with especially moralistic suitable-home rules and retained protective labor laws especially restrictive of women's roles in the work force. Such rules tied women's social provision most firmly to their ascribed gender role.[28]

From the late 1930s through the 1950s, states expanded their efforts in intergovernmental social programs only to the extent that they were effectively goaded by financing arrangements. UI underwent the most substantial and widespread improvements, but the reforms did little for women. OAA was enhanced in states where citizens' groups exerted pressure on lawmakers for more generous pensions for the elderly. The majority of states continued to be sluggish, however, regarding programs for which they were either left with a relatively high degree of responsibility, as in the case of ADC, or where they retained total autonomy, such as in labor regulations for jobs in "intrastate" commerce. The joint national-state programs in the SSA were hindered further by the multiple opportunities for state and local agendas to displace the intentions of national policymakers.[29] Consequently, the states persisted for decades in governing in a

---

[27] Paul E. Peterson, *The Price of Federalism* (Washington, D.C.: Brookings Institution, 1995); Paul E. Peterson and Mark Rom, *Welfare Magnets: A New Case for a National Standard* (Washington, D.C.: Brookings, 1990); Patterson, *New Deal and the States.*

[28] See Winifred Bell, *Aid to Dependent Children* (New York: Cambridge University Press, 1965); Judith Baer, *The Chains of Protection* (Westport, Conn.: Greenwood, 1978); Russell L. Hanson, "Liberalism and the Course of American Social Welfare Policy," in *The Dynamics of American Politics: Approaches and Interpretations*, ed. Lawrence C. Dodd and Calvin Jillson (Boulder, Colo.: Westview, 1994), pp. 132–59.

[29] Russell L. Hanson, "Federal Statebuilding during the New Deal: The Transition from Mothers' Aid to Aid to Dependent Children," in *Changes in the State*, ed. Edward S. Greenberg and Thomas F. Mayer (Newbury Park, Calif.: Sage, 1990), pp. 93–114; Theodore J. Lowi et al., *Poliscide* (Lanham, Md.: University Press of America, 1990), pp. 27–28; Jeffrey L. Pressman and Aaron Wildavsky, *Implementation* (Berkeley, Calif.: University of California Press, 1973).

manner that set citizens apart from those incorporated into the liberal promises of national citizenship.

Divided Citizens, Separate Participation

The manner in which citizens are incorporated into the polity in turn determines the institutional framework within which their subsequent participation occurs and influences the choices of political goals and strategies they pursue. Accordingly, the restructuring of citizenship by gender in the New Deal organized men and women within distinct sovereignties, encouraged their organizations to seek different goals in politics, and separated groups that might otherwise have formed political coalitions.

In the wake of the New Deal, labor organizations, which continued to be dominated by men and to represent primarily men's interests in the work force, focused their political efforts at the national level, where they urged policymakers to expand social citizenship. Organized labor emerged from World War II full of optimism, with the CIO advocating the adoption of tripartite industry governance along the lines of the corporatist model utilized during the war. On behalf of the CIO, Sidney Hillman began to organize the first "political action committee" in the United States. The organization sought to influence Democratic leaders to promote fiscal Keynesianism and social reform.

Efforts to improve the conditions of women in the work force occurred mostly at the state level. Because most women's occupations were omitted from coverage in the FLSA, the National Consumers' League, which had struggled for improved conditions for women workers at the state level before the New Deal, once again turned to the states to try to make minimum wage laws covering women's occupations more widespread. There, together with other women's organizations and with the support of well-known Democratic women such as Eleanor Roosevelt, Frances Perkins, and Molly Dewson, the NCL engaged in difficult and often futile state-by-state campaigns. State legislatures still resisted the passage of gender-neutral labor standards, and laws for women only remained the most viable strategy for reformers. Meanwhile, the groups that had promoted mothers' pensions during the Progressive Era had disappeared from the civic landscape, leaving ADC without the support of an organized and vocal constituency to work for its improvement.

The separation of citizens in the polity and the particular goals that they were influenced to pursue in turn affected the shape and size of political coalitions. First, the return of some women's organizations to the struggle for labor laws for women perpetuated the divisions that had plagued the women's movement since the 1920s. The National Women's Party and affiliated groups resumed their attempts to block the NCL's efforts, advocating instead a liberal agenda with the Equal Rights Amendment as the centerpiece. Second, although men's and women's organizations participated in some joint efforts to improve the minimum wage at the national level in the late 1940s, for the most part their activism remained quite separate. The disconnection between such groups both prevented the formation of a unified social movement that might have pressured politicians to expand the New Deal and preempted the development of a powerful, broad-based labor movement.

Labor power peaked in 1945, when 30 percent of the work force was unionized, then began to decline. Even with labor's numbers falling, however, organizing efforts continued to ignore most women's occupations, including service and clerical jobs. By 1956, women were 32.0 percent of the labor force but still only 18.5 percent of organized labor. Among the male labor force, 32.3 percent were organized in contrast to only 15.7 percent of the female labor force.[30] The weakness of labor left it defenseless against the growing power of the conservative coalition in Congress, which was solidified through the enactment, over Truman's veto, of the Taft-Hartley Act of 1947. The law placed new constraints on unions and returned a measure of autonomy to the states by permitting state laws to ban union shops in which nonunion workers could not be hired. By 1954, fifteen states, mostly in the South, had responded by passing right-to-work laws. During the same period, organized labor rallied behind full-employment legislation and the Wagner-Murray-Dingell bill, also without success.[31]

As a result of declining political strength, labor organizations adopted a defensive posture and retreated to the private sector to focus on collective bargaining. They pursued social welfare protections at the level of the individual workplace or industrywide rather than through the political system. Workers in oligopolistically structured core industries fared best: those in competitive sectors such as textiles and electrical products, which tended to employ more women, struggled to hold their ground. Such trends reinforced the division of social citizenship, as unionized men, who enjoyed new leverage vis-à-vis management, gained privileges denied most working women and minority men, who were left out altogether.[32]

Men had been cycled through the public sphere by New Deal provisions;

---

[30] Blau and Ferber, *Economics of Women, Men, and Work*, p. 273.

[31] Nelson Lichtenstein, "From Corporatism to Collective Bargaining: Organized Labor and the Eclipse of Social Democracy in the Postwar Era," in *The Rise and Fall of the New Deal Order*, ed. Steve Fraser and Gary Gerstle (Princeton: Princeton University Press, 1989); Steve Fraser, *Labor Will Rule: Sidney Hillman and the Rise of American Labor* (New York: Free Press, 1991); Katznelson, Geiger, and Kryder, "Limiting Liberalism"; Amenta and Skocpol, "Redefining the New Deal."

[32] Lichtenstein, "From Corporatism to Collective Bargaining," pp. 144–45.

they were subsequently ushered back to the private sphere; but they gained a significant dimension of social citizenship: now they could organize and engage in collective bargaining with the sanction of national government. Women, conversely, continued to have their citizenship defined by the states, often in a paternalistic and scrimping manner. Women reformers concentrated most of their efforts in the 1940s and 1950s on wage issues, but with the multiple targets presented by state policies, they achieved very little. Only with the 1960s would the boundaries of divided citizenship begin to become more permeable.

Blurring the Boundaries of Divided Citizenship

Even under divided citizenship, the first glimmers of change began. The *Brown vs. Board of Education* decision in 1954 indicated an emerging skepticism on the part of the Supreme Court about states' classifications on the basis of race.[33] The civil rights movement was gathering momentum, pressuring states and municipalities to dismantle Jim Crow segregation.[34] Increasingly, the Court began to hold states responsible for granting equal protection of the law, guaranteed by the Fourteenth Amendment, to all their citizens. In time, a second constitutional revolution would alter, in some ways more fundamentally than the New Deal, how states governed.

In the 1960s and 1970s, the culmination of the civil rights movement, Democratic Presidential victories, and the new women's movement combined to extend national social citizenship to groups left out in the New Deal arrangements. Policymakers expanded the FLSA in 1966 to include agricultural workers and in 1974 to cover domestic service workers, retail and service workers, and most other categories of employees.[35] The Equal Employment Opportunity Act of 1972 improved women's status in UI, and the Pregnancy Discrimination Act of 1978 forbid states from denying UI to pregnant women.[36] Other laws also served to improve women's status in the workplace: the Equal Pay Act of 1963 and the Civil Rights Act of 1964, which prohibited discrimination on the basis of sex as well as race.[37] In social policy, policymakers dissolved OAA in 1974 and created a new program, Supplemental Security Income, for the elderly poor and blind and

[33] 349 U.S. 294 (1954).
[34] C. Vann Woodward, *The Strange Career of Jim Crow* (New York: Oxford University Press, 1974), pp. 150–88; Frances Fox Piven and Richard A. Cloward, *Poor People's Movements: Why They Succeed, How They Fail* (New York: Random House, Vintage Books, 1977), pp. 207–11.
[35] Weiner, *Federal Wage and Hour Law.*
[36] Pearce, "Toil and Trouble," p. 454.
[37] Hugh Davis Graham, *Civil Rights and the Presidency* (New York: Oxford University Press, 1992), pp. 67–86.

disabled persons. Unlike OAA, SSI operated according to national standards with uniform minimum benefits and mandatory cost-of-living increases. Gradually, with both the increasing likelihood that women were covered by OASI and the elevated standards for SSI, the unequal treatment of men versus women within OASI became a more critical issue than the divergence between the contributory program and public assistance. Feminists, charging that OASI discriminated on the basis of sex, pushed the courts to examine the policy. Some of the more overt gender-based distinctions regarding wives and widows were found to violate the equal protection clause of the Fourteenth Amendment. Attention then turned to less obvious issues, especially the tendency of the program to offer higher benefits to married women who had never worked for pay than to women who had participated in the labor force throughout their lifetimes.[38]

As national social citizenship expanded, the oppressive qualities of state governance for marginalized groups lessened. National government and social forces pushed states to reform, transforming various of the critical political-institutional features that had characterized state governance for so long. The Civil Rights Act of 1964 restrained the states' use of the police power by striking down Jim Crow laws and by barring discrimination by states in activities that used funds from the national government. The reapportionment decisions of the Supreme Court in the early sixties forced states to reallocate membership in their legislatures in accordance with the one person-one vote principle and to repeat the process after every census. As states with outmoded districting plans, especially those in the South, refigured their districts to make them equal in population, state legislatures became increasingly responsive to urban concerns.[39] The Voting Rights Act of 1965 dealt a further blow to entrenched state interests by ending state autonomy in determining voter registration and voting procedures, thus bringing to an end those measures that had disenfranchised southern blacks for decades. In turn, states experienced increased party competition. These changes helped awaken state legislators to broader concerns in the realm of social policymaking, and they stimulated the development of professional administrative procedures at the state level.[40]

Lawmakers and the courts, prodded by an insurgent welfare rights movement and its lawyers, changed the ADC program to make it significantly more nationalized, at least in terms of administrative procedures and eligibility rules.[41] The program, renamed Aid to Families with Dependent Chil-

---

[38] Barbara A. Mikulski and Ellyn L. Brown, "Case Studies in the Treatment of Women under Social Security Law: The Need for Reform," *Harvard Women's Law Journal* 6 (spring 1983): 33–41.

[39] *Baker v. Carr*, 369 U.S. 186 (1962) and *Reynolds v. Sims*, 377 U.S. 533 (1964).

[40] Ann O'M. Bowman and Richard C. Kearney, *The Resurgence of the States* (Englewood Cliffs, N.J.: Prentice-Hall, 1986).

[41] Martha F. Davis, *Brutal Need: Lawyers and the Welfare Rights Movement, 1960–1973* (New Haven: Yale University Press, 1993).

dren when amended in 1962, was transformed most dramatically through changes wrought by the judiciary through statutory review. The states lost a substantial measure of their autonomy and discretion when the Supreme Court made individual state eligibility rules invalid unless they were explicitly authorized by the federal statute or deemed to be consistent with the Court's understanding of the underlying purpose of the program.[42] Thus many of the long-standing rules that had enabled states to limit eligibility for AFDC were abolished, including the most restrictive residence requirements, suitable-home rules, and the man-in-the-house rules that had allowed social workers to conduct midnight raids on the homes of female beneficiaries to ensure that no adult male was living there.[43] Financial eligibility rules and the tremendous variation in AFDC benefits from state to state persevered, but at least some of the worst aspects of state administration were alleviated. Through such changes, AFDC began to approximate an entitlement, a benefit assured to those who fit nationally uniform, standardized eligibility criteria.

In sum, the boundaries of divided citizenship became much less distinct as policymakers expanded national programs to cover persons previously neglected, and as state and local officials lost much of the discretion through which they had been implementing programs. Just as the civil rights and women's movements were prompting the Democratic Party to act on behalf of African Americans and women, however, white men—the original, primary beneficiaries of the New Deal—began to defect from party ranks. This shift continued during the 1980s, leading first to the revitalization of a Republican Party anxious to limit once again the power of national government, second, as government deficits grew, to the reposturing of the Democratic Party to do much of the same.[44]

Reinventing Divided Citizenship

Even before the last vestiges of dual federalism had disappeared, new momentum was building for a return to state and local governance. Great Society Democrats believed that decentralized arrangements would assure democratic representation and results, and they shaped the War on Poverty

---

[42] *King v. Smith*, 392 U.S. 309 (1968); *Shapiro v. Thompson*, 394 U.S. 618 (1969); and *Goldberg v. Kelley*, 397 U.S. 254 (1970).

[43] R. Shep Melnick, *Between the Lines: Interpreting Welfare Rights* (Washington, D.C.: Brookings, 1994); Gilbert Y. Steiner, *Social Insecurity: The Politics of Welfare* (Chicago: Rand-McNally, 1966); Blanche D. Coll, *Safety Net: Welfare and Social Security, 1929–1979* (New Brunswick: Rutgers University Press, 1995).

[44] Thomas Byrne Edsall and Mary D. Edsall, *Chain Reaction: The Impact of Race, Rights, and Taxes on American Politics* (New York: Norton, 1992); "Williamsburg's New Federalists," *Economist*, November 26, 1994, p. 32.

programs accordingly.[45] Subsequently, Republican presidents from Richard Nixon through Ronald Reagan adopted the approach themselves and pledged to return authority to states and localities as a means of scaling back the size, tax burden, and invasiveness of national government. The push to dissolve power continued through the 1996 enactment of welfare reform that decentralized responsibility for poor women and their children to a degree unknown in the United States since 1935.

Efforts to dismantle the national standards that made welfare approximate an entitlement began in a serious manner during the Reagan administration, which achieved a partial victory through the Family Support Act (FSA) of 1988.[46] To encourage states to devise their own "workfare" plans for women on welfare, the FSA permitted states to acquire waivers from federal standards for AFDC. By the mid-1990s, numerous states had responded by enacting a variety of work requirements for program recipients and time limits on assistance. Once again, the implementation of welfare began to vary with local political and cultural norms and economic imperatives. In an effort to trim the rolls, state legislatures enacted a patchwork of rules regulating the behavior of women on welfare. Some states established "learnfare" stipulations in the form of deductions in benefits for families in which children were truant from school; others imposed time limits on assistance, mandated that teenage mothers on AFDC live with their parents, or prohibited additional assistance to women who became pregnant with a second child while on welfare.[47] Moreover, in implementing workfare programs, local officials regained the discretion they had lost in the 1960s. One of the effects of this change was the restoration of racial bias in program implementation: white women tended to receive preferential treatment in work programs while black women were marginalized.[48]

In 1996 the Congress and President Clinton acted in concert to more fully reestablish divided citizenship. Although the several proposals under consideration for altering the financing and benefit arrangements for Social Security, now the premier public system of social provision for middle-class Americans, all leave national administrative authority untouched, the Per-

---

[45] Jill Quadagno, *The Color of Welfare* (New York: Oxford University Press, 1994), pp. 33–59. Theodore J. Lowi, "Europeanization of America? From United States to United State," in *Nationalizing Government*, ed. Theodore J. Lowi and Alan Stone (Beverly Hills: Sage, 1978), pp. 15–29; David B. Robertson and Dennis R. Judd, *The Development of American Public Policy* (Glenview, Ill.: Scott, Foreman, 1989), pp. 160–62; 231–39.

[46] Steven M. Teles, *Whose Welfare: AFDC and Elite Politics* (Lawrence: University Press of Kansas, 1996), pp. 119–46.

[47] "Rowland Seeks to Cut Welfare for Parents of Truant Children," *New York Times*, February 15, 1996, p. B6; "Welfare Revamp, Halted in Capital, Proceeds Anyway," *New York Times*, March 10, 1996, pp. 1, 20.

[48] Susan T. Gooden, "Race and Welfare: Racial Disparities in Treatments and Outcomes among VIEW Participants" (Ph.D. diss., Syracuse University, 1996).

sonal Responsibility and Work Opportunity Reconciliation Act of 1996 goes well beyond the FSA in returning the governance of poor women and their children to the states. In fact, the law does away with AFDC entirely, dissolving even the very modest national standards established back in 1935. The old grant-in-aid arrangements have been replaced by federal block grants for states to use for welfare purposes. Although the new law requires that states operate a welfare program in all political subdivisions to qualify for federal moneys, the program need not be uniform across the state. Most important, gone are the features of AFDC that, at least since the 1960s, made the program bear some resemblance to an entitlement: no longer must states guarantee assistance to families that meet certain basic eligibility requirements. Rather, states are free to determine who will qualify for assistance and under what circumstances. States are not required, furthermore, to provide cash assistance to families and may opt to provide in-kind benefits instead. Thus social provision is once again subject to the particular rule of the states, with an important deviation: paradoxically, as observed by Martha Derthick, the new law fosters devolution, but at the same time contains unprecedented exercises of coercive national government power, forcing states to regulate the behavior of welfare recipients through time limits and work requirements.[49] Whether such features signal a transition toward yet another form of intergovernmental relationships, with national government shedding the neutral, professional character of the New Deal administrative state and assuming a strong, moralistic role, is yet to be determined.

In any case, public expectations that poor, single mothers with children will support their families through paid work have grown as women have continued to increase their numbers in the work force. Yet the marketplace has by no means provided an equal playing field for men and women. Although the median hourly wage gap between men and women has declined over the last decades (in part because wages of less-skilled male workers have fallen), women still earn, on average, only seventy-five cents for every dollar earned by men.[50] While the wage structure has undergone a downward shift for most workers, more women than men have been finding employment only in low-wage work. In 1993, 33 percent of women workers compared with 21.4 percent of men were earning poverty-level wages.[51]

---

[49] Martha Derthick, "Crossing Thresholds: Federalism in the 1960s," *Journal of Policy History* 8 (1996): 78–79.

[50] Sheldon Danziger and Peter Gottschalk, *America Unequal* (Cambridge: Harvard University Press, 1995), pp. 113–16.

[51] Lawrence Mishel and Jared Bernstein, Economic Policy Institute, *The State of Working America, 1994–1995* (Armonk, N.Y.: Sharpe, 1994), pp. 124–27; see also Rebecca M. Blank, "The Employment Strategy: Public Policies to Increase Work and Earnings," in *Confronting Poverty: Prescriptions for Change*, ed. Sheldon Danziger, Gary D. Sandefur, and Daniel H. Weinberg (New York: Russell Sage, 1994), pp. 168–204.

Adult women still constitute 64.3 percent of workers earning the minimum wage, the real value of which had declined sharply during the 1970s and 1980s. In 1996 Congress finally enacted a 90¢ per hour increase in the minimum wage, bringing the standard to $5.15 per hour by mid-1997.[52] Even with the increase, the minimum wage barely enables even single full-time working persons to live above the poverty line, though the Earned Income Tax Credit adds a modest supplement to such wages. Finally, though women's unemployment rates have fallen to parity with men's, unemployed women are far more likely to slip into poverty because UI benefits are proportional to previous wages and thus continue to be lower for women.[53]

Although organized labor has finally turned toward organizing women, promoting women in its leadership, and offering attention to women's particular concerns at the workplace, the ability of the labor movement to improve the well-being of workers appears to be diminishing. The increasing internationalization of the economy, technological changes, and critical court decisions have placed labor organizations on the defensive and rendered them especially weak politically.

Reflections for the Future

Broad governing principles can endure for long periods, but time and again public officials and citizens must rework the particular details of their social contract. According to Michael Walzer, "The social contract is an agreement to reach decisions together about what goods are necessary to our common life, and then to provide those goods for one another." [54] The particulars of that contract are subject to continual political determination as a political community reconsiders its fundamental character.

Today's social and economic circumstances are far less daunting than those that confronted policymakers during the Great Depression, but citizens, now as then, are disenchanted with both "government as usual" and the dislocations in the economy. Middle class Americans feel squeezed; poverty has persisted even as the economy has performed well in the 1990s. Most sobering, 19.7 percent of children are living in poverty. Rates of children in poverty are especially high in female-headed households, and more than half of the current generation are likely to be living in such a household for some period before reaching age eighteen. The poverty rate in

---

[52] "Clinton Signs a Bill Raising Minimum Wage by 90 Cents," *New York Times*, August 21, 1996, p. B6.

[53] Sheldon Danziger and Peter Gottshalk, "Unemployment Insurance and the Safety Net for the Unemployed," in *Unemployment Insurance: The Second Half-Century*, ed. W. Lee Hansen and James F. Byers (Madison: University of Wisconsin Press, 1990), pp. 47–68; Pearce, "Toil and Trouble," pp. 452–54.

[54] Michael Walzer, *Spheres of Justice* (New York: Basic Books, 1983), p. 65.

families headed by single women is 53 percent, much higher than that of other western industrialized nations.[55] At the same time, the hands of policymakers are tied by the threat of government deficits and reluctance by the public to accept new taxes to balance the budget. Federal funds are strained by growing obligations for upper-tier entitlement programs—Social Security and Medicare—yet such programs must be altered or they will be insufficient to meet the demands of aging baby boomers in the decades ahead. More fundamentally, the modern polity is plagued by diminishing social trust and low respect for political officials which combine to create a sense of civic disconnection.

Under these circumstances, policymakers need to consider how citizens can be incorporated into the polity in ways that might best promote the sense of social solidarity so fundamental to civic life. As shown throughout this book, both the logic of inclusion in public policies and the institutional administrative framework for policies shape the experience of citizenship in critical ways. The New Deal provides some lessons for renegotiating both dimensions of policymaking to meet changing demands and expectations.

Today, the liberal, work-oriented approach to inclusion in public policies, which was one part of the New Deal legacy, has nearly supplanted the more traditional legacy that New Dealers inherited from earlier social reformers. Women's work-force participation rates have risen enough that women now fare better under work-based policies than in the past. Indeed, social security, as the central work-based program, has evolved to approximate a "universal" policy that performs redistributive functions while still treating beneficiaries with dignity.[56] Still, women do lack parity in benefit levels. Meanwhile, to the extent that policies based on a nonliberal rationale did perpetuate ascribed gender roles and racial hierarchy, as in the implementation of ADC, their demise is to be celebrated.

Yet the negation of a policy agenda that recognizes the social value of unpaid activities, particularly parenting and care for children and elderly family members, ignores the circumstances of women's lives far more blindly than even New Deal policies. In spite of changes in gender roles, women still typically bear primary responsibility for the care of children and must juggle employment with domestic commitments. With the exception, however, of the Family and Medical Leave Act of 1993, which guaranteed unpaid leave for the care of family members, policymakers fail to fashion policies that permit women—or men—to balance employment with caring and nurturing activities. Indeed, work-force participation is treated as the

---

[55] Irwin Garfinkel and Sara McLanahan, "Single Mothers, Economic Insecurity, and Government Policy," in *Confronting Poverty*, ed. Danziger, Sandefur, and Weinberg, p. 208.

[56] Theda Skocpol, "Targeting within Universalism: Politically Viable Policies to Combat Poverty in the United States," in *The Urban Underclass* (Washington, D.C.: Brookings, 1991), pp. 425–28.

exclusive route to economic well-being, with little heed paid to the other tasks vital to the health of the community.

The change in the logic of inclusion in policies is epitomized by the new welfare law's requirement for mothers to participate in the work force, even if they have very young children. This approach overlooks the dim prospects of low-skilled women workers, who are at the bottom of the wage scale and are ill prepared to compete for jobs that would enable them to support their families. Moreover, the work-oriented approach has lost sight of best aspects of the maternalists' vision: a concern for children as the political community of the future, and a focus on the needs of those adults charged with the responsibility of raising children. Under the new policy, states may provide assistance with childcare but are not required to do so. Low-income women are being taught to understand their responsibility to work as a primary civic obligation,[57] while policy officials ignore the inherently civic dimension of raising children, the obligation that maternalists kept central in their focus.

The lessons of the New Deal for policy inclusion, are, therefore, two-pronged. First, liberal, work-oriented policies can go far to foster social inclusivity, but they require constant attention to remedying or compensating for gender inequities in employment status. Social security has evolved to play a particularly important role today in keeping elderly women, who rely on it as their sole means of subsistence, out of poverty. Suggestions for partially privatizing the system threaten to relegate such women, who are much less likely than men to have sufficient funds to invest, disproportionately into a lower tier of social citizenship.[58] As well, job training and education is essential for low-skilled women to improve their status in the labor market and, simultaneously, in work-oriented social policies.

Second, policies that recognize the civic value of various forms of unpaid work, particularly the care for children, can serve an important function in the polity. The critical caveat is that such policies must be designed to treat recipients with fairness and respect, and not to institutionalize social inequities. Work requirements in the new welfare policy should, therefore, be modified to recognize the demands of parenting. More broadly, policymakers should consult with educators to develop a broad-based plan for high-quality, accessible, and affordable early childhood programs that will both foster the development of young children and permit women of all economic classes to work if they so choose. Government could also provide incentives to businesses to establish guaranteed paid family leave time. Such policies should be extended regardless of sex, allowing responsibilities for parenting to be shared more equitably between men and women.

---

[57] The notion that welfare should be reformulated to teach the civic obligation of work was articulated in Lawrence Mead, *Beyond Entitlement* (New York: Free Press, 1986).

[58] Jerry L. Mashaw and Theodore R. Marmor, "The Great Social Security Scare," *American Prospect* (November–December 1996): 30–37.

New Deal policies also suggest important lessons for policymakers today about the institutional administrative arrangements for public policy. Certainly, Americans now appear supportive of decentralizing governing responsibility. To the extent that state and local officials are more keenly aware of market forces, they may be best poised to forge innovative means of improving women's labor market status. They may be most aware, for instance, of needs for new modes of public transportation or housing that could connect low-skilled women in urban or rural areas with job possibilities in the suburbs. They may also be best able to develop job training and educational opportunities that prepare citizens in their domain to adapt to the demands of a changing economy.

As such innovation is encouraged, however, standards for social citizenship must be broad, inclusive, and national in scope if they are to endow citizens with the dignity befitting those with political membership. The New Deal legacy of divided citizenship demonstrates that when such standards are determined by the states, citizens become subject to political geography, to the cultural and racial agendas of elected officials and administrators and the condition of the economy in the states in which they live. The message given to citizens affected by such policies is that they are marginal to the polity, unworthy of the provision and rights that unite national citizens. By contrast, nationally administered policies of the New Deal, those that grant rights regardless of state of residence, have helped to knit citizens together as a political community. This lesson suggests that the new welfare policy should also be altered to require that states meet national guidelines, both in fairness in determining eligibility for assistance and in benefit levels.

In a speech in 1932, Roosevelt said, "Government is a relation of give and take, a contract. . . . The task of statesmanship has always been the redefinition of these rights [in the contract] in terms of a changing and growing social order. New conditions impose new requirements upon Government and those who conduct Government." [59] He and other New Dealers took up the political task of reformulating that contract through policies they hoped would meet the circumstances of their time. Today, citizens and public officials must engage again in the reformulation of governance, this time to address different circumstances and social norms. In so doing, the manner in which social provision is rearranged will have vast implications for the meaning and experience of citizenship and the possibilities for community and social equality in the highly diverse American polity.

---

[59] Franklin D. Roosevelt, "Campaign Address on Progressive Government," Commonwealth Club of San Francisco, September 23, 1932, in *Public Papers and Addresses of Franklin D. Roosevelt* (New York: Harper, 1936), p. 753.

Index

Italicized page numbers indicate pages on which tables or illustrations appear.